"A must-read for those who are
and deliberate erosion of child
legal culture."

Jerzy Kwaśniewski, attor
Ordo Iuris ("Legal Order")

"Excellently done! Stolen Childhood maps out the terr horror that many children, mothers and fathers have experienced in Norway, including our family. The grotesque use of the term 'in the best interest of the child' has become a euphemism for 'overlooking children's rights and destroying able and caring families'."

Inez Isabel Arnesen, mother and human rights advocate

"A timely and necessary book that champions children's needs while exposing a system that continually overlooks them."

Suranya Aiyar, mother, lawyer and author

"Well-researched, intensive and alarming. Systemic abuse and human rights violations by Norway's Barnevernet are meticulously exposed."

Dr Chris Prunean, physician and musician

"A masterly collection of essays, stories, testimonies and quotes, with a thoughtful opinion that provides insight into Norway's child welfare services."

Jan Aage Torp, pastor and president of European Apostolic Leaders (EAL)

"Cleverly weaved together, unbeknown that you are walking through the process that leads to the removal, separation and destruction of the child and the family unit."

Trine Overå Hansen, journalist at IDAG and TV host at Visjon Norge

"I'm delighted to see the authors and contributors bring their special skills together to show the world the truth. Ignore this book at your peril."

Dr Daniela Mariş, psychiatrist

"A remarkable book that poignantly shows what happens when a country creates 'inferior groups' and rallies the hangers-on for their support."

Margaret Hennum, paediatric nurse

"Our people have succumbed en masse to the belief that children's rights are adhered to in Norway. We need to remove the blinkers and stop needlessly putting families through terrifying trials that lead to disastrous consequences for children and their families."

Berit Aarset, nurse, foster mother and leader of Human Rights Alert – Norway (HRA-N)

"In Stolen Childhood an articulate and factual case is made on why the Norwegian child welfare service should be thoroughly investigated from top to bottom, disbanded and started anew."

Peter Costea, attorney

"An important book that proves that there is a case for Norway to answer."

Preben Kløvfjell, lawyer at Norwegian law firm Tveter and Kløvfjell

"A fair and accurate account of the Norwegian child welfare service. It is not out of control; it follows the course the government and the politicians have decided."

Ruby Harrold-Claesson, lawyer and president of the Nordic Committee for Human Rights

"The systematic violation of children and family rights is real, and it is happening today in my country, Norway."

Sverre Skimmeland, lawyer at Norwegian law firm Advokatconsult

Stolen Childhood

The truth about Norway's child welfare system

Steven Bennett
with Tomáš Zdechovský
and Jan Simonsen

Emira Press

ISBN 978 1 9160 2600 1
e-ISBN 978 1 9160 2601 8

First edition 2019

Acknowledgements

Scripture taken from the New King James Version. Copyright © 1982 by Thomas Nelson, Inc. Used by permission. All right reserved.

Cover design © Andi Negrei/Clair Lansley

A special thanks to my editor, Joy Tibbs, for your diligence and belief in the importance of this subject. It encouraged me so much from the moment you caught on fire, passionately and patiently using your talent to make this book even more compelling and readable. I'm eternally grateful for your care and support with the hundreds of hours you poured into this book.

This book is dedicated to my supportive wife Daniela for loving and accepting me for being me, and for being a virtuous wife and mother to our children.

And to all the children and their families who are needlessly torn apart for no good reason.

Contents

Foreword

This book is a wake-up call. The children of Norway need a welfare service that works in their favour; a service that treats them with the respect they deserve. Unfortunately, the current child welfare system (NCWS) does not fit this description. Respecting children's rights in theory is of no worth if their rights are not respected in practice.

Alarm bells providing warning after warning have been sounded at the highest level in the Norwegian government, but still our politicians do not act. The lack of concern from the Norwegian media, organisations working to protect children, human rights organisations, other professionals and the general public is shameful.

It is rather shocking that there is no interest in or demand for basic facts to back up the strong and persistent criticism of NCWS. Hopefully this book will shine a light into the dark places in which many children and families are currently finding themselves.

Children are suffering as a result of this dysfunctional system. Some are taken away from their families for no legitimate reason, while others who really need help are either actively ignored or go unnoticed. In far too many cases there is a lack of respect for children's needs, and the harsh way in which children are removed from their families causes unnecessary childhood trauma.

I am very concerned for the children who are suffering; not just from trauma in the aftermath of being taken away, but also from the abuse they experience in care. A child should be protected, kept safe and made to feel secure. Under the current regime, NCWS' focus is on inspecting parents and the quality of their parenting skills. Children are overlooked in this process and are not treated like human beings by the system.

I recommend *Stolen Childhood* to anyone who is interested in or concerned about our obligation to respect and comply with children's basic human rights, not only in theory, but also in practice. What we need is a safe, competent and child-respecting child welfare service.

This book is dedicated to the children of Norway.

Gro Hillestad Thune
Norwegian lawyer, author, and former member of the European Commission of Human Rights (1982-98)

Preface

"Thank you so much for the time and effort you put into saving our children and helping our families."

"Spot on! I am so grateful for all your work!"

"Thank you for being a voice for all the families!"

"Thank you for speaking the truth. You are giving all the innocent families and their children a voice. Thank you! And God bless you!"

Like most children's and families' rights supporters, those of us who have spoken up for families in Norway have experienced our fair share of appreciation, and it's heart-warming to receive comments like these.

Statements like this, and the obvious need for a new child welfare service in Norway, have ultimately led to the writing of this book. I became involved after a friend forwarded a petition to me requesting the immediate release of the Bodnariu children, who had been removed from their home by NCWS. I started to investigate, encountering many Norwegian professionals and victims of child welfare overreach in the process.

During this time I have been grateful for the opportunity to lend a voice to many families and their children who have found themselves in a terrifyingly helpless position; a position that is not of their own making. It has also been incredibly fruitful and encouraging getting to know many wonderful people in Norway from various professions who are trying their hardest to make a real difference: professionals in healthcare, education and training, public and government administration, legal services, law enforcement, the arts and entertainment, and so on.

This has been a roller coaster ride that has taken my emotions from one end of the spectrum to the other. Without ever being in the same position myself I have come close to feeling the darkest, most terrifying moments many families in Norway have experienced, having been separated from their loved ones for no good reason.

Words cannot describe the torture parents go through each night as they pass their children's bedrooms and find no little ones to tuck in, read a story to or kiss goodnight. Let's hope the international effort will prove fruitful sooner or later, but in the meantime we need to provide vital care and support for the families that are suffering deeply in Norway.

At the beginning of my research I had a fair number of 'system defenders' (those connected in some way with NCWS) contact me. Among other things, they tried to convince me that those who wanted a new child welfare service were, in fact, child welfare haters. This type of thinking couldn't have been further from the truth. What most children's and families' rights proponents hate are the injustices and legal uncertainties so many children and their parents experience at the hands of NCWS. Far too many children are having their childhoods stolen each and every day, and this urgently needs to change.

Steven Bennett
Children's and families' rights proponent

Introduction

This collection of essays, articles, interviews, testimonies, reports, quotes and poems will take the reader on a journey from an overview of the current child welfare situation in Norway to the process of child removal, character assassination and dehumanisation many experience, and to the history of child welfare systems around the world. Stolen Childhood highlights ideologies that support the abuse of human rights, detailing the devastation this brings to children and their families. It also offers practical ideas for the implementation of a new family-friendly welfare service in Norway.

With contributions from children, parents, lawyers, psychologists, psychiatrists, healthcare workers, education personnel, foster carers, doctors, politicians, human rights commentators and those within the arts and entertainment industry, it gives readers a window into the current Norwegian child welfare system and its practices.

I have been dealing with the topic of children being removed from their parents in Norway for some time now in the European Parliament, ever since the widely publicised case of Czech mother Eva Michaláková came to my attention. Since the number of complaints about NCWS' actions addressed to the European Parliament is on the increase, I continue to take this matter very seriously.

I have encountered Norwegian families who have had their children removed by NCWS and were prohibited from seeing them with no reason given. These families were offered no help and had no opportunity to prove their parental abilities or love for their children. I am aware of a few hundred cases like this in Norway, and I am sure this is just the tip of the iceberg. I dearly hope this book will assist in bringing about real change for children and their families in Norway.

As an MEP I am deeply worried about the way Norway, in many areas under the rule of law, and particularly in child welfare cases, violates its human rights obligations. I am not surprised to see tens of thousands of people across the world marching in protest against

Norway's human rights abuses. Along with colleagues from many other countries I have decided that these abuses must come to an end.

Tomáš Zdechovský
Czech politician and MEP

1

Stolen

In 2011, award-winning Norwegian film-maker Kathrine Haugen's world fell apart while she was filming in Cyprus.[i] In immense distress, one of Haugen's best friends rang to inform her that Norway's child welfare system (NCWS), also known as 'Barnevernet', had taken her children away with the help of the police. This experience led Kathrine on an eight-year film-making journey.

Miscarriage of justice

During the research process for her forthcoming film, Haugen had the privilege of meeting up with Eva Michaláková, one of the best-known victims of injustice at the hands of NCWS. Haugen writes:[ii]

> Eva Michaláková is the mother of two sons, David and Denis. To ensure that the two boys grow up to become solid and productive Norwegian citizens, the Norwegian authorities have decided that both David and Denis are to break all bonds with their mother Eva and the rest of their Czech family. They are to be brought up in two separate Norwegian homes, even though both are citizens of the Czech Republic.
>
> The system of child welfare has a long and solid tradition in Norway. As the first country in the world to pass a law that gave the Norwegian state permission and responsibility to take care of children (namely children from the lower echelons of society) in 1900, the tradition continues to gain momentum today. An enormous growth in the Norwegian economy over the last forty years or so is one plausible explanation as to why the number of children taken from their parents by force has exploded in Norway over the past decade.

Another reasonable explanation is that Norway continues an over-100-year-old tradition of strict social control. The laws that apply in these cases prove this point. They are written and interpreted in a way that leaves no room for the family to object to state interference in their private lives.

The government-appointed expert group on the matter, Raundalen-utvalget, stated in 2012 that its ethical stance is "to weaken the family's power and freedom, and to enable society to rescue the most vulnerable children".

Given this viewpoint, it is no wonder that around five children are taken away from their parents without warning each day in supposedly the "best country on earth" to live in. Raundalen-utvalget states that one of the reasons for this "ethical" stance is to make sure that children grow up to become "solid and productive members of society in the best interests of the nation".

The fact that this policy breaks with basic human rights is not an issue for the Norwegian government, which blindly continues its offensive campaign against families living in Norway. The idea behind this policy is the same today as it was when the law was first written: control over the working class to protect society against children who might threaten the social order. Today, Norway has the resources to implement this ideology to its full potential, and to finalise an experiment that started well over a century ago.

One can also read into the state's premise of the goal to eliminate all social problems: to be the first nation in the world to create "the perfect state". The means to achieve this goal include an extremely tight-knit system of laws, and subsequently the effectiveness with which these laws are enforced.

Today we see that a very high number of foreign citizens under the age of eighteen are taken into custody by the Norwegian authorities. It is as if the mantra is: "What we don't understand is considered a danger to our way of life."

This process of assimilation is not new in Norway. In the summer of 2015, an official report stated that Norway had indeed conducted an assimilation process against the Tater-Romani Romani people;[1] a process that the report states is in breach of human rights. It is interesting that the actions of the state that are condemned as a criminal act against the Tater-Romani people are the same actions Eva Michaláková has been subjected to. It is no wonder that this form of politics has created protest movements all around the world.

In July 2015, Eva came to visit me and my family in the small town where we live. We did some interviews, had meals together, and talked about her children and how her case has impacted her and her family. During the time we spent together, one of the days was spent on the beach. Eva connected well with my daughter Alma, and it is sad to think about what her sons are missing out on.

I first met Eva in Prague in October 2014 during a session held at Charles University. I was there shooting footage for my documentary about the Norwegian child welfare system. It was my first time in Prague, and I went on a boat trip to get some footage of this beautiful city. I also spent time at the Franz Kafka museum, and the striking similarities between The Trial by Kafka and Eva's experience with the Norwegian repressive state apparatus cannot be ignored.

To first be accused of something and, in the background of these vague suspicions, which have been constructed by strangers, moved to the next step in the process, this is the massive dehumanising process Eva was, and still is, being subjected to. Norwegian philosopher and author Prof Dr

1 Tater people are thought to be an earlier branch of the Romani people, having entered Scandinavia between 1100 and 1400. They are believed to have originated from India (not to be confused with the Tatar people, a people from Turkey who lived in Russia and also travelled). The Tater people in Norway did not come from Turkey, but Norwegians didn't care to distinguish between the different people groups 'polluting' the roads, as we will see with the Sámi people later in this book.

Arild Linneberg states suggests that when one conducts a character-assassination on the accused this is a clear indication of a miscarriage of justice.

Eva was first noticed by an employee at the preschool, who thought she was 'strange'. The seed of suspicion was planted, and with this gaze of mistrust that was cast upon Eva the suspicions led to accusations that subsequently grew, both in number and in severity, until she ended up becoming a 'monstrous mother'. Without being in a position to prove that the accusations were false, Eva lost the right to have any contact with the two boys she had carried in her heart and given birth to.

This is a predicament that is impossible to fully convey in a documentary. I think one has to turn to Franz Kafka to comprehend what it feels like to be put in this situation. It is important for me to demonstrate that it's not the parents who are the criminals in these cases.

The pattern that repeats itself in all of the cases in this documentary are constructed beforehand. First of all, there is a story constructed at a national level; a narrative developed over the last century in which scientists, strongly influenced by the Positivist school of criminology, have gained control. Since this version of reality won the battle on how to view the world, the consequence has been an enormous growth in professions relating to detecting, diagnosing and treating children. It is also important to emphasise that all professions connected with children in Norway – from the midwife to medical doctors, nurses, preschool teachers and school teachers – are constantly reminded of their obligation to report any form of 'abnormality' to the authorities.

Civilians are also – through massive, paid-for campaigns and via editorial pieces in newspapers and TV – reminded how vulnerable children are, and that we all have an obligation to contact child welfare if we have the slightest suspicion of anything being wrong with a child or its parents.

We are told that this campaign is to ensure help for children in need, but when one studies the texts, laws and ideology behind this social construction the premise is still based on the nation's need to maintain a high degree of social control. The state has a special obligation to ensure that the 'gold of the nation' – the workforce – becomes as solid as it can be.

The fact is, the apparatus constructed to 'help' these children boasts a workforce that the state itself has, on several occasions, acknowledged does not have the educational level or the personal ability to do their jobs properly and in accordance with the law. But this does not stop the authorities from increasing the number of children subjected to this peculiar form of assistance to 'help' them become well-functioning adults.

The Franz Kafka Museum displays a board with a text that reads:

> *Franz Kafka was born into a myth called Prague. A city with three human groups (Czechs, Germans and Jews) at work, brought together there centuries ago, yet separated by cultural, racial and linguistic differences. The conflict leaves its mark on the city's physiology, turning the districts into hermetic compartments, drawing out invisible borders, but it does not determine the ultimate nature of the cage. We also have to discern this from the bird's point of view.*

Eva's two sons were born into a myth called Norway. Comprehending the time we are living in is hard, and it might be impossible to understand the invisible borders the different people groups migrating to Norway now have to face. To be part of a society and still be a stranger within it are experiences I believe everybody can relate to. One need not be a foreign citizen in a strange country to feel like an outsider; one can feel estranged even from one's own family at times. These feelings are not to be considered a diagnosis, nor is it a hindrance to a nation's growth that people from different cultures, races and languages live together. On the contrary, diversity brings creativity and innovation.

It is understandable that Norway – as an extremely homogeneous nation with a long tradition in practising what one can say as a severe form of social control – feels the need to use force to uphold peace and stability when the demographics of the country change dramatically. But there are limits to what the state can allow itself to do in this regard, and human rights are among the statutes Norway has agreed to enforce and uphold.

Forceful integration of individuals is assimilated. It is interesting to witness the lack of patience the authorities in Norway have regarding those who deviate from the standard settings. And it's fascinating to experience the breach in what is said and what is actually done in Norway regarding those who are labelled 'different'. Norway proclaims that it is a tolerant and understanding nation, but if a child wears the wrong kind of clothing to preschool alarm bells go off and the authorities are notified.

As there are so many families that deviate from the 'norm', the number of families reported to child welfare is rapidly growing. Around 50,000 families are being subjected to thorough investigations by the authorities each year. The lack of trust in parents' ability to care for their own children will have long-term consequences, and what this kind of policy will do to a nation as a whole is hard to predict. The protest movements and demonstrations in Norway and abroad are indications that the state is, in fact, in breach of its own population's view on what is acceptable.

The title of my documentary film is taken from an utterance made by a social worker. She said that every child living in Norway has the right to live under the 'Norwegian standard'; this standard being something very definite. It is clear to me when I read the texts constructed around Eva and her family that the preschool's employees, and later the child welfare service's view of these Czech immigrants, implied that Eva's sons did not live under what they considered to be a high enough standard. The border that kept Eva and her family isolated from the rest of society was perceived to be so strong that the authorities had an obligation to take the children out of their 'isolation' and place them with two different Norwegian families.

It must be pointed out that Eva's sons did not live under conditions that in any way justified the state's actions against them. As I said earlier, and as my film proves, the pattern in all these cases is the same. Whether the children taken come from, in a material sense, a wealthy Norwegian family or an immigrant family with less money, the system acts in the same way. If someone in the state system feels concerned, the families and children will be repressed. Eva's two boys are now separated from their parents and their respective families. They are separated from each other as siblings, but they are 'becoming Norwegians'. The social order is being maintained.

It is by no means easy to live in an airtight container where there are invisible borders between those who are born into the Norwegian standard – economically, socially and linguistically – and immigrants like Eva, who had to work long hours in the textile industry to secure her right to stay in Norway. Even though her sons were born in Norway the family was perceived to be different from the majority.

This may make children of foreign nationals feel like outsiders, but it should not be an argument for the state of Norway to forcefully remove David and Denis and assimilate them, depriving them of their mother's love, and their Czech identity and language, so that the state can be in control of the process that is to turn these two boys into 'good, productive Norwegians'.

The text at the museum asks us to imagine Franz Kafka's childhood and see it through a veil of fear and guilt. The texts in Eva's case describe her sons' experiences when they were taken from their family without any warning and placed in foster care. The total lack of understanding these children have met with from those within the state apparatus is almost unbearable when one discerns the children's point of view. These texts are documentary evidence that one can use when imagining what Eva's two little birds might have felt – both fear and guilt – when captured in the golden cage of the Norwegian standard.

The downside to this kind of politics is a lack of understanding of the individual and the rights of the individual. There is a strong consensus in Norway; a monophony that is surprising to researchers. Perhaps one can interpret protests in the Czech Republic against the treatment of Eva and her sons as a form of disbelief. To strip two underaged Czech citizens of their right to have contact with their biological family without proof of neglect is not what one expects from a democratic nation in Europe. It might be something one would expect from a totalitarian regime, but not from the democratic nation we perceive ourselves to be.

I think maybe the protests and a closer look from other nations that are now taking on Norway will reveal the actual social machinery – the state apparatus – hidden beyond the beautiful exterior. Perhaps we will discover that the official presentation of Norway is in conflict with what Norway really is. The official (fairy)tale showing Norway as a harmonious nation may just be an illusion that is used to cover up the system to the outside world. We may discover that Norway is not worthy of the status and standing it has as a perceived upholder of human rights.

If one tries to answer the old questions – who, what, where, when, how and why – in view of child welfare services and the nation's obligations and ethical stance to "weaken the family's power and freedom" there is a consensus in this country that the greatest danger a child is subjected to is its parents. And strangely enough, it is the mothers who represent the greatest threat to their children. As is shown, both in the single cases and the national narrative, it is a great fear among the social scientists – the architects behind the politics – that the mother's psychological conditions might influence the children in a negative way.

Here one must take an even larger construction of stories and narratives into consideration when one tries to find out why this is so. I keep thinking of a book by Salman Rushdie I read many years ago, Shame, and how the need to control women´s sexuality stems from the need to control resources. Controlling the 'machine' that produces 'the nation's gold' – the most valuable product we know, children – is not a new invention in society. What might not be obvious is that the policy of controlling children by forcefully taking them away from their mothers is considered normal in a country like Norway.

In Eva's case, it is both fascinating and deeply frightening to see how her narrative has been constructed. And for me as a writer, the hardest thing with working on these cases – and what upsets me the most – is the obvious prejudice behind the construction of texts that form the evidence against parents and children like Eva and her sons. The total lack of sobriety and decency in the forming of sentences that are to prove these people are guilty of whatever the repressive apparatus have accused them brings me back to the witch-hunting era. Any sign is to be interpreted in the worst kind of way. Also, signs of love and affection are filtered through what one might call a delusional system until the world is turned upside down. For me, this is a process that makes the accusers become the criminals.

Eva Michaláková has decided to fight for her and her sons' rights. She has taken on a system that, for over a century, has systematically taken children away from their families to be brought up by the state. "The road to hell is paved with good intentions" is a saying that could apply to official Norwegian family politics. But this only applies if the intention is, in fact, to rescue children from abusive parents, and in turn this intention has failed to secure the children's rights.

If the goal is to secure a stable workforce and uphold strict social control the premise changes. There is a huge difference between an ideology constructed to protect the individual from an abusive power structure and the opposite: an ideology that defends the power structure against an individual. In this case, a child.

This is, of course, also a philosophical question: who has ownership of a human being? It might be that the majority of Norwegians actually find that it is the state that owns the children, and that the majority think it is OK to give up parental rights to the state apparatus so that society as a whole can decide how, where and by whom children are to be raised.

But this has not been a clear political idea discussed and voted on in a democratic fashion. Therefore, one can state that the parents have ownership of the child, and that this principle is applicable to all parents. This means that the parents have a say in the purpose of the child's life. It might be that the parents find it problematic that the child is to be born into a state to become a mere productive part of the apparatus. It might be that parents make room for their children to develop into individual human beings with wants and needs of their own.

In Prague, lawyers, politicians and academics from all over Europe were discussing these matters. Some of the families that had lost their children to the authorities, both in the UK and in Norway, were also present to share their stories.

At the start of the event I was not aware that Eva's two sons had been taken by the Norwegian state, so I was not prepared to film her. But when she took to the podium I did my best to catch her speech on tape.

After her speech, Eva Michaláková broke down into tears, as did many participants at the event. As a Norwegian I felt ashamed. Eva's father and I talked during a break. He reminds me of my father, and I can only imagine the hurt this family has endured for years now. The press was present at the event and Eva had to give interviews. The Norwegian lawyer attending the event was also interviewed by two TV channels. They wanted answers as to why Eva's children could be taken from her in this matter. This is a question I have tried to answer in my film.

I spent time with Eva in 2015 and visited her where she now lives. I have talked to people who know her very well. I know the texts that construct her story, and I have seen how she connects with children.

Eva Michaláková's case is what we consider a miscarriage of justice (a *Justismord*). There is no doubt about that, and this will be proven in my documentary film. In the meantime, the years pass by and Eva's two boys have been away from their mother for so long now. The damage that has been done to her and her children cannot be rectified, but this does not mean that we should give up the fight against what comes across as an undemocratic regime. It is very important that an alternative version of the official story is constructed, and it is important that this version is based on factual and proven incidents, which is not the case with the version the Norwegian court system upholds as the truth.

Prof Linneberg says that a lie does not become more truthful even when it is repeated again and again. This utterance is indeed valid in this particular case.

Eva works as a teacher's assistant here in Norway, and she does a great job for our children. It's too bad that the Norwegian state doesn't grant Eva's two sons the privilege and pleasure of her presence, which our children have the advantage of.

Eva Michaláková's tragic case is just one example of a justice system that rarely delivers justice. More than 100 attorneys from around the world wrote to the Norwegian prime minister in 2016 regarding another heartbreaking injustice.[iii] Has the system suddenly become uncontrollable, or has this type of abuse against the family been going on for a long time, as Haugen claims?

In 1999, Norwegian lawyer Sverre Kvilhaug commented (text translated):[iv]

For many years the family has been regarded by Barnevernet as something very negative and destructive; as something one would rather keep the child far away from. The 'solution', which will supposedly fix all the child's problems, both in the short and long term – and which child welfare considers relevant to a very large number, with the support of presumptuous experts – is to remove the child from the family and preferably keep contact between children and parents at as low a level as possible; often for just a few hours a couple of times a year.

At the same time, it is a paradox and typical of Barnevernet that, despite such limited visitation arrangements, one constantly finds that parents are blamed for all negative developments while the child is under the 'care' of Barnevernet, while foster parents are praised for anything that goes well.

Children's human rights

Norwegian lawyer Gro Hillestad Thune was a member of the European Commission on Human Rights for sixteen years. She is regarded as Norway's leading expert on human rights, and her name is recognised internationally.

In September 2015, an article written by Thune was published in *Aftenposten* (Norway's largest printed newspaper). The heading read: "Barnevernet's many players lack knowledge and understanding of their duty to comply with children's fundamental rights."

Thune insightfully describes the inaction of the authorities regarding this dysfunctional child welfare system in her article. The result of this inaction is that voices have started to grow louder and become more direct. She clearly elucidates that families are being exposed to serious abuse by the authorities, and that NCWS' lack of competence is very concerning. Thune writes (text translated):[v]

> In a debate in *Aftenposten* on the sixth of September, Jan Storø suggests a common commitment to ensure quality in child welfare cases. This is an idea that definitely ought to be followed by actual measures.
>
> He is right when he claims that criticism, which brings people into their trenches, is not very constructive. Therefore, it would have been better if those of us who wrote the 'Notice

of Concern about Barnevernet' had not been forced to play rough. However, when it is impossible to get through to our most prominent politicians with articles, interviews, lectures and meetings there is no other way, unfortunately, than to provoke a reaction by calling a spade a spade.

My personal concern is that for many years I have witnessed children and families being exposed to serious abuse, to abuse of power and to violations of their human rights all over Norway. Those responsible are the people paid by our public system to take care of children with a certain need for safety, care and love.

The professional Notice of Concern [the report we wrote] may get slaughtered for both its content and its form. Nevertheless, this must not overshadow the essence of this matter. A large number of professionals have, through their professional experiences, witnessed this abuse perpetrated by the system and have had enough of it. They can no longer accept the inaction of a society that is justified by the excuse "all major systems have their errors".

Today's situation is a disgrace

The experiences differ, and we don't necessarily agree on what changes are specifically required. However, we are perfectly clear that the situation we see today is a disgrace.

Children who struggle because their parents are having difficulties are far too often exposed to the very opposite of what they need. The children and their parents have value as human beings, which must be safeguarded when public servants, with enforced decisions placed in their hands, step into their homes. Due to the parents' and children's vulnerability, it is particularly important that the human rights provisions included in our Norwegian laws are respected.

My personal motivation is simple: the lack of knowledge and understanding among the many Norwegian child welfare representatives regarding the duty to comply with children's fundamental rights, as determined by our constitution, the Human Rights Act, the Human Rights Court's practice and the notes from the UN Children's Committee.

Many fail

Many are failing in this. To be just, the criticism must be directed toward many: parliament, the political parties and their think tanks, several government ministries, colleges, county boards, Bufetat[2], research communities, consultants and experts, the Norwegian Board of Health Supervision, the Association of Local Authorities, the Ombudsman for Children, and the National Institute for Human Rights [NIM]. Ensuring that children's human rights do not only exist on paper is a responsibility many have to share.

I wholeheartedly support Storø when he proposes an open debate on improvements, and I would urge him and others to come up with specific suggestions for topics to debate.

Here are a couple of suggestions from me:

1. Finding ways to establish a quality assurance system for the child welfare system based on user experience: both the good ones (best practices) and the bad ones.
2. Finding realistic and affordable ways to ensure that the children's rights in the European Convention on Human Rights/case law of the European Court of Human Rights (ECtHR) in Strasbourg are respected in child welfare cases.

Arm's length

A seminar is occasionally set up with the stated aim of finding ways to improve child welfare protection in Norway, and time and time again these seminars are dominated by NCWS' own people, including government bureaucrats and union officials within NCWS, its own employees and 'expert psychologists' connected to the system.

All the above are 'system defenders', and are allotted plenty of time to speak. They pretty much sing from the same hymn sheet. It seems that system defenders are not particularly interested in the best interests of the child, but are primarily concerned with protecting themselves and their position.

2 The Office for Children, Youth and Family Affairs (Bufetat) is a government body responsible for the 'practical' aspects of child welfare (management of child welfare institutions, recruitment and training of foster families).

Lucy Smith's Children's Rights Day is an annual event, which was held in the Old Festive Hall at the University of Oslo. Internationally renowned human rights lawyer Ruby Harrold-Claesson wrote the following comment just before the pro-NCWS event, hosted by Barneombudsman, the Children's Ombudsman, took place on November 22, 2018:[vi]

> Be aware that this conference is propaganda for Norway's child welfare policies, which are very strongly criticised by the Council of Europe. However, attendance could have the positive effect of exposing the Norwegian government's child welfare policies.

In an article titled "Norway's deceptive 'Barnevernet' seminar", Jan-Aage Torp, a pastor from Oslo who is also co-founder and executive chairman of Christian Coalition World ("Kristen Koalisjon Norway" or KKN) – a people movement based on Judeo-Christian values – wrote:[vii]

> "Norway is attempting to deceive the world about Barnevernet," states Einar C Salvesen, psychology specialist and founder of KIB[3], the nation's only professional network of psychologists, lawyers and other specialists within the field of NCWS that is presenting a concerted and long-term criticism of the scandalous child welfare services.
>
> The outrage from Salvesen and numerous other professionals who have contacted KKN this week comes in response to the seminar Ms Linda Hofstad Helleland, Minister of Children and Equality, was to host in Oslo on Thursday 22 October 2018 on the subject of NCWS.
>
> In the program set up by the ministry, lawyer Thea Totland was scheduled to speak on behalf of KIB, in spite of the fact that she was never part of the organisation. Despite being a mild critic of NCWS, she represents another organisation.
>
> When the organisers of the seminar were made aware of this fact, they were still not willing to give any KIB

3 KIB is the Competency network for quality in NCWS ("Kvalitet i Barnevern KIB Norge"). Its specialist focus is on the way psychological knowledge is managed within the system, and how to safeguard children's and families' human rights.

> representative an important role, either as a speaker or as a member of the panel. An overwhelming majority of the people who are to present their views on NCWS at the seminar are known to be sympathetic to the system, and they do not have sufficient knowledge of the criticism presented internationally against NCWS.
>
> KIB is the only organisation that has studied the content of the international criticism thoroughly, and that consists of professionals with a broad psychological background who can recognise the way the misuse of psychological theory can lead to wrong decisions when it comes to removing children from their biological families. Therefore, the seminar launched by the new minister will not contain any enlightening or informative criticisms that the ministry can make use of to address the deeply disturbing current situation within NCWS.
>
> "Tim Whewell from the BBC has been invited to contribute in a panel, but he does not know the real NCWS. He has produced two excellent documentaries about certain aspects of it, but he is not able to give any substantive analysis and criticism of the faulty practices," comments Salvesen.

As Torp points out, many experts in this field are not currently being given a voice. With all this potential help at hand, NCWS could turn 180 degrees and truly act in the 'best interests of the child'. At the same time, it could become a light for other nations and end up becoming Norway's greatest success story of all time! Hundreds of Norwegian professionals with the necessary expertise and love for families are queuing up to radically improve the system, but is anyone listening?

Chapter 1 notes

[i] Haugen, K., "Focus on child abuse", Barnefjern: http://www.barnefjern.org/kathrine-haugen

[ii] Haugen, K., "Eva Michalakova", Barnefjern: http://www.barnefjern.org/eva-michalakova

[iii] Kumar, A., "100 Attorneys: Norway Violated Humanitarian, Moral Laws Seizing 5 Kids from Parents Over Christian Faith", *The Christian Post*: https://www.christianpost.com/news/100-attorneys-norway-violated-humanitarian-moral-laws-seizing-5-kids-from-parents-over-christian-faith-163896

[iv] Kvilhaug, S., "Dagens barnevern knuser familiene og reduserer barnas livskvalitet" ("Today's child welfare system breaks down families and reduces children's quality of life"), BarnasRett: http://www.barnasrett.no/sverre_kvilhaug/dagens_barnevern_knuser_familien.htm

[v] Thune, G. H., "Debatt om barnevernet: Alle gode krefter må gå sammen" ("Debate on Barnevernet: All forces for good must work together") *Aftenposten*: https://www.aftenposten.no/meninger/i/v6vw/Debatt-om-barnevernet-Alle-gode-krefter-ma-ga-sammen--Gro-Hillestad-Thune

[vi] Bennett, S., "BE AWARE – Propaganda conference to push Norway's child welfare policies", Step Up 4 Children's Rights: https://stepup4childrensrights.com/be-aware-propaganda-conference-to-push-norways-child-welfare-policies

[vii] Torp, J.-A., "Norway's deceptive 'Barnevernet' seminar", Christian Coalition World: https://christiancoalition.world/news/read2/norway-deceptive-barnevernet-seminar

2

Crisis

As a signatory of the European Convention on Human Rights (ECHR), Norway appears to be a fine example of a country that respects the rights of its citizens. This is exactly what the outside world sees when it looks through the lens of all the promotional material that ranks Norway as a role model; as a country to emulate. However, what we saw on paper is rarely adhered to, especially with regard to NCWS. Several Norwegian lawyers and psychologists have observed that the laws and conventions Norway has signed up to are often ignored, abused or used against children and their families. It's very much a case of smoke and mirrors.

Morten Ørsal Johansen, a Norwegian MP based in Oppland, wrote an article titled "Barnevernet: a state within a state", which was published in the Norwegian newspaper *Gudbrandsdølen Dagningen* (*GD*), and subsequently in *The Sunday Guardian Live*. Johansen highlights the clear legal understanding within the system but explains that the law is often ignored. He alludes to recordings he heard, in which a case worker plainly said that he or she was not working toward returning children to their families. When questioned about this, the case worker replied that he or she knew the law but didn't follow it. The staff member went on to state that the Child Welfare Act was just a guide.

Johansen writes: [i]

> I know of countless examples of how representatives of NCWS conduct themselves. In my view it has become a state within a state, which does not comply with current

laws and regulations. It seems to me that it has only one goal, and that is to make as many emergency care decisions as possible. This is not the way NCWS should operate.

The happiest country?

In 2018, Norway took second place in the UN's "World's Happiness Report 2018.[ii] Mercer's twentieth annual Quality of Living survey in 2018 compared 231 major metropolises, examining factors such as crime, healthcare, education, public services, recreation, housing and personal freedom. Vienna ranked highest in terms of quality of living for the ninth year in a row.[iii]

But is it really possible to measure happiness? And are these reports meaningful, aside from being used as a useful tool in the world of politics? It isn't strictly possible to measure the happiness of a people group, such as a country. There is no such thing as a happy or unhappy country; happiness is too subjective. It's also worth noting that some of the top-ranked countries in the survey have the highest suicide rates and consume the highest volumes of antidepressants.

In his article, "That world happiness survey is complete crap", Kyle Smith notes that happiness surveys don't even agree with one another, with different surveys giving completely different answers. For instance, Gallup's World Happiness Report in 2012 placed Panama first, followed by Paraguay and El Salvador. Meanwhile, Pew Research Center's Life Satisfaction survey in 2014 placed Mexico first, followed by Israel and Venezuela.

Smith commented:[iv] "In Scandinavia, meanwhile, there is immense societal pressure to tell everyone how happy you are, right up to the moment when you're sticking your head in the oven."

Time for change

Jan Simonsen was a Norwegian MP from 1989 to 2005. He was also a member of the Parliamentary Assembly of the Council of Europe (PACE), where he sat on the Committee on Legal Affairs and Human Rights. Simonsen has been advocating for a new child welfare service to replace the existing one for many years.

In his article, "The state is lying about Barnevernet", he argues that the Norwegian authorities have been communicating a false picture to the rest of the world with regards to the behaviour of the country's child welfare system. He writes (text translated):[v]

> In Poland, a Norwegian woman has become a folk hero after fleeing from NCWS with her child and pursuing asylum there. In April 2016, around 75,000 people in more than fifty-six cities in twenty-six countries around the world demonstrated after NCWS had taken four children and a baby from a Norwegian-Romanian family. In the Czech Republic, the removal of a child from a Czech mother living in Norway led to fierce criticism of Norway, both from the country's president and many politicians, as well as prompting several demonstrations outside the Norwegian embassy.
>
> Barnevernet and the Norwegian Ministry of Foreign Affairs complain about misleading arguments and lack of understanding of the Norwegian system, and have, in recent years, launched fire-extinguishing attempts to prevent further destruction of Norway's reputation abroad. Among other things, the Norwegian embassy in Bucharest published an article in English, which was probably also used by other embassies.
>
> The Ministry of Foreign Affairs claims, in writing, that care orders only occur "when the child is subject to serious neglect, maltreatment or abuse" and adds that it only happens as a last resort.
>
> Czech journalists I have spoken to say this is also the answer they have received from the Norwegian Directorate for Children, which is responsible for NCWS, and from the Department of Childhood, Youth and Family Affairs. This explanation is a pure lie, obviously presented by those who know otherwise. NCWS' statistics show that most children are deprived of their parents because it feels the parents lack "caring skills", which of course is completely different from "neglect of care", and which can be corrected with support measures.
>
> A recent case the *247 Avisen* newspaper covered this Saturday proves that the Norwegian authorities are lying

about Barnevernet. Two children were taken from their parents. After two-and-a-half years the case came up in the county board, which deals with child welfare cases, despite the fact that the law states it will take no longer than three months. The 14-year-old daughter had come home to her parents, but the four-year-old son had to stay with his foster parents. The NCWS argued, among other things, that it had been so long that he had become accustomed to his new surroundings, and this was agreed by the judge.

According to the newspaper, this case was not a matter of substance abuse or violence, but a lack of attention and of knowledge about care and stimulation. In other words, the reason for the care order was neither "serious neglect, maltreatment or abuse". NCWS accepted the return of the daughter but not the son. According to *247 Avisen*, the county board stated that the mother requires special guidance, and that it would therefore be the father who had to bear the bulk of the care. The expert thought the father had the "caring skills" but not the "caring capacity". Taking care of two children was considered too much for a father.

However, according to NCWS' top management and the Norwegian Ministry of Foreign Affairs, it is only in the cases of serious neglect, violence and abuse that children are taken from their parents.[vi] As we see here, this is a pure lie. Some brave MPs should confront the Norwegian authorities responsible with the way they are trying to lie their way out of the reality. The Norwegian reputation abroad cannot be corrected by lies, which will eventually be discovered and will further impair the reputation of Norway. It can only be rectified if one first manages to 'correct' NCWS so that it starts to function the way the authorities untruthfully claim that it does today.

International attention

In the following commentary, Simonsen highlights some well-known child welfare cases that have received significant media attention, especially in the international arena. He has observed tragedy after tragedy, and a constant unwillingness from the Norwegian authorities to admit that they are going in the wrong direction, destroying family after family. Simonsen writes the following (compiled from various translated commentaries and used with his permission):

> My twin brother, Åge Simonsen, DSc., is one of Norway's leading experts on child welfare systems and has frequently been used as an expert witness in favour of the parents when child welfare cases have ended up in court, even though his formal education, including a doctorate, was in natural sciences and not in sociology. He has for many years been a member of organisations that have raised critical concerns about the child welfare system.

India

Åge Simonsen confirms that other countries have been scandalised by the brutal behaviour of Norway's child welfare system. Some years ago, there was a case concerning the children of an Indian family in which the father was working within the oil industry in Stavanger. Barnevernet took the children away because of accusations that the mother breastfed the newborn baby girl too much and that the toddler boy's tantrums signified an attachment failure with the mother.

The parents and their lawyer suggested a solution whereby the children would be temporarily cared for by the children's relatives in Calcutta, a solution opposed by Barnevernet. Instead, the children were taken from the parents and placed with a Norwegian foster family. However, the family appealed to the Indian Minister of Foreign Affairs. The case led to demonstrations against Norway in India, to many articles appearing in Indian newspapers, and finally to the Indian Minister of Foreign Affairs taking the case up with Norway's Minister of Foreign Affairs at the time, Jonas Gahr Støre. Following immense pressure from the Indian government, the Norwegian authorities agreed to give the children to their uncle in West Bengal, India.

Åge Simonsen also highlights a case where Norway lost in the European Court of Human Rights (ECtHR) in 1996; a case concerning the state taking responsibility for the children away from the parents. In this case a child was taken from its mother immediately after birth and placed in a foster home. By the time the case reached court the child had lived with foster parents for seven years, but the mother still won against the Norwegian authorities. Her win in the ECtHR was of little value to the mother, however, since after losing in Strasbourg the Norwegian authorities let the foster parents adopt the child and refused to follow up on the ECtHR's decision.

Russia

It is also worth mentioning something the Russian ombudsman for children's rights reported in 2013: that Norwegian authorities had committed abuses against Russian families in fifty-five cases. According to the national Norwegian broadcasting company, NRK, he says that the plight of Russian children in Norway will be taken up by the Council of Europe and by the United Nations. The serious denunciation of Norway came, NRK says, at the same time that Russian TV channels were showing hour-long programs about the plight of Russian parents and their children in Norway, in which the Norwegian child welfare system was the main focus.

Åge Simonsen holds the opinion that Barnevernet takes many children away from their parents without any documented failure to care on the part of the parents. Examples of arguments used are that the parents do not have "good enough ability to give care", and that there is a risk of future care failure if the parents are allowed to keep their children.

Poland

The Polish government is working on a new law that will make it easier for Polish authorities to provide assistance for citizens who are subjected to abuse from child welfare systems in other countries, such as Norway. Several Norwegian families are currently applying for asylum in Poland, and one family's asylum request was officially granted in December 2018.

Czech Republic

Eva Michaláková will remember May 2011 until she dies. Eva was living with her husband, who is also Czech, and two children, David (six) and Denis (two), in Steinberg, a small village in Norway with around 1,000 inhabitants. When Eva's husband was at work one day the police suddenly called her on the phone, telling her it concerned her eldest son. The mother was upset and feared he had been involved in an accident at preschool.

Instead, the police informed her that the preschool's employees had told the police her son had been sexually abused by his father. The son allegedly told the preschool nannies that his father had "fumbled with his hand over his pyjamas". Just a couple of days later the parents were informed that their children would be taken away from them. "I broke down completely," Eva Michaláková told a Czech magazine.

The children were sent to a local hospital for an assessment, which did not confirm any abuse. But Barnevernet reiterated its accusation after interviewing the mother, one of the preschool employees and the son. A Norwegian court, which later backed the parents' rights to the children, rejected these interviews as evidence because the court held that the boy had been interviewed in a coercive and unacceptable way.

The police dropped the case due to a lack of evidence of any abuse having taken place. However, in February 2012 Norwegian authorities decided to take away the rights of the parents to care for their children and sent the children into foster care. According to TV Nova, a Czech television station, the mother was promised that she would have them back in her care if she divorced her husband, which she did, but the sons were not returned. Before being deprived of her parental rights, the mother and her sons were only allowed to meet each other twice a year, for two hours each time, under the strict supervision of child welfare employees. The boys were not even allowed to hug their mother or speak Czech, according to Czech news outlet iDNEZ.cz.

Romania

While the Michaláková family's ordeal was still taking place, another widely publicised story shocked the world between 2015 and 2016. It involved a Norwegian-Romanian family from the small village of Naustdal in central Norway, who were unfairly and brutally torn apart, which resulted in multiple protests around the world.

Barnevernet employees are obliged to obey a rule of confidentiality, and media sources excuse themselves by stating that there is insufficient knowledge of each case to be truly objective. It's a closed system.

The answer given to international media by Barnevernet is that it only takes children away from their parents as a last resort, when absolutely necessary, in connection with a serious care failure, violence or abuse. Such an answer throws serious suspicion on parents who lose their children.

When the press communicated that the parents in Naustdal had also been reported to the police and accused of violence against their children, many people will have believed that they were bad parents. But is this so? Or does Barnevernet distort the facts, blowing everything out of proportion so that it bears very little resemblance to the actual facts? Is Barnevernet causing the children more harm and trauma rather than helping them?

Smacks on the bottom and light twisting of an ear were completely normal within child-raising in Norway just a few years ago, as well as during my own childhood, and are still common in many countries. But in Norway these are now punishable crimes. Shouldn't the parents be fined instead, or, in more extreme cases, receive a suspended prison sentence?

Is it really in the children's best interests to remove the most beloved of all things a mother and a father have? Moreover, is it reasonable to punish the children, who most likely feel that being torn away from their parents is far more traumatic than being lightly spanked on the bottom? It goes without saying that this practice probably could have been stopped by a quick chat with a child welfare employee.

Norway was previously considered by countries across Europe to be a humane nation fighting for human rights. Now a picture is emerging of a brutal nation with a system called Barnevernet, which is cold, cruel and inhumane; a system that is destroying families instead of helping them. The name 'Barnevernet' is now associated with the term 'abuse', and rightly so.

The Naustdal child welfare office received thousands of letters, emails and telephone calls demanding the release of the Bodnariu children. This caused many problems for this office, but the problem was of its own making. But it is not the lone target for criticism. It has probably just followed rules and ordinary practice based on the education and training it has received. Common sense is long gone from this closed system, and not only in Naustdal.

The brutal, legal removal of these children in Naustdal caused many Romanians in Norway to flee or send their children back to their own country out of fear. The Nausdal case garnered enormous attention in Romania and triggered protests all around the world.

Who was responsible for this uprising? The Romanian politicians and thousands of idealistic individuals in countries all over Europe demonstrating against a Barnevernet they claim acts inhumanely, or Barnevernet itself, which has developed a system many have found to behave in an unnecessarily brutal way toward parents and their children, when they could instead be helped through guidance and support, if any is needed at all?

The protests also caused problems for Norwegian embassies. Communications officer Frode Andersen from the Ministry of Foreign Affairs told the *VG* newspaper: "We have tried to come out with factual information stating how Barnevernet functions, and under which rules. That is no easy task, as the campaign is based on an accusation of it twisting facts on purpose."[vii]

Maybe a humbler attitude on the part of the Norwegian authorities would have been more appropriate, rather than accusing Romanian and Czech politicians, and Christian leaders, of "twisting facts on purpose". An allegation like that will hardly improve the strained relationship between Norway and other countries, who are fighting for their own citizens to have their children returned to them.

Czech MEP Tomáš Zdechovský reacted strongly to Andersen's VG statement, which criticised foreign politicians and supporters of a Romanian family that have been robbed of their children, accusing them of deliberately misrepresenting the facts. Zdechovský contacted the Norwegian embassy in Brussels and asked for an explanation for the accusations that he and other protest leaders are deliberately lying.

The Naustdal case, which Norwegian newspaper *Bergens Tidende* has written extensively about, confirmed the problems in Barnevernet's practices and has added new fuel to the protests. If Barnevernet does not change its practices of tearing families apart and taking the children away on relatively feeble grounds the protests will continue, and Norway will eventually become a despised nation internationally. The illusion of Norway as a humane nation is sadly in the process of being torn down, revealing the raw truth and reality of a nation at war against the family.

The Naustdal tragedy involving married couple Marius and Ruth Bodnariu was a breakthrough for the struggle against a child welfare system that is out of control. Due to the massive demonstrations abroad it received a lot of publicity, which had been missing in the Norwegian media. Everyone who appeared in the media and knew the Bodnarius talked about a very good family with a lot of love between the removed children and their parents.

Friends and relatives of the family established their own web page. They stated in one commentary:[viii]

Marius and Ruth touched many lives in a very positive, life-changing way before they met each other. Then, after they met and got to know each other's passion for helpless, homeless children, Marius and Ruth fell in love, got married and started a family of their own.

Marius and Ruth's parental, and their collective family's, rights were grossly violated via the unwarranted confiscation of the Bodnariu girls from school and the boys (including the youngest and still nursing three-month-old baby) from home; the arrest of the father, Marius, from work; the unsuccessful coercion of the mother, Ruth, by Norwegian authorities; interrogations of the parents (Marius and Ruth) without access to a lawyer; and the interrogation of Marius without permitting him access to an interpreter.

Despite Norwegian authorities grossly abusing their power in tearing this family apart, Marius and Ruth Bodnariu, as loving and concerned parents, have transparently and openly complied with all Norwegian authority investigations for the return of their children. Throughout this ordeal Norwegian authorities have employed intimidation tactics and overly excessive zeal, interrogating the Bodnariu children with leading questions designed to inculpate and secure incriminating evidence against the parents, and to cover up evidence supporting the parents in their defence against the irrational, extreme and unsubstantiated allegations brought against them.

Norwegian authorities have outright admitted, and clarified, that they are unfamiliar with, and uncertain of, the nature and quality of parental care Marius and Ruth have provided to their children. Yet these same Norwegian authorities spitefully and malevolently insist on the revocation of Marius and Ruth's parental rights and vindictively continue to expedite proceedings for the reprehensible adoption of Marius and Ruth's children.

The Bodnariu family eventually won their battle against Barnevernet, but it took more than half a year for the family to be reunited. The massive demonstrations around the globe obviously affected the outcome. The day before the case was raised in court, Barnevernet proposed a compromise: the children could be returned to the family if the family agreed to receive 'help' from the child welfare office in their home.

From experience, this 'help' has often been used to spy on the family with the ultimate goal of moving the children out of their homes. This was a major concern for the Bodnariu family. Once all the children had been returned the family went on holiday to Romania. There, safely away from Barnevernet, the children begged their parents not to return to Norway. They were terrified of being stolen from their beloved parents once again.

Unfortunately, there is a strong indication that the children have been seriously affected by this unnecessary and brutal intervention, and possibly traumatised for life. Norwegian psychologist Einar C Salvesen has been involved in numerous child welfare cases over a period of many years. After reading the papers from this case, he told Norwegian TV that he did not doubt that Barnevernet was wrong when it took the children. He feared the injuries the children may have received and said the case had been a tragedy for them. He stated: "This case is so painful and heartbreaking that it's almost unbearable."

In May 2017, the Bodnariu family was honoured by an important, family-centred Christian organisation in Norway called Christian Coalition World, and awarded the Family Defense Award.[ix]

Tragedy after tragedy

Why does Barnevernet continue to create tragedy after tragedy for families? These cases from the Czech Republic and Romania are not unique. They are representative of a system in crisis. Norwegian children are also affected daily in the same brutal fashion. Therefore, we should be forever grateful for international action taken against Barnevernet.

Norway's ruined reputation regarding child welfare action is justly deserved. The international community has been shocked to discover how easy it is to take children away from their caring and able parents in Norway. The sense of humanity seems far more prevalent in Europe than in our own country. One of the leaders of a demonstration in Prague said to me: "It was a good thing that you were here and held an appeal, because even a lot of Czechs do not believe it can be true."

The world is in the process of discovering that Norway has a system that, in a brutal way, destroys families and individuals, creates tragedies and increases the suicide rate among children and parents. The picture revealed to the world is not a pretty one, and Barnevernet employees in Naustdal are not alone in being responsible for it.

The consequences of such a dysfunctional system are huge and deeply tragic for children and their families. A few years ago I visited the leader of the Democrats in Norway, Vidar Kleppe, in Kristiansand. His party is small and outside parliament but is highly critical of Barnevernet. Kleppe worked to help a man who had lost his children to the system. This man was a resourceful person, who had previously had an important job within Norwegian sport. The children were taken because his spouse had some minor psychological problems. Even though they divorced he never got his children back. The politician worked hard to help but was unsuccessful.

Two years later I asked a friend of this man, from the same hometown, how his case had turned out. "He gave up and took his own life" was the answer.

During a demonstration against Barnevernet in Oslo, my brother Åge Simonsen received a phone call just before it was his turn to speak. He was told that a young girl he had tried to help in fighting against Barnevernet had taken her life.

In July 2016, a woman wrote in a Facebook post that her daughter had given up the fight for her children. She had taken her life. The bereaved mother and grandmother expressed her sorrow that her granddaughters were not even allowed to attend the funeral.

There was another story about the father of a ten-year-old son. Crying, the son told the father he had been bullied at school. When the father complained to the school, the school denied there were any problems and claimed the son had problems because of the father. The school contacted the local child welfare office.

A similar story was told on Norwegian television a few years ago. A boy was doing so well at school that the parents felt he should move up a class or get a special education for highly accomplished students. He had top marks in all subjects. The school contacted Barnevernet because they felt the father was being difficult. Barnevernet started its investigations at the family's home and the parents had to talk to a psychologist. However, there were two other complaints. One came from a tenant the father had to throw out because he had not paid the rent. The other came from the tenant's girlfriend.

Barnevernet received support from the county board (the special court for child welfare) to place the boy with foster parents. Barnevernet proposed that the boy should be placed in a temporary home until the case came to court, and the boy's aunt and uncle agreed to take care of him until a decision had been reached. When the boy, who was only ten years old, was taken away by a child welfare representative, together with three police officers, he asked why he had to leave his father. When the child welfare representative began to answer, he looked at her and said: "Get to the point." Then he said: "You have no idea how much my dad has helped me." In the end, he willingly left, but said: "I'm only going with you because my father has promised to do everything he can to get me back." The outcome of this case is not yet clear.

Subjective assessment

How did the Norwegian authorities tackle the problem of the Naustdal tragedy? The Norwegian embassy in Bucharest published a long statement about Barnevernet on its website. Here is an excerpt:

> *In 2014, approximately 53,000 children received measures from the child welfare service in Norway. More than eight out of ten of these cases were voluntarily assistive measures for children and families.*

The number of children receiving assistance from Barnevernet is of course completely irrelevant in relation to the problem that many children in Norway are taken away from their parents. Statistics from the Norwegian Directorate for Children, Youth and Family Affairs show that 11,200 children and young individuals were living in Norwegian foster homes in 2014. That year, 1,665 children were taken from their parents involuntarily, and three to four children were taken away from their parents every day.[x]

The embassy wrote that an order for transfer of care is issued by a special Norwegian court or an ordinary court "only when the child is subject to serious neglect, maltreatment or abuse", and adds that "placing a child outside the home without the parents' consent is always a last resort". This is a serious allegation, indirectly reinforcing grave accusations against the parents, who have a scant chance of defending themselves.

The embassy's claim that children are only taken away from their parents when there is "serious neglect, maltreatment or abuse" is so far from the truth that it could be characterised as a serious lie.

Several hundred cases were examined by Åge Simonsen, whose conclusion was that few of the transfers of care were motivated by genuine care failure; rather that they were carried out after a subjective assessment by a bureaucrat within Barnevernet that the parents "lacked the ability to care". They were not considered able enough to be parents.

This also accords with statistics from the Norwegian Directorate for Children, Youth and Family Affairs regarding the twenty most frequent reasons why Barnevernet takes action. At the top of the list we find: "The parents lack parenting abilities." In an interview with Norwegian newspaper *Verdens Gang*, lawyer Thea Totland says she has noted an increasing number of cases over the last few years in which there is no question of evident care failure, "but that the ability to care is judged on the basis of opinion and on the basis of a number of demands which many are not able to fulfil". Many Norwegian lawyers are in agreement with Totland's assessment.

What, then, are the criteria imposed by Barnevernet as a diagnostic for parents having an insufficient ability to raise their children?

Professor Marianne Skånland has arguably monitored our child welfare services with critical eyes for the longest period of time and studied the field most thoroughly. In one of her articles she lists arguments used by child welfare agencies. From the sixty-nine examples she gives I have selected five as representative:

1. The psychologist recorded that the mother could not make an omelette to his satisfaction and that she cuts the bread into slices that are too thick.
2. The child looks eagerly at strangers around it and smiles at them. This means that it is not attached to its mother.
3. The baby turns its face the wrong way when its father washes it.
4. The mother wants to let the children's grandmother bring them to and from physiotherapy and other medical treatments they need instead of taking them herself. In this regard, the mother is putting her own interests before the children's.
5. When visiting the children, the grandmother wanted to embrace them. Child welfare had to stop that, since it can create an unwanted attachment.

The embassy writes that: "Parents are entitled to a due process – including a lawyer paid for by the government – the right to be heard and the right to appeal the decision."

On paper that is correct, but the judicial process is illusory. Case law shows that it never succeeds. Norwegian lawyers confirm that this is so. While the cases run in the courts the children are in the hands of foster parents, and the child welfare services therefore advance as an argument against the biological parents that the children have adapted to their new 'parents' and that it would be traumatic for them to be torn away from their new environment. This argument is asserted even more strongly over time and is approved by the courts.

In summary, it must be said that in most cases the child welfare services take children from their parents on the basis of a subjective judgment of a "lack of ability to care", using very flimsy arguments. The attitude right from the start is that the major responsibility for our children lies with the state, not the parents. Parents and children are subjected to these abusive actions from the child welfare services daily. They affect Norwegian and foreign parents in Norway. The children of asylum seekers – children who have been confiscated by Barnevernet – are kept on permanently with Norwegian foster parents, while their parents are expelled from Norway.

In Barnevernet's wake we have seen human catastrophes, destroyed families, and in some cases parents who have taken their own lives or ended up abusing drugs in their desperation at having lost that which is most precious to them. A report from the Norwegian Institute for Urban and Regional Research shows that foster children in Norway take their lives eight times more frequently than other children do.[xi]

This is the truth about Barnevernet that the Norwegian embassy in Bucharest did not want to inform the Romanian public about.

Humility please

In Norway we tend to have a high self-image. We are very good at winter sports; one of the best countries in the world, in fact, especially taking into account the small population.

But that does not mean we are the best at everything. It is difficult to obtain certified essential medicines used in comparable countries – even in our neighbouring countries – and a little while back Norwegian students at a university in Hungary were informed that their education was certainly not good enough to give them accreditation in Norway. This is the same ineptitude we have seen in situations where Norway has been criticised for child welfare violations and abuses.

After a major demonstration in Oslo involving more than 1,000 participants, former State Secretary (*Viceminister*) of the Ministry of Children and Equality, Kai-Morten Terning, said that he was hurt by the unreasonable criticism of Norway's child welfare system abroad.[xii] He did not even try to distinguish between the serious and well-thought-out criticism from foreign colleagues and the media, and the common misunderstandings held by the majority of people.

Jahn Otto Johansen is one of Norway's most famous personalities. He has been a correspondent in Russia for many years and has written several books. In a letter to debate website Verdidebatt he calls for greater humility:[xiii]

> *Norwegian politicians and bureaucrats have an elevated self-image. Criticism from outside is usually rejected because nobody should tell a Norwegian national that he could possibly do anything wrong. Anybody caught having done something really reprehensible will immediately respond with, 'I am completely devastated', and that is the end of the matter.*
>
> *One such matter is the fact that some of the accusations against Norway are exaggerated, which is not to say they are clearly wrong. It is quite a different matter, however, that even though there are sure to be well-intentioned and good people in Barnevernet, there is widespread authoritarianism. This has not only affected foreign families with children but Norwegian families as well.*

Our problem with Barnevernet and other Norwegian authorities is that they are so intensely convinced that whatever they do is always right. You shouldn't come here and criticise. We Norwegians get our backs up, especially if foreigners are the ones to criticise us.

Chapter 2 notes

[i] Johansen, M. Ø., "Norway's child-confiscation policies are disastrous, unjust", *The Sunday Guardian Live*: http://www.sundayguardianlive.com/lifestyle/11055-norway-s-child-confiscation-policies-are-disastrous-unjust

[ii] Staff writer, "World Happiness Report 2018", World Happiness Report: http://worldhappiness.report

[iii] Staff writer, "Vienna tops Mercer's 20th annual Quality of Living Ranking, Mercer: https://www.mercer.com/newsroom/2018-quality-of-living-survey.html

[iv] Smith, K., "That world happiness survey is complete crap", nypost.com: https://nypost.com/2017/03/22/that-world-happiness-survey-is-complete-crap

[v] Simonsen, J., "Staten lyver om Barnevernet" ("The state is lying about Barnevernet") *247 Avisen*: http://www.247avisen.com/2017/10/29/staten-lyver-om-barnevernet

[vi] Staff writer, "Removing children from their families always the last resort: Minister of Children and Equality Solveig Horne", *The Oslo Times*: http://www.theoslotimes.com/article/removing-children-from-their-families-always-the-last-resort%3A-minister-of-children-and-equality-solveig-horne

[vii] Skevik, E. "Varsler ny protestbølge mot norsk barnevern" ("New wave of protests against Barnevernet announced") *VG*: https://www.vg.no/nyheter/utenriks/i/xnj4G/varsler-ny-protestboelge-mot-norsk-barnevern

[viii] Staff writer, "Bodnariu family", bodnariufamily.org: http://bodnariufamily.org

[ix] Staff writer, "Family Defense Award given to the Bodnariu family", Christian Coalition World: https://christiancoalition.world/news/read2/article/1421773

[x] Staff writer, "Statistics on Child Welfare Services", the Norwegian Directorate for Children, Youth and Family Affairs: https://www.bufdir.no/en/English_start_page/Children_under_the_care_of_the_child_welfare_services

[xi] Kristofersen, L. B., "Foster children suicide statistics" in *Infertility and mortality in the period 1990-2002* (pages 12-13), Norwegian Institute for Urban and Regional Research: http://www.hioa.no/extension/hioa/design/hioa/images/nibr/files/2005-12.pdf

[xii] Simonsen, J., "Tok Et Oppgjør Med Solveig Horne" ("Setting the record straight with Solveig Horne"), Barnefjern: http://www.barnefjern.org/tok-et-oppgjor-med-solveig-horne

[xiii] Johansen, J. O., "Det selvgode Norge" ("Excessive self-image") Verdidebatt: http://www.verdidebatt.no/innlegg/11639586

3

Concerned

Statistics show that respect for human rights, including children's rights, deteriorated alarmingly in Norway between 2008 and 2015. An enormous increase in emergency placements has, in many cases, put the authorities in a position of not only breaking the law, but also of violating the basic human rights of children and parents.

Around eighty-five to ninety per cent of all 'care orders' executed in Norway today come via an urgent resolution, which represents a significant shift compared with just a few years ago. The rule of law has diminished drastically since 2008. This means that only ten to 15 per cent of all care placements in Norway constitute mainstream placements under the Child Welfare Act's 'Decree to take care of a child' stipulation § 4.12 (a type of care placement that gives the child a significantly greater rule of law).

Emergency decisions should only be used if children would be significantly harmed by remaining at home with their parents. They should only be used in extreme and exceptional cases, for example if there is an immediate and significant threat to a child's health or development.

Emergency decisions are processed by the county board. However, the county board doesn't directly consider the parents' ability to competently care for their children. Instead, it relies on the report from NCWS and checks whether it is in line with the law. The review of an emergency decision happens first in court, often three to four months after the emergency decision was made and executed, and after the child has been placed in a public institution. Of all emergency decisions, the county board upholds around ninety-five per cent, which means that if a case gets to the county board stage children only have around a five per cent chance of staying with their parents.

The most worrisome thing is the extensive use of emergency orders. In 2008, 945 emergency decisions were made, representing an increase of twenty per cent year-on-year. Concerned about the increased incidences of emergency decisions at this time, the Norwegian Ministry of Children, Equality and Social Inclusion allegedly sent the circular below to all the local authorities, urging caution (text translated):[i]

> The ministry sees the sharp increase as a cause for concern because emergency placements create poorer legal protection for the affected parties than the ordinary position after bvl. § 4-12, and because an emergency placement may represent a disproportionate intervention for children and parents if it later turns out that there was no basis for relocation. An extensive use of emergency placements could conflict with Norway's obligations under the European Convention on Human Rights Article 8 and practice for this.

Although the Norwegian Ministry of Children, Equality and Social Inclusion asked local authorities to restrict the implementation of emergency decisions in 2008, Norway saw a rapid increase during the seven years that followed. Statistics show that 1,504 emergency decisions were made in 2015, an increase of sixty per cent.

What is the reason for such an astonishing rise in emergency placements? Are there significantly more serious issues today? Is there a greater need to protect children that might justify this? Are parents more wicked compared with a few years back, or compared with other countries around the world?

Sadly, this trend is set to continue as a newly proposed child welfare law that would exercise far greater control over children and their families in the future is being considered by the Norwegian government.[ii] This proposed new law would represent a huge setback for human rights and democracy in Norway. Why is the existing moral framework being firmly swept away, and why is the rule of law being shoved into the gutter, causing the family to be woefully brushed aside?

Has NCWS become a family bulldozing business? Barnevernet

literally means 'child protection', but is this a good translation, considering the trail of devastation and trauma this agency creates for so many normal families?

NCWS is a very good example of an agency displaying systemic failure. Thousands of children have been taken away from good parents over the years and placed with strangers in foster homes. Around 55,000 children received some form of 'help' from NCWS in 2016, and the number is growing year on year. This is an extremely high volume for a population of around five million, and it is worth noting that many of its stakeholders – including psychologists, lawyers and county boards – are economically dependent on the child welfare system.

Autocracy

Many people ask how it is possible to take children away from capable and caring parents without any abuse, neglect, violence or drugs involved, as in the Bodnariu case and those of thousands of others in Norway.

NCWS is regulated by the Child Welfare Act (1992). It uses Section 4-12, (a) – (d) of this law to justify the removal of children:

> A care order may be issued:
>
> (a) if there are serious deficiencies in the daily care received by the child, or serious deficiencies in terms of the personal contact and security needed by a child of his or her age and development
>
> (b) if the parents fail to ensure that a child who is ill, disabled or in special need of assistance receives the treatment and training required
>
> (c) if the child is mistreated or subjected to other serious abuses at home
>
> (d) if it is highly probable that the child's health or development may be seriously harmed because the parents are unable to take adequate responsibility for the child
>
> An order may only be made under the first paragraph when necessary due to the child's current situation. Hence, such an order may not be made if satisfactory conditions can be

> created for the child by assistance measures under section 4-4 or by measures under section 4-10 or section 4-11.
>
> An order under the first paragraph shall be made by the county social welfare board under the provisions of Chapter 7.

Section 4-12 (a) is the most commonly abused rule by NCWS. It enables the agency to remove a child if its physical and psychological conditions don't live up to the agency's expected standards. Most children are taken away from their parents after being accused of lacking in emotional care, which is loosely implied in this clause. When the law changes, this should be the first clause to be repealed, as it is nearly impossible for parents to defend themselves against such vague and abstract allegations. Just about anything can qualify as a lack of emotional care. For example, one mother was accused of giving her baby milk that was too warm. In court, the NCWS worker was asked how she knew that? She said that she could see it on the baby's face. The mum argued that she had checked the milk first and then held the baby in her arms in such a way that it was impossible for the NCWS worker to see the baby's face or how it reacted.

Section 4-12 (d) was originally intended to apply to parents with significant learning difficulties, but the threshold has since been lowered. Now if parents have a mild learning difficulty or a slightly-below-average IQ their babies can be removed just after birth. This section of the law is often used against parents who are perceived to have psychological challenges, or who are suffering from mild depression or ADHD. If someone asks for psychological help because they were abused or have experienced some form of trauma this may also be recorded and used against them.

Section 4-12 (d) can also be used to take a child away if NCWS suspects he or she may suffer neglect or abuse at some point in the future. Even if the children are lovingly cared for by their parents, NCWS can raise a point of concern if it foresees that the parents will not be capable of giving their children sufficient care as time goes on. In order to predict the parents' future caregiving abilities, NCWS use theories, methods and psychobabble that are based on guesswork and speculation. They are not only unscientific but are also unreliable.

Time and time again, children are removed from their families for no justifiable reason other than the ambiguous theories NCWS has concocted or its biased predictions about the future. These vague speculations are incredibly difficult for parents to disprove, and therefore they often become the final judgement.

Section 4-12 (b) can be used if the parents keep their children out of school for a while because of bullying, for example. Although the parents may feel that it's in their child's best interests to have a break from school, NCWS will often run straight in with an emergency takeover and make up a story afterwards, accusing the parents of not being able to solve the problem and failing to cooperate with the school.

Section 4-12 (c) is very rarely used, as it relates to violence and sexual abuse. When this clause is enforced it is often misused, especially regarding physical abuse. To make it look more serious than it is, NCWS will report an incident to the police and order them to investigate it once an emergency decision has already been made. In the meantime, a legal decision is agreed by the county board. More often than not, no one is prosecuted by the time the police are finished with their investigation because no abuse has occurred, so the parents are acquitted. But because it has taken so long for the initial hearing to take place at the county board, NCWS refuses to release the children. This method is often used when there are accusations of sexual abuse but no sexual abuse has actually taken place. NCWS repeatedly refuses to release the children until they turn eighteen.

NCWS should practise administrative discretion and professional standards, but when parents ask why their children have been taken, it is usually unable or unwilling to explain the legal thresholds that allowed them to take such drastic action. In fact, NCWS is often unable to answer questions even from the start of a case. If the parents ask how the law works they are labelled as uncooperative, and this can be used against them. NCWS may deliberately keep this fact a secret to make parents more vulnerable and the situation less predictable. To some, this is tantamount to an act of terror, and it violates Article 6 of the European Convention on Human Rights.

NCWS is legally obliged to process all material in such a way that families are able to predict the schedule for any judicial proceedings. Legally, there should be a very high threshold when it comes to confiscating children, and section 4-12 should only be used in exceptional cases. This is not what is happening in Norway, where section 4-12 is used to prove just about any point NCWS wants to make.

Notice of concern

In 2015, a National Notice of Concern was sent to the then Minister for Children, Equality and Social Inclusion, Solveig Horne, addressing the following:[iii]

> The current situation within Norwegian child welfare services gives rise to deep concerns. As professionals and responsible citizens we consider ourselves accountable for clearly warning as follows: under the current laws in Norway, an unknown number of children are suffering due to incompetence and abuse on the part of the authorities.
>
> As a society, we should no longer accept the prevailing situation. Our opinion is that it requires mobilisation of a stronger commitment among all those dealing with the challenges facing NCWS. This applies to child welfare professionals, politicians, media and the general social debate. We all have to ensure that children and their families are not exposed to breaches of their human rights caused by incompetence or decision-making processes within welfare and care organisations. This is especially so, given that these same organisations are meant to create welfare and take care of actual needs.
>
> An increasing number of professionals in interaction with NCWS are increasingly understanding that the system, in many situations, falls short of promoting the interest of children, and that there is a need for comprehensive change. Experience suggests that initiatives so far being launched or planned are insufficient or inadequate. Ministers and department heads have promoted change, but obviously this is not enough.

We would prefer to have confidence in the professional expertise and discretionary decisions of the NCWS, and that these would help to ensure well-founded actions and decisions. Similarly, we would like to believe that the legal rights of children and families are being maintained by the courts and their expert witnesses. Professionals who have examined individual cases all too often discover a completely different reality.

We know that there are many cases where statutory services have had to intervene in family conflicts and take over the care of children. Many NCWS offices address this extremely demanding task in the best way possible. At the same time, we regularly observe examples where NCWS appears to be a dysfunctional organisation performing erroneously with subsequent serious consequences.

We observe cases where NCWS is failing to recognise obvious child abuse and serious lack of care within families. Thus it does not act in a timely way with adequate interventions, which might have saved children from an unacceptable life situation. In such circumstances, developing and agreeing on better methods of assessment will help children suffering due to lack of care to get adequate help quickly.

On the other hand, there are cases where NCWS transfers children from their homes based upon very weak evidence characterised by speculative interpretation, discrepancies between assessments and conclusions, and missing quality of measures [for example supporting the child to take up a new sport or to complete homework, or sending the parents on a cleanliness course] that might otherwise have brought about change.

A serious matter is the lack of legal rights for families resulting from the close link between many expert psychologists and NCWS. NCWS is their principal and employer, and frequently engages the same psychologists for assessments of the same case as were initially related to sanctioning emergency decisions to take over childcare.

When the parents appeal decisions at the county boards and on through the court system, they learn that NCWS has appointed the same expert witnesses as in earlier parts of the proceedings. For the experts these are well-paid assignments, and for many professionals these child protection cases are their only source of income. Thus the assigned expert witnesses may easily prefer to state expert opinions that support decisions already taken by NCWS. Thus we encounter a serious conflict of interest, which may constitute impaired legal protection of the vulnerable families involved in NCWS decisions.

When expert witnesses submit their reports and give evidence in the courts, we often see that the observational basis upon which they are reporting is very weak. Hence, their assessments are often weak and abstract. Nevertheless, statements from experts appointed by NCWS are given excessive emphasis when presented in court. Judges are frequently entrusting these decisions to the expert witnesses. In some cases, the biological parents have sufficient financial resources to appoint their own expert witnesses. In these cases, judges appear to place less emphasis on these alternative conclusions. Witness statements from privately appointed experts are not given the same status as those made by the experts appointed by statutory services. Far too often we observe that biological parents without sufficient financial resources do not have any chance of a fair hearing when faced with a large and powerful statutory service. Consequently, we see that once decisions have been made based on weak observations and unverified interpretations, they are applied through all levels of the legal system.

On the basis of the portrayed representation above, we contend that care arrangement decisions in an unknown number of cases fail at all professional and legal levels, and that devised safeguard mechanisms do not function as intended. For the families concerned, the consequences are serious. Immigrant families are particularly vulnerable. They lose their children without opportunity to understand

Norwegian culture, such as zero tolerance for physical punishment in child-rearing. Many immigrants have grown up with physical punishment through generations, and they sincerely believe this to be in the best interests of their child.

Trust, respect and dialogue are the most necessary tools in order to change what in Norway is considered unacceptable child-raising violence. In the absence of these tools, a crisis of confidence between NCWS and minority groups will emerge. We have closely observed this situation in many Norwegian local authorities. When conveying the explicit Norwegian view of success and failure in building good childcare, a more self-critical stance is needed. At the same time, we need to develop increased insight into specific expressions of emotional attachment and care, as these are exposed in other cultures.

At times, there is a shocking disagreement between the competencies found within the local NCWS and its power, which this public institution is authorised to exert over families. It is hard to envisage any other area in our society where public service interferes so radically in people's private lives.

Today's situation shows that many of the functions and services of NCWS are not functioning at a standard that justifies its use of power. Within NCWS, examples show that authoritarian and closed systems/cultures are nurtured, thus exposing children and vulnerable families to the risk of being abused by community decisions. Legal protection in Norway is challenged when the voices of children and vulnerable families stand little chance of being heard.

Hardship is felt particularly strongly by families that have insignificant financial or social resources to initiate their own legal cases and to support these cases through the legal system. A naive belief held by many is that NCWS protects all children in the best possible way, and that the checks and balances built into the system are adequate. Unfortunately, this reinforces a sense of powerlessness felt by the children and families who experience the opposite.

Ripped apart

Without warning, a young family's life was torn apart one Monday morning in November 2015. Two black cars drew up at the farm where Marius and Ruth Bodnariu lived with their children in a beautiful Norwegian setting.

Ruth was waiting for her daughters, Eliana (nine) and Naomi (seven), to arrive home by bus, while her sons, Matei (five) and Ioan (two), were playing in the living room. Ruth's three-month-old baby, Ezekiel, was also in the house at the time. The five children were forcibly removed by NCWS and placed in foster care.

KKN's Jan-Aage Torp commented in January 2016:[iv]

> For almost two months, the devastation of a Romanian-Norwegian family has taken place in the little West Norwegian village of Naustdal in the province of Sogn and Fjordane.
>
> Marius and Ruth Johanne Bodnariu have five children, who have all been taken away from them because of 'concerns' regarding 'family care and violence'. All their efforts to get their kids back home have been futile.
>
> I have today talked with them, and my sources in Romania for several weeks have given me extensive reports.
>
> ### What is regarded as 'family violence' in Norway? Even a light smack or slap!
>
> Until 2009, the Norwegian Supreme Court's ruling of 2005 stating that 'a light slap' is acceptable in the discipline of children was the norm. But then parliament passed a law stating that even such a slap is 'violence'.
>
> Personally, I have never slapped my six kids, who are now all grown up. But I have always defended the rights of a family to include a light smack as a disciplinary measure within an environment of respect, honour and love.
>
> Now, even a mother who physically stops her child from doing something harmful can lose her kids at the hands of NCWS. This is what is really happening. I know!
>
> In November 2008 I was called in to receive an official reprimand by the Norwegian government's Children's Ombudsman for having defended the right to give a light slap on national radio. I did not budge. His threats did not work.

Ostracised families

Norwegian children enter the school system as pupils and emerge as employees for the state, according to the standards Norway has set. To ensure that all children turn out the way Norway desires the government has created a complex system in which many public entities are involved: teaching services, health services, school assistants, NCWS and child psychiatrists to name but a few. The aim of these institutions is to catch those who differ from that which the state has defined as the norm.

The concept appears good, at least for everyone who fits this standard. On the other hand, the individual's unique characteristics are diminished, so unfortunately many children fall outside the picture of the perfect or archetypal Norwegian child. Those who do receive no help at all. Instead, families are often hunted by a power-hungry state and experience a system that abuses its power. It is a system they cannot trust; one that works against its stated purpose.

As we discussed earlier, children should only be removed from their parents in extreme and exceptional cases. Originally, the criteria revolved around violence, sexual abuse, substance abuse and psychiatric issues. Now, however, 'precision measurements' relating to the parents' caring abilities have been introduced. But is it possible to measure this ability? Surely an NCWS staff member, or a psychiatrist who makes one or two home visits, is not competent enough to make such assessments. As a result, these evaluations often go tragically wrong.

Children who are placed in foster homes have an uncertain future. They are afraid of losing their parents and grandparents, and they may also be separated from their siblings, as in the Bodnariu case. The children who are taken away do not know what will happen tomorrow, next week or next year. They do not know how long they will have to stay in their temporary foster homes or where they will be going next.

Many of these children feel like shuttlecocks, where frequent relocation between foster homes becomes part of their everyday life. Such unsafe parameters create nervous and insecure children, and it is very detrimental for children to live their lives 'on hold'.

Instead of creating a safe and decent society, the child welfare system is dividing and ruling over the community.

Numerous children who were previously active in the local community and may have performed well in academic, sport or cultural activities have been moved to new geographical areas where they no longer have the same opportunities, and this seriously hampers their development.

Laurence Wilkinson, legal counsel at ADF International based in Strasbourg, wrote an opinion piece back in 2017, which included the following:[v]

> Norway has a reputation for being a world leader when it comes to providing social services and respecting human rights. However, allegations of 'child-kidnapping' perpetrated by a powerful and well-funded government agency called Barnevernet have recently sparked angry protests around the globe. International news teams flocked to the country to investigate while the Norwegian government was quick to assure the international community that it was complying with international law.
>
> If you talk to Norwegians, many feel as though the recent international scrutiny is due to one or two isolated incidents that have been blown significantly out of proportion. Nevertheless, the allegations have now reached the Council of Europe, the continent's principal institution for safeguarding human rights, democracy and the rule of law throughout its forty-seven member states, and home of the European Court of Human Rights. While it is Norway's child protection services that are currently in the spotlight, the findings of these investigations will have ramifications for families across Europe.

Families that are exposed to a public assault at the hands of NCWS are usually segregated from society. The parents are afraid for their children, for their careers and for their social status. Nobody has any interest in being associated with people who are not perceived to be taking care of their children, either at work or socially. This can have disastrous consequences for people who live in small villages, where everybody knows everybody. Many are scared away from their jobs and social circles. Moving away from the area is often the only option.

It is not only parents who are denied contact with their children, but also grandparents and the rest of the family. As an example, there was one case where parents and grandparents hid at the back of a church to see their children or grandchildren being confirmed. Parents and relatives have also been known to dress up during the official national holiday observed on May 17 each year[4] just to get a glimpse of their children. Relatives say they are afraid to talk to the children in cases like this in order to avoid losing the meagre visitation rights they have left, for example the two hours they are permitted to spend with the children four times a year. This appears to be one method NCWS uses to control the parents.

Mind games

Parents cannot expect any support from their children's 'new parents'. The foster parents are often instructed by NCWS to keep their distance from the biological parents and to speak negatively about them to the foster children. Fostering is very lucrative, earning foster parents around €50,000 a year, plus other grants and supplements. Foster parents can visit the website of the Norwegian Directorate for Children, Youth and Family Affairs (Bufdir) and start the process of picking out a child or several children. On the page for Trøndelag (Trondheim), site visitors can pick a child by name and age, or even according to their advertised behaviours and preferences, almost as if the children are being traded at a cattle market or sold in a shop window.[vi]

Foster parents are often fed one-sided information, and this is where small details can be blown out of proportion. For example, someone who takes regular medication might be viewed as a drug addict, while sending a child to school with an empty lunchbox

4 Norwegian Constitution Day, referred to as *syttende mai*, *Nasjonaldagen* or *Grunnlovsdagen* in Norwegian. Ironically, a semi-official 'Children's Day' is also celebrated on this day. Children appear in parades waving their Norwegian flags, eating ice cream, and celebrating to show how happy they are to be citizens of this great democracy. Parents and grandparents proudly line the streets to greet and support their little ones.

might be considered evidence that the parent doesn't care about the child and lacks parenting skills. NCWS cites confidentiality rules whenever it is asked to explain why it is unable to give foster parents further details about the child's family.

NCWS often portrays the biological parents as being extremely incompetent or abusive, and has strict rules about how the foster parents must deal with them in the child's 'best interests'. The foster parents are often told that the child does not want to speak about their biological parents because the parents have traumatised them, and therefore it would be damaging to the child to bring the parents up in conversation. The real reason – the fact that NCWS has already traumatised the child by forcefully removing him or her from the home – is hardly ever mentioned.

Children are often told they have been taken away because their parents would undoubtedly harm them in the future if they continued to live at home. Children quickly assume their foster parents are forbidden to talk about their biological parents because they are never mentioned. As a result, the children appear confused, and the foster parents take this as confirmation of what NCWS has told them. It's not a case of teamwork between the foster parents and NCWS; most of the time the foster parents are simply placing blind faith in NCWS' 'expertise'.

NCWS also emphasises its goal of bringing the biological family back into the child's life once the parents have received enough help to change and the child has had enough time to settle into a safer environment within a good home. This is upside-down information. It makes foster parents believe the child welfare service is really considering the child's best interests, and since that is often the foster parents' genuine concern they try to cooperate as best they can, which just gives NCWS more time to avoid doing what they are pretending to do.

NCWS rarely helps biological parents. It wants the parents to admit to things they have not done. When they refuse to go along with a fabricated chain of events and outright lies, the biological parents are called uncooperative and the foster parents believe the biological parents are incapable of changing for the better. They even start to see the biological parents as selfish; putting their own needs before those of the child. In this way, NCWS convinces the foster parents that they are the best possible carers for the child.

When children turn seven in Norway they have the right to express where they want to live. If the child is over twelve their wishes should be given even more credence. Prosecutors and psychiatric experts often claim to have talked to the children, but if the children's wishes do not match up with NCWS' they will not be heard.

NCWS spends a long time preparing each emergency decision, and usually it is the result of a collaboration between many different units. The parents are not supposed to know anything, so all parties involved work in secret. The intervention finally takes place when the police and NCWS attend the school or home to pick the children up.

Children are often told this has happened in consultation with their parents, and that they are being picked up because their parents can no longer care for them. Fearful fellow students are given no information about what has happened, and this is left to their own parents to communicate. NCWS often speaks negatively to children about their parents without offering a reasonable explanation as to what is happening or why.

After a 'care takeover', all communication between parents and children takes place on NCWS' premises. The parents are completely defenceless when they see that NCWS is trying to turn their children against them, and are not allowed to talk about the case during these meetings. To be on the safe side, NCWS often decides the meetings must take place under continuous supervision so the parents cannot say anything disadvantageous about the organisation to their children. This is a very serious invasion of privacy. In this way, NCWS has full control over the parents. If the parents protest or refuse to follow its rules, NCWS often starts reducing access to the children.

In an article titled "Lawyer claims experts are bought and paid by the child welfare services", lawyer Louis Anda argues that NCWS works far too closely with certain experts, such as psychologists.[vii] He notes that this closeness – or collusion – between the child welfare office and the expert often means that any report written about a family is anything but an independent opinion. Anda comments that the child welfare system should not be allowed to choose its own experts.

He criticises NCWS, suggesting that the agency often dictates to experts what it requires them to write about the family. An example Anda gives involved one expert who believed a particular child did not need to be removed from the parents. Nevertheless, NCWS solved this problem by bringing in another expert who was prepared to write what it wanted, thereby justifying the removal of the child.

Growing concerns

In his article, "Not everyone will be celebrating May 17 this year", Norwegian lawyer Olav Sylte writes about a family that had their two small children taken away by NCWS in spring 2017, with a permanent takeover effected in the autumn at the county board. [viii] The parents appealed, and in March 2018 an expert report supported the return of the children. The parents were delighted and expected their small children to be returned a few weeks later.

NCWS ignored this expert report and a new hearing date was set for August 2018. By this time these small children had been thrown from pillar to post within a very lucrative foster care industry, which is also advantageous for the lawyers and other professionals who support everything NCWS says. After coming face to face with such inhumane behaviour at the hands of the child welfare system, this precious family was unable to hold their Constitution Day or Children's Day celebrations on May 17, 2018.

According to Sylte in his article "Relocated by force, bully victim allowed to move back home", children who are bullied at school are repeatedly taken away from their parents by NCWS.[ix]

In one particular case, Sylte notes that the district court concluded unanimously that a child who had been taken away from his family in the summer of 2018 and returned in December 2018 was wrongfully taken. Sylte writes:

> This bullying case is not unique. It is constantly happening that the Norwegian child welfare service is convicted of making such 'misplacements'… The court's courageous and,

> in our opinion, absolutely correct decision, was also contrary to the recommendation of an expert psychologist who had investigated the matter on behalf of the child welfare service.

At the beginning of 2018, *The Christian Post* reported on another case regarding a 12-year-old boy who was forcibly removed from his home. The boy in question was being temporarily homeschooled because of bullying.[x] The boy's parents uploaded a video to Facebook showing their son being removed by three NCWS employees and six police officers. In just over a week the video had been viewed more than 600,000 times before a deal was struck that allowed their son to return home.

Some parents do not inform the school authorities when their child is being bullied at school for fear of NCWS getting involved. They are afraid to run the risk of being perceived as struggling parents, which can result in an investigation and the possibility that the child will be taken away.

According to an article written by preschool magazine editor Øyvind Johansen entitled "Those who have not applied for a kindergarten place will find the local authority at the door", the Norwegian 'preschool police' may start knocking on families' doors very soon. More money (1.4 million kroner; around €150,000) is being provided to local councils to fund a taskforce that will knock on people's doors and offer compulsory 'guidance' to parents who have not yet applied for preschool. This has been alluded to before in Norway, but it seems the 'family police' idea is alarmingly being brought to life in Drammen, a city not too far from Oslo.

A mother in the Johansen article expresses concern about this taskforce force. A qualified preschool teacher, she has chosen to keep all three children at home. She states (text translated):[xi]

> It's very crazy that they will impose on us the provision of a preschool space when we have taken a conscious decision not to go that way. The vast majority of people living in Norway are informed that there is an offer of preschool.

Where will this lead?

An article written by the Bulgarian News Agency (BTA) in June 2018 records the concerns of Bulgaria's Foreign Minister, Ekaterina

Zaharieva, for Bulgarian children who have been taken away from their families in Norway:[xii]

> We are aware that each country tries to protect children's rights according to its own rules. However, we are strongly concerned about the cases of children who are Bulgarian citizens and are taken away from their parents. We also find it perplexing that a brother and sister can be separated by hundreds of kilometres and stopped from seeing and talking with their mother, which will inevitably break their bond and tear them away from their roots and mother tongue. That is why we want to work in close cooperation with Norway's institutions and help the affected families.

Meanwhile, Norwegian lawyer and human rights expert Thune is quoted as saying (text translated):[xiii]

> With disbelief, I hear descriptions of babies being ripped out of their mother's arms; the siblings from immigrant backgrounds, who, without warning or explanation, are collected from the school for police questioning; a whole family arrested by police in uniform with bats and shields, in the presence of neighbours; fathers taken and arrested; youths taken by force into aircrafts and left at institutions that prohibit contact with the world; and siblings sent to different parts of the country without the right to contact each other.

Chapter 3 notes

[i] Bennett, S., "Emergency placements sky rocket in Norway", Step Up 4 Children's Rights: https://stepup4childrensrights.com/emergency-placements-sky-rocket-in-norway

[ii] Staff writer, "Forslag til ny barnevernslov overlevert barneministeren" ("Proposal for a new child welfare act handed over to the Minister of Children"): https://www.regjeringen.no/no/aktuelt/forslag-til-ny-barnevernslov-overlevert-barneministeren/id2512893

[iii] Salvesen, E. C., Thune, G. H., Nwoso, T. E. and Witoszek, T. N., "Notice of Concern – The situation within Norwegian Child Protection Services": https://christiancoalition.world/news/read2/national-notice-of-concern-barnevernet

[iv] Torp, J.-A., "The Devastation of a Romanian-Norwegian Family", European Apostolic Leaders: https://europeanapostolicleaders.eu/structure/jan-aage-torp-president/president-blog/read3/article/1374419

[v] Wilkinson, L., "Norway's Government-Abducted Children, and Ramifications for Europe", *Forbes*: https://www.forbes.com/sites/realspin/2017/02/27/norways-government-abducted-children-and-ramifications-for-europe/#24be7bac4f73

[vi] Staff writer, "Children who need foster homes: Do you have room for another in your family?" Bufdir: https://www.bufdir.no/Fosterhjem/Alle_kontorer/Trondheim/Barn_som_trenger_fosterhjem

[vii] Anda, L., "Lawyer believes that experts are purchased and paid for by the child welfare service", NRK: https://www.nrk.no/sognogfjordane/_-for-tette-band-i-barnevernet-1.11311342

[viii] Sylte, O., "Noen skal ikke feire 17. mai i år" ("Not everyone will be celebrating May 17 this year"): http://advokatsylte.no/artikkel/9/barnevernsaker/769/noen-skal-ikke-feire-17-mai-i-ar

[ix] Sylte, O., "Tvangsflyttet mobbeoffer får flytte hjem igjen", ("Relocated by force, bully victim allowed to move back

home"): http://advokatsylte.no/artikkel/9/barnevernsaker/811/tvangsflyttet-mobbeoffer-far-flytte-hjem-igjen

[x] Smith, S., "Norway Forcibly Removes 12-Y-O Son After Christian Family Decides to Homeschool", *The Christian Post:* https://www.christianpost.com/news/norway-forcibly-removes-12-y-o-son-after-christian-family-decides-to-homeschool-video.html

[xi] Johansen, Ø., "De som ikke har søkt om plass i barnehage, kan få kommunen på døra" ("Those who have not applied for a kindergarten place will find the local authority at the door"), Barnehage: https://www.barnehage.no/artikler/de-som-ikke-har-sokt-om-plass-i-barnehage-kan-fa-kommunen-pa-dora/432120

[xii] Staff writer, "Foreign Minister Zaharieva, Norwegian Ambassador Discuss Cooperation on Bulgarian Citizens' Problems with Norway's Child Welfare Service", Bulgarian News Agency (BTA): http://www.bta.bg/en/c/DF/id/1815028

[xiii] Thune, G. H., "Kronikk: Det er noe grunnleggende galt med barnevernet" ("Chronicle: There is something fundamentally wrong with child welfare"), *Aftenposten*: https://www.aftenposten.no/meninger/kronikk/i/vp9l/Kronikk-Det-er-noe-grunnleggende-galt-med-barnevernet

4

Misunderstanding?

In May 2011, NCWS took two children away from Indian couple Sagarika Chakraborty and Anurup Bhattacharya, who had moved to Stavanger. All members of the family were Indian citizens. Dr Nandita Chaudhary, who taught at the University of Delhi for more than thirty years, wrote the following harrowing account of this family's experience entitled "Nightmare in Norway: How a mother lost her children to the State (and fought to get them back)":[i]

> Finding the strain of being parents for the first time, added to the stress of lingering differences in the absence of a strong family network, can leave a person isolated, anxious and even angry. In such a situation, when support is offered by an agency it is likely to be accepted. Unbeknownst to this couple, the support that was offered on account of some signs of marital difficulty and their son's developmental challenge, became the instrument with which their children were ultimately taken away from them.
>
> In a recent conversation with Team Masala Chai, Sagarika revisits her nightmare in Stavanger, a time when she lost her own children to an organisation that promised her support for their care. But she, with the support of her family and some friends, did not give up until she got them back. This is her story.
>
> **About the family**
>
> According to news reports Mr. Bhattacharya migrated to Norway in 2006 to work as a geophysicist and IT specialist at

an oil company. In December 2007, he returned to India to marry Sagarika Chakraborty. Sagarika was born and brought up in Kolkata, and this was her first trip overseas. She looked forward to a comfortable and happy life in her new home.

Soon the couple was expecting their first child, for which Sagarika returned to India to her natal home, as is customary. The care that an expectant mother can receive with her natal family is believed to be an important reason for this practice, especially for the first child. Their son was born in Kolkata in October of the same year, and Sagarika stayed on in India for some time. Her son was fourteen months old when she returned to Norway. There are some reports of the fact that the relationship between the young couple was not smooth sailing, and perhaps Sagarika's extended stay in India after the birth of her son was related to some trouble between the two families, and also between the husband and wife.

Her husband worked long hours and was not able to give much time to the home and family life. Sagarika was a full-time mother and was responsible for all the housework, which her husband perhaps felt he did not need to share. He was also compelled to take language classes to add to his existing load of work, making him even busier than he was at work.

Soon the couple was also expecting their second child, and she reported having had a difficult time with this pregnancy, so they decided to enrol their son into a local nursery. The morning sickness was severe. She found herself quite isolated with the struggle of caring for her son and a difficult pregnancy, but she successfully managed through this difficult phase and gave birth to a daughter in December 2010.

The relationship with her husband, however, was not thriving, to say the least. He was extremely busy at work, and the challenges of being young parents in an unfamiliar place engulfed them. With the new baby in the house, the workload escalated, and her husband was not able to make time to help her out. With the older one just over two years of age and a new baby, Sagarika was overworked. Barely able to recover from a difficult labour, she also had the task of making daily trips to the school to pick up and drop her son. At this point, the school teachers commented on the fact that their son tended to have tantrums and the mother appeared a bit disorganised, as she was sometimes late in arriving for the morning class. The family was placed under scrutiny, as is common practice when something that doesn't fit well with the local image of family life is encountered.

At home they continued to speak Bengali and lived in accordance with the traditions they were familiar with. Because of the difficulties they were perceived to be facing, the school advised the couple to take Marte Meo counselling for dealing with their son and handling their relationship and household better. This was initiated when the daughter was a young baby and professionals from NCWS paid visits to their home for observations. These visits also involved several video recording sessions.

Matters took a turn for the worse in the summer of 2011. After several home visits and prescribed consultations, NCWS took the decision to separate the two children from the parents based on their home observations and the son's conduct at school. One of the episodes related to Sagarika's handling of her son's distress when she picked up the daughter to breastfeed her.

Already uncomfortable about being watched and filmed at home, sometimes during the breastfeeding session, Sagarika did what Indian parents commonly do. She raised a threatening palm to her son and asked him firmly to stop what he was doing since there were people in the house. Without understanding the context or communication intended by the gesture, this was taken as a direct threat of physical abuse, and was perhaps the final reason for separating the children from what was seen as an 'abusive situation'.

Other allegations were made about peculiarities in sleeping arrangements. The mother slept with the baby and the father with the son, more to ensure that the son would sleep undisturbed. And about 'force-feeding', when the mother fed the young boy with her hands to ensure that he finished his food. On another occasion, Sagarika closed a kitchen door to pick up some broken glass while NCWS authorities were observing her to make sure that her son didn't hurt himself on the broken glass. Unfortunately, this was read as 'locking' the son in another room, when actually she had asked one of them to watch him! Also, they said that the four-month-old daughter didn't look her mother in the eyes, and that was peculiar.

Furthermore, Sagarika's perceived unwillingness to accept her son's assumed 'disorder' was also seen as a sign of being an inappropriate caregiver. Her understanding of the situation with the son was that he was jealous of the baby and his tantrums and disruptive behaviours were linked to that. This is not how the school and NCWS saw it. Sagarika was unable to comprehend why these interpretations were being attached to her handling of her children. Being unaware of the language and culture of the local people, she was taken completely by surprise at the outcome of these observations.

The son and daughter, then two-and-a-half and five months old, respectively, were taken from their home and placed in state custody until they were eighteen years of age. The decision was taken that they should have minimal contact with their parents no more than three times in a year. Both parents were stunned by the sudden decision, as from their perspective the observations and sessions had been going well. The allegations of inappropriate care were levelled against them. The mother was traumatised by the grief of losing and not being able to meet her children, and the stress of the situation also took a toll on their relationship. Noted activist and lawyer Suranya Aiyar argues that Sagarika's was a case of a woman being caught with "the worst stresses of Indian family life combined with the worst stresses of Norwegian/Western family life."

After a long battle with NCWS and the intervention of the Indian government, Sagarika, by then legally separated from her husband, was given custody of her children. She now lives in Kolkata and both children are with her.

> **Extracts from our conversation with Sagarika**
> *You know, life is not easy in Western countries. I had to manage everything on my own. I had to take care of the house, and both my children. Abhigyan, my son, was a difficult child, so disciplining him was always a challenge. He started going to nursery. We had to stay with him in the nursery for long hours as they did not agree for us to leave him. I used to go to the nursery with my baby because they wanted me there. At the nursery they never said anything about him to me. He was adjusting well, I thought. Then suddenly one day an official at the nursery suggested that* ***someone from CWS will come home to help you take better care of your daughter and will also help you with some housework****. I did not know why she was coming. I merely agreed, thinking it might help me.*

The highlighted portion of Sagarika's narrative clearly identifies how cleverly she was misled into believing that the agency was on her side; there to make her feel comfortable and safe enough to open up her home and her life to them. However, as indicated in this and other reports, they spent most of their time evaluating her and keeping detailed notes about their understanding of her gestures and actions, since they did not understand the language she was using. Due to the language barrier between her and the NCWS personnel, there was no opportunity for any conversations about the children and there was no attempt on their part to access a Bengali-speaking translator to better understand what was going on. She recalls that the personnel came with files in hand and spent their time just looking at her and her children, often making her very uncomfortable in her own home. There were hardly any exchanges between them and her. We try to imagine such a situation in our own homes and cannot shake the sense of deep violation at this intense scrutiny of personal life.

> *The lady officer from the agency came often to observe us. She used to come at any odd time, while I was cooking or feeding my baby. She just used to sit and keep looking at me. I didn't understand their language very well, so wasn't able to talk too much. But they never even indicated to me at any time that there was any problem; never gave me any warning about what they were writing. I never imagined that they could do such a thing as taking away my children. I was shocked when that happened.*

NCWS was involved with the family for more than seven months, and for the entire period of observation and counselling there was no indication of any attempt to advise or suggest anything to the mother or father regarding their interpretations, not even checking if they had correctly understood what was going on. Neither of the parents had any idea where these sessions were headed. As far as they were concerned, these people had come to help them with their son, and to help them deal with his difficulties. At no point did they even imagine that they were being scrutinised and secretly being held responsible for what was going on with their son. No warning signs were issued by the officers. We asked Sagarika if they ever approached her husband about these matters, since he would have been able to communicate with them easily given that he was studying the language.

> *I had no idea what they were thinking and planning. Neither me nor my husband were expecting this consequence. We were never informed that there was any problem with us, or that the children could be taken away by NCWS. Both of us knew about the counselling and observation part, and we had openly agreed to it for the sake of our son. But I remember*

very clearly that when I did request a cancellation or a rescheduling of the home visits I was told that this would not be possible. Even on days when I wasn't feeling well they insisted on coming. I remember being extremely uncomfortable on such occasions and I wanted to be alone with the baby, wanting to rest when the baby slept, but they sat there through everything, just sat there and observed everything, constantly writing things down in their files. Some days I felt awful. I didn't know what to do.

Even during this conversation, so many years later, Sagarika is still puzzled about why exactly they considered her actions so bad that they would take her children away from her. She believed she was a caring and devoted mother who was willing to do whatever was necessary for her children.

After my daughter was born, me and my husband were sleeping in two different rooms. My husband used to sleep with my son and I used to sleep with my daughter. You know, little babies keep getting up in the night to feed, so we thought that this was best for all of us. I think now that NCWS thought it was wrong for us to do this; that it was wrong for me to sleep with my baby. I just cannot understand why they would think that.

Many times I could see them frowning at me, but they never said anything. Like when I was preparing food, I could see they did not approve of what I was cooking, and when I was feeding the children I think they made many notes about that. I know later they did say that I used to feed the children with my hand, and I think they said that is wrong. I think they found fault with most of the things I did. As a child, my son did not play with many toys, and when he was a baby and I was cooking I used to let him play with the utensils in the kitchen. This is something we all do in our families. I think this also became a point of complaint about me, as they felt a child should play with toys and not kitchen utensils. I did sometimes get angry with him and would threaten him by raising my hand, but it was only a threat. I would raise my voice only when there was something unsafe, like a hot surface. I wanted to prevent him from getting hurt. I think they put me down as an abusive mother, and I cannot understand how they came to that conclusion.

Whenever they came, they spoke only in their own language. Whereas we tried our best to speak English in their presence, a similar request from us was not accepted. Therefore, I had no clue about how they were interpreting what was going on. I think they were also aware that we did not have much support from the community since we didn't know many people there.

Through their recordings, observations and interpretations, NCWS was building up a case against the family; a case that would eventually lead to a sudden and complete removal of the children one fateful day. There was no warning or negotiation allowed. They just turned up at their door, came in and took the children away.

On May 9, 2011, two days before NCWS took my children away, I went to the health centre for my daughter's vaccinations. She got injections in both legs and was in pain and had developed fever. I was not able to sleep those two nights. My husband was also very tired. I still went to the kindergarten for the sake of my son, and I thought that when I got him back from nursery the whole family could relax. At this time, the NCWS people again insisted on coming to our home. I was very stressed due to the lack of sleep and didn't want anyone at home. I tried to tell them about the vaccinations, the pain, the fever and our sleepless nights. They insisted on coming.

I started to prepare breakfast and they started asking some questions about household duties and

> *who does what. I told them that this was not the right time for them to ask us questions as we hadn't slept and needed to finish the household tasks. The officer then took my daughter out of the house saying, "You are tired, we will take your daughter for a walk outside."*
>
> *When we had completed our work we waited for the child to be brought back. After about an hour we were told that our children have been taken to a care home and we would not be allowed to see them... I don't have words... I cannot tell you... I cannot explain what I felt... I remember I was crying, hysterical, shouting... I asked how they could do such a thing... But I was not heard. Later, I heard that they had recorded my behaviour as hysterical and taken that as further proof of my unsuitability as a mother. Tell me... how would you react if your children were taken away from you?*

After months of effort, Sagarika's parents were able to get the government of India to intervene in this ruling. This was followed by negotiations between NCWS and the Indian government. However, when they did release the children it was the young unmarried brother of her husband to whom they gave custody of the children. After a long battle, in the January of 2013, Sagarika and her children were legally reunited by the order of the Kolkata High Court. They have been together ever since.

Sagarika's husband stayed on in Norway and has never visited Sagarika or his children again. Sagarika has been subjected to repeated psychiatric and psychological assessments by experts appointed by the Indian government to ensure her mental well-being and her capacity to care for her children adequately. She was never found lacking in any way. Her nightmare was finally over.

NCWS tactics

Suranya Aiyar, a mother and lawyer educated at the University of Oxford, identified a number of characteristics relating to the treatment the Bhattacharya family suffered at the hands of NCWS:[ii]

- The low threshold for confiscation of children from their parents
- The absence of a fair and independent hearing for the parents
- Cultural bias in evaluating parenting practices and a lack of understanding of the culture of the children being confiscated
- Findings of parental abuse or neglect based on woefully inadequate evidence, including hearsay, conjecture and speculation that would not be admissible in other types of legal proceedings
- Preventing members of the extended family from stepping in as guardians when parents are deemed unfit
- Children being confiscated for months under interim orders
- Children being confiscated without any prior notice or court process, even where there is no emergency situation
- Confiscation being ordered by lay tribunals who have no legal expertise and whose members include employees of the agency recommending the confiscation
- Failure to provide an interpreter to parents or children who do not know the local language, and the denial of the right to have court or investigative proceedings explained in a language they understand
- Rubber-stamping by courts and lay tribunals of the findings of care workers who function for all practical purposes as adversaries of the parents in care proceedings
- Monetary and other incentives for care agencies who place children in foster care or give them up for forced adoption
- Termination of parental rights and the placing of children for adoption after the child has spent a certain period in state care, even while the parents are contesting the confiscation of the children in the first place
- A systemic preference for removing children from families rather than enabling families to provide better care for them
- Administrative heavy-handedness on the part of care agencies empowered to confiscate children from their parents

- Parents being blamed for developmental and other disorders in their children, even though there is no scientific rationale for doing so
- The misinterpretation of medical evidence or the application of medical theories that are vigorously contested within the medical community in findings of abuse and neglect against parents
- Mothers not being allowed to continue breastfeeding their babies upon confiscation – even under supervision, and even where the baby has been exclusively breastfed and is therefore not accustomed to bottle feeds
- No attention being given to helping infants and young children adjust to their new environment in state care by allowing parents to spend time with them and care for them under supervision

Authoritarianism

Here is an excerpt from an article written by father-of-four, physician and musician Dr Chris Prunean in December 2015 under the subheading "Go nuclear, investigate later":[iii]

> NCWS has been billed as a progressive organisation that ultimately knows best what is best for children. But this monster is an anti-family bully in the business of destroying families.
>
> It is a feared organisation that has gone unchecked. People are afraid to come out and support victims of NCWS because of the looming implicit threat that their own children will be snatched away in return. A Romanian pastor living in Norway expressed his reluctance to sign petitions and take to the streets because his seven-year-old might be confiscated. The Czech president has gone as far as to label NCWS as a "Nazi organization"... The Nazis snatched away the Jews. Barnevernet snatches away children.

In recent years, NCWS' purpose has changed from helping families to becoming family controllers, or 'family police'. As a result, it is now a powerful machine with the authority to implement serious action against families, especially those in vulnerable and difficult situations.

Dr Jørn Eikemo, a medical doctor in Oslo, stated the following:[iv]

> I can only confirm the dreadful story of the Romanian Bodnariu family with similar, horrible cases I myself handle as a medical doctor in Norway. NCWS is in many ways a fascistic official government organisation one could compare to Hitler's '*Jugend* organisations', only in Norway with a communistic ideology. NCWS hates families, and men in particular. And, they see the mother and father of the child almost as an enemy, with a bad influence over the child. It is a terrible situation where children are kidnapped from their parents without law and order. Please come and help us. The authorities in Norway will never admit to or change anything without pressure from abroad.

Berit Aarset, a Norwegian nurse, mother of an adopted foster child, grandmother and leader of Human Rights Alert – Norway (HRA-N) and author of *Maktovergrep og Justismord* ("*Abuse of Power and the Miscarriage of Justice*") observed:[v]

> The authorities and its system defenders will always defend the decision to take children away from the Bodnariu family and others alike. The Norwegian authorities cannot be told, and are convinced that everything they do is excellent, and that every country should follow their lead. Tragically, this is the reality of the situation in Norway. The Bodnariu case represents thousands of other similar cases where children are taken away from their families for purely ideologically driven and trivial reasons. If the authorities admit that a great injustice was done to the Bodnariu family, which it clearly was, then thousands of other cases could be reopened as well, and the image of Norway would sink in the sand. NCWS, the self-proclaimed number one image of Norway, is like a god, and for many it is worth dying for before the truth is allowed to see the light of day.

In her article, "Barnevernet has become the family controller", Thune explains that the messages of concern NCWS receives about children or parents from members of the public are often related to very trivial matters. Although NCWS has the potential to help people who are in need, she believes it creates more problems than it solves in many cases.

According to Thune, the notes preschool employees make are very often inadequate and full of errors, therefore giving a wildly inaccurate picture of the child's home life. Staff are simply not qualified to question children about their home care situations. She writes (text translated):[vi]

> A message of concern from a preschool provides open access to a family. NCWS can call them, visit them and demand that they come to the office. They can talk to children and parents separately. They have a free pass into the family's life.
>
> The 'interrogations' are often initiated with a number of leading questions, and the children feel compelled to answer in some way to satisfy the caregivers in the preschool, and then the imagination is fuelled. Often what the children are talking about is also misinterpreted. This can have disastrous consequences for the child and the family.

During the Bodnariu scandal, when four children and a baby were unfairly taken away from their parents, we heard time and time again from the Norwegian authorities that the worldwide demonstrations against Norway were based on a cultural misunderstanding.

Has the rest of the world misunderstood Norway's cultural traditions? That is certainly possible. The question is, are we talking about different cultural norms from country to country, or are we missing something that explains the situation more accurately? Can a country's unique norms and standards justify such an abuse of power, the daily violation of human rights and the targeting of family groups that don't quite live up to the Norwegian standard?

Aldous Huxley warned the world through his classic book *Brave New World* of a society that relies on economic security; one that venerates state-proclaimed 'experts' and is totally controlled by bureaucracy, actively discouraging individualism and encouraging collectivism in its place.

These foundational concepts have led to the worship of the Norwegian state and its image at all costs, and particularly at the cost of children and families. Did Huxley accurately predict a modern-day Norway populated by 'slaves of servitude'?

Huxley's *Brave New World* and Orwell's *Nineteen Eighty-Four* paint a very bleak picture of the future. Orwell wrote about a tyrannical rule forced on a population, and many families in Norway have experienced and are still experiencing a reign of terror against them at the hands of NCWS. Huxley visualised a world in which most of the population became slaves to the state in a completely hedonistic society. He also wrote about a new form of totalitarianism that did not resemble the communist dictatorships of old. A totalitarian state that uses firing squads is obviously inhumane, while this new form is just as barbaric, only in a way that is subtler and more difficult to prove.

The foundations that have been established through the veneration of 'experts' and a lust for pseudoscientific theories (for example those of Kari Killén, who we will come across later in the book), which have propelled Norway away from the biological principle (the inherent connection between a parent and child) and into a dangerous place that is causing great distress for tens of thousands of families every year.

There is no denying that most Norwegians love servitude and enjoy the economic security that comes with it. The question is, what price will they have to pay for their love of servitude? Will it come at the cost of truth? At the cost of good families being completely destroyed?

Over the last forty years or so the indoctrination of its population via media outlets, public institutions and the education system have given the Norwegian authorities very effective control over their population.

Ádám Szabados, a Christian pastor in Hungary, made a valid point that may move us closer to understanding the real reason why so many children are taken away from normal and functional families in Norway. In a televised discussion in Norway during the Bodnariu abduction, Peter Saunders, Ádám Szabados, Terje Gilje, Einar C Salvesen and Paul Susman discussed family life and the Norwegian state. Szabados said:[vii]

> Why is it that many, many people around the world feel very deeply about this? I think the answer is that we are dealing with something here that is fundamentally wrong; something that is evil at a very fundamental level.

Why has Norway become such a frightening place for so many families? The Norwegian approach is authoritarian in the sense that it demands that parents fit within its utopian model as a means of reaching its own ideological goals. Norway demands not only obedience from its population, but a conversion to its ideology. When NCWS encourages parents to lie (for example, when a parent is told to make something up about their spouse and agree to divorce them), they are often promised that everything will work out for the best and that they will get their children back if they comply. Rarely are these promises fulfilled.

One example of this can be seen in the case of the Bodnariu family, according to an article written by Prunean titled "More Dishonesty from Barnevernet in Bodnariu Case".[viii] During their arrest and interview, Marius and Ruth were repeatedly threatened and coerced into saying and doing unethical things, and to admitting to things they had never said or done. In fact, two NCWS social workers tried to coerce Ruth into saying that Marius was a violent man, which was untrue. They promised that if she testified to this and divorced Marius the five children would be returned to her.

Parents are expected to think that the 'truths' and ideologies presented by NCWS will benefit them; that the only way forward for society is to blindly accept its belief systems. It is not enough to simply *obey* the ideology; citizens must wholeheartedly *believe* in it.

Berit Aarset of Human Rights Alert – Norway writes:[ix]

> Norwegian authorities have built up an image abroad that human rights (ECHR and UN conventions) are respected here in Norway. They have managed this by acting as peacemakers, fighting for human rights in other countries, investing millions in social welfare programmes (in reality, social order programmes) around the world, and awarding the Nobel Peace prize annually. At the same time,

> Norwegian authorities are causing children and families great harm through the way the child welfare system works in Norway. From the hundreds of cases we have witnessed, one characteristic is that everyone is expected to report everyone else to NCWS for the slightest of 'misdemeanours'. This is very similar to how the Stasi operated in East Germany between 1949 and 1990.

Those who buy into NCWS' ideology often attack those in the community who don't, such as the minority of lawyers, barristers, doctors, judges, writers and other professionals who stand up for the genuine rights of children and the family. Those who religiously follow this ideology hate the fact that others may have a different opinion, or a better, more creative way of doing things.

Does Norway's population have the right to hold a different opinion? Those who persist in disagreeing with NCWS' ideology may have their reputations smeared, or may be forced out of their usual social circles. Some may even lose their jobs. Can this really just be a 'cultural misunderstanding'?

From joy to hell

In 2016, Australian television network SBS broadcast a *Dateline* documentary called *Norway's Stolen Children?* In it, Natasha and Erik Olsen, who had their twins taken away from them at birth, were interviewed by investigative reporter Georgina Davies. Below is the transcript:[x]

> **Narrator:** Norway has a dark secret that's tearing families apart. In this progressive, wholesome country, hundreds of parents are fighting against the state – fighting for the right to raise their own children. I'm on my way to meet a couple whose battle with this country's child protection services has changed their lives forever. Their babies were taken just hours after they were born.
>
> **Natasha Myra Olsen (mother):** We'd been so looking forward to seeing these girls for so many months.
>
> **Narrator:** Natasha was due to give birth to twins.

Natasha Myra Olsen: We sang to them, we talked to them…

Narrator: Erik was about to become a new father. It was going to be one of the happiest days of their lives.

Natasha Myra Olsen: We had seen them on ultrasound. I felt all the movements in my tummy.

Narrator: But they were robbed of everything they had looked forward to when Norway's child protection service, known as Barnevernet, showed up at the hospital.

Erik Myra Olsen (father): After the girls arrived, we had a very nice time with them at the hospital for about four hours before Barnevernet came and took them away. And from there it turned to hell.

Natasha Myra Olsen: The hardest thing was coming home empty-handed after all the pain. It's a sadness and a sense of loss that no one can understand.

Narrator: So what reason did Barnevernet give for taking away the baby girls?

Natasha Myra Olsen: Barnevernet told me that I had been diagnosed as mentally disabled, and that I could not take care of the children.

Narrator: When Natasha was 13, her adoptive mother claimed she had a mental disability to get welfare payments. Barnevernet then used this fraudulent document against her.

Natasha Myra Olsen: At first, I was very sad that they used this… that they used this as a reason to take my girls, because that is absolutely not what I was like.

Narrator: The twins, only hours into the world, were placed in foster care. The plan for them was permanent adoption. Natasha was determined to rewrite the past. She set about proving she was a capable mother with the help of lawyer Astrid Gjoystdal.

Natasha Myra Olsen: We've lost so many months with the girls, and this first year of their lives is extremely important.

Erik Myra Olsen: The girls were kidnapped. Barnevernet should apologise. It's common courtesy to admit your mistake when everyone knows something is wrong.

Narrator: As I prepare to head home, I discover that the day after my interview with Natasha and Erik they went into hiding. They have now fled the country with their twins and are all over the news in Norway.

News report: Over the past few weeks the local police have conducted a comprehensive investigation. They have been looking for nine-month-old twins and their parents.

Narrator: They suspected Barnevernet was building a case against their parenting skills. They were afraid of losing their twins for a second time, so they are claiming asylum in Poland. They sent me this footage and told me the twins are happy and doing well. Poland is protecting them, but they are also wanted by Norwegian police for kidnapping their own children.

The story of Erik and Natasha is unusual; not all cases are this dramatic. But Barnevernet has announced a review of 200 cases to see what they can learn and improve on. Those who have been involved in these cases first-hand are worried that Norway will one day look back with shame.

Possible racist motives

Samson Dejene's three children were taken away by NCWS in 2014. Samson believes the fact that he originally hails from Ethiopia played a part in their removal. He has spent most of his life in Oslo serving as a social worker and even working for NCWS. The following transcript is part of the same SBS *Dateline* documentary:

Reporter: So this is where you live?

Samson de Jene, (father): Yes. This is my house, and I have been living here for four months.

Narrator: Samson's originally from Ethiopia, but Oslo has been home for most of his life. He moved into this small bedsit to save money so he can keep fighting through the courts to win his kids back.

His kids were taken away two years ago. Like most cases it's not a simple story, but Samson feels at the centre of his battle is racism.

Samson de Jene: But unfortunately, there [are] people who misuse their power and who don't have enough knowledge of other cultures, other people, who are very judgemental. This is very, very sad.

Narrator: He became the main carer for his kids when his marriage broke down. But when the kids were living with their mum temporarily, Barnevernet turned up and took them away.

Samson de Jene: The reason they have given is that the kids need help and the situation for the kids they are living in is not good enough. That's the reason they have given me and that's why they had to take them from their mum. But they haven't given me any reason why they didn't consider me for the full-time custody of the kids. When I see kids on the street, when I hear, especially when kids say "Papa", then it's like something struck my heart. Everything reminds me of my kids, yes.

Narrator: Samson's educated, Christian and has a good job as a social worker. In fact, he used to work for Barnevernet. But he's having a hard time convincing them that he's a good parent, because of something his daughter said. She told her new foster family that her parents had spanked her at home.

Samson de Jene: The mum has admitted that she has slapped on the bottom. But in my case I have never slapped them. Never. My background plays a big matter, when it comes to violence, because automatically when a person is from Africa it's very common that people think that, oh, these people spank their kids. But that's not the case.

Killing the family

In an online article published by ABC Nyheter titled "We need to discuss what constitutes good care", Norwegian lawyer Thea Totland argues that Barnevernet's microanalysis of parental care results in erroneous psychological reports and recommendations that often become the deciding factor in whether a parent can keep their children or not.

As general manager of the Children's Rights Foundation (CRF), Totland insists that a child welfare debate should be set up, given that she and other professionals are witnessing serious mistakes that are having catastrophic consequences for children and their parents. They have observed psychologists emphasising details such as eye contact and perceived attachment issues between the parent and child, but argue that this strategy has been implemented without any official discussion.

Totland observes that the court often places more emphasis on the supposed experts' conclusions than on those from other professionals, even if the other professionals have much more experience with the family (text translated):[xi]

> If the preschool, healthcare and psychiatric nurses who have had contact with the family for the last two years say, "Yes, it's lacking, but the overall situation is OK", we cannot go in and pick up children due to bad eye contact. Unfortunately, it's happening today.

According to Totland, it's unrealistic to expect all parents to offer their children the same type of care:

> It is impossible to implement. An anonymous tip from someone who dislikes you means that child welfare can intervene and find something that could indicate the emotional care given is not good enough.

In Totland's opinion, when emotional care from the parents is insufficient, it may be better for the child to remain with their parents, siblings, extended family and friends, and in the school and local community – possibly with support from child welfare – rather than taking children away from their parents.

She highlights the high risk of misinterpretation in using this microanalysis alongside an unclear intervention threshold and a lack of professional scrutiny. Totland notes that child welfare is a very difficult field to work in, and that it some areas it works well, but she adds that it is very unpredictable, and that Barnevernet's reputation is a problem.

> It's a shame because it means people who have a real concern and people who really need help do not dare to report or ask for help. It may be vital for some children that the reporting process is working.

Totland concludes that ideal development cannot be guaranteed for all children, and that children who are removed from their families must receive a very high standard of help in the areas it is needed.

Meanwhile, in another ABC Nyheter article, expert psychologist Sverre Asmervik criticises NCWS for taking a boy away from his parents even though he was described as gentle, well-functioning, polite and kind, and was very popular with other children at the preschool.[xii] The parents had been described as "warm and loving" toward their two-year-old son by a preschool teacher who knew the family well. Asmervik notes that the boy's home was visited by an expert who found it to be very nice and reported that the parents gave the boy a lot of attention and good guidance. Asmervik believes this type of situation is "killing the family".

Chapter 4 notes

[i] Chaudhary, N., "Nightmare in Norway: How a mother lost her children to the State (and fought to get them back), Masala Chai: https://masalachaimusings.com/2018/02/02/nightmare-in-norway

[ii] Aiyar, S., "Humanitarian Crisis for Indian children and their families in confiscatory child care proceedings abroad": http://dokument.r-b-v.net/india/nhrc-petition-121012.pdf

[iii] Prunean, C., "Barnevernet is Ruining Norway's Reputation", Delight in Truth: https://delightintruth.com/2016/01/01/barnevernet-is-ruining-norways-reputation

[iv] Eikemo, J., "Dr Jørn Eikemo asks the International community for help", Step Up 4 Children's Rights: https://stepup4childrensrights.com/dr-jorn-eikemo-asks-the-international-community-for-help

[v] Aarset, B., "The Bodnariu case represents thousands of other similar cases", Step Up 4 Children's Rights: https://stepup4childrensrights.com/the-bodnariu-case-represents-thousands-of-other-similar-cases

[vi] Opheim, B., "Barnevernet er blitt familiekontrollører" ("The child welfare services have become family controllers"), Norges Kommentar Avis: http://www.kommentar-avisa.no/Artikler-Startside/Hovedoppslag-2018/Rettssak_mot_Midt-Agder_Barnevern-29.07.2018.pdf (originally featured in *Dagen*: http://www.dagen.no/Nyheter/barnevern/%E2%80%93-Barnevernet-er-blitt-familiekontroll%C3%B8rer-617494)

[vii] "Family Life and the State: The Case of the Bodnariu Family in Norway", Forum of Christian Leaders: https://youtu.be/Q9tC1d5Xg-M

[viii] Prunean, C., "More Dishonesty from Barnevernet in Bodnariu Case", Delight in Truth: https://delightintruth.com/2015/12/29/more-dishonesty-from-barnevernet-in-bodnariu-case

[ix] Aarset, B., "Norway's Stasi characteristics", Step Up 4 Children's

Rights: https://stepup4childrensrights.com/norways-stasi-characteristics

[x] Davies, G., Scott, C. and Tozer, J., "Norway's Stolen Children?" SBS Dateline: https://www.journeyman.tv/film_documents/6850/transcript

[xi] Brækhus, L. A., "Vi må diskutere hva som er god nok omsorg" ("We need to discuss what constitutes good care"), ABC Nyheter: https://www.abcnyheter.no/nyheter/2015/06/25/194407770/vi-ma-diskutere-hva-som-er-god-nok-omsorg

[xii] Brækhus, L. A., "Sakkyndige i barnevernssaker: Opprørende å se at denne typen arbeid blir gjort på en såpass dårlig måte" ("Specialists in child welfare cases: Outrageous to see that this type of work is done in such a bad way"), ABC Nyheter: https://www.abcnyheter.no/nyheter/2015/06/23/194407393/opprorende-se-denne-typen-arbeid-blir-gjort-pa-en-sapass-darlig-mate

5

Courageous

Billy Graham once said: “Courage is contagious. When a brave man takes a stand, the spines of others are often stiffened.”[i]

In 2016, Norwegian mother Cecilie Bedsvaag travelled to Romania, where she was given the chance to briefly tell her story.[ii] Cecilie also lent her support to the campaign for the release of the Bodnariu children, reminding the international community that the Bodnariu tragedy was in no way unique.

In an article that appeared on the Delight in Truth website, Cecilie Bedsvaag states:[iii]

> I can testify that everything said about Barnevernet is how it is in Norway today. Barnevernet is an evil organisation that removes children permanently from good parents.
>
> It has been eleven years since the first time I came into contact with this demonic institution. On February 21, 2005, my mother reported me to *Vinderen barneverntjeneste* [Barnevernet]. It was her birthday. Only a few days before I had given her a portrait of my beautiful daughter, five months old, as a birthday present. She betrayed me, and in the meeting with the social workers told the most disgusting lies.
>
> I got a telephone call the next day. The social workers were on their way to my house. They were coming in a taxicab. I was devastated, and when they read me the notice of concern aloud I started to cry. Of course, this was taken as proof of mental instability by the two imbeciles from Barnevernet.

My case was finally dismissed eight months later that year, after I had endured two so-called investigations.

Barnevernet left my family alone for almost two years when my mother decided to report me for sexually abusing my daughter. This time my daughter was taken to an emergency shelter where she stayed for two months. **I won in the county board** (*fylkesnemnda*) and got her back.

Barnevernet persevered and a new trial was scheduled in January 2008. **Again, I won.** However, I was pressured into having my daughter examined, which I did. Nothing was wrong with her. She had an intelligence well above average. But Barnevernet was not satisfied. My mother continued sending false notices of concern, and in October that year I lost 2-3 in the county board.

Next, I was pressured by the judge to have a psychological examination. One clinical psychologist and one psychiatrist were appointed. I did not accept the psychologist, who was infamous for always siding with Barnevernet. She was biased. The psychiatrist was a communist who had bought himself surrogate twins from India. He was going to raise the children alone, without a mother.

The judge tricked me into coming to Oslo after she had disclosed the report to Barnevernet, and my daughter was confiscated without a court decision. The trial lasted four days and took place behind closed doors. **I was not represented by a lawyer. Barnevernet's witnesses were mostly anonymous.** Their identity was not disclosed to me. During the trial the judge kept laughing. It was a trivial case for her. "*En sånn barnevernsak*" ["such a child welfare case"] she said the first time I met her.

It was only three weeks since my daughter had been taken away from me, and I was in psychological pain. Still they expected me to shake hands with the social worker who had taken my daughter. I did not, and the visitation was reduced from four to two hours every second month. I saw my daughter six times, then all visitation rights were denied.

Today my daughter lives in England with a surrogate family. The address has been secret for seven years and we are not allowed any direct contact. I send letters and gifts every month and Barnevernet reads my letters and opens the packages. My daughter is doing well at school and she is fine. She wrote me a letter telling me that she would like to speak with me. Barnevernet will not let us meet until she is eighteen years old.

They have also threatened me with forced adoption. I am treated like a criminal. The leader of Barnevernet keeps telling everyone that I have battered her. When I go to London on shopping trips Barnevernet alerts the UK police. All the female passengers on my flight on October 22, 2015, from Rygge in Norway had to show their passport to two waiting police officers at Stansted Airport because of Barnevernet's paranoia of kidnapping.

This is my story so far. I give my full support to the Bodnarius. I am not broken but fit for the fight, and I will continue to use my pen, not a sword, in the fair war against this tyranny.

So help me God.

The Norwegian Church

Courageous Christians and others who share Christian values are very much in the minority in Norway, but there certainly are some, and this is enough to offer the country a glimmer of hope.

To a certain extent, the silence from the Norwegian Church has been deafening. When church leaders do talk, some blindly support the authorities without any understanding or desire for knowledge of child welfare cases from the perspective of a child, parent or professionals who are supporting the family. Some have even gone on record stating that they are shocked at the suspicion, fear and false accusation levelled against NCWS. Other church leaders simply naively support the system, often going as far as to advise their members not to help families who have been targeted or victimised.

It's worth noting that many of these church organisations, who have most likely skipped over the Bible story of "The Good

Samaritan", are well subsidised by the Norwegian government. The vast majority of courageous Christians who stand up for victims of NCWS abuse do not, on the whole, receive state subsidies.

Family Defense Award

KKN's Pastor Torp is a man who exhibits love and authority, and is one of the few people in church leadership who hasn't succumbed to the lust for popularity and position. He has a heart for the family and, like anti-Nazi German pastor Dietrich Bonhoeffer, contends that Christians should not retreat from the world but be active within it.

According to the KKN website, Marius and Ruth Bodnariu and their five children were awarded the Family Defense Award on June 8, 2017.[iv] They received the award in recognition of the faith and love at the core of their family, and the way they handled this battle in such an exemplary way. It also recognised the extended Bodnariu family on both the Norwegian and Romanian side, which is spread across many nations and fought together with the family in Naustdal; as well as the tens of thousands of supporters worldwide who demonstrated against NCWS' wrongful intervention.

Marius and Ruth Bodnariu were not able to attend the award ceremony as they feared they would be arrested by Norwegian police after they had chosen not to attend their court hearing in January 2017, at which they were charged with alleged "family violence". They were represented by Norwegian and Romanian family members in their absence.

Romanian senators Titus Corlatean and Ben-Oni Ardelean spoke during the award ceremony. They also came to Norway to support the Bodnariu family during the heat of the battle in January 2016. Senator Corlatean is former Foreign and Justice Minister of Romania, while Senator Ardelean is Vice-President of the Chamber of Deputies in Romania's parliament. There were also contributions from victims and activists in the battle against NCWS. Addresses were given by leading politicians in Norway, and various nations were represented by their ambassadors.

In the same month, a seminar focusing on NCWS was held in central Oslo, at which Corlatean, Ardelean and various Norwegian leaders gave lectures. Representatives from NCWS were invited to express their views but chose not to attend.

Ten commandments

The prize the family received was named the Family Defense Award in honour of former MP Vice-Chairman of the Progress Party, John Alvheim, who chose to speak out against the dangers of NCWS even while he was chairman of parliament's Social Committee between 1997 and 2005. Torp writes:[v]

> John Alvheim (1930-2005) was chairman of the Norwegian Parliament's Social Committee between 1997 and 2005, and was undoubtedly regarded as the most trustworthy politician in Norway on social issues across party lines. He was particularly known for his defence of the elderly and his warnings against NCWS' abuses.
>
> After his death, Norwegian politicians chose to ignore his warnings against NCWS, which have become even more radical in ideology and methodology since 2012 thanks to the backing it has received in parliament. Solveig Horne opposed everything Alvheim stood for [even though she was representing the same party].
>
> Alvheim was a devout follower of Christ and I was privileged to work with him on several occasions with regard to family issues. Here are his 10 Commandments for those who are targeted by NCWS:

1. Shut up. Everything you say will be used against you.
2. Contact a lawyer immediately.
3. Get a psychologist, even if you are healthy. You might need it.
4. Don't accept help, it will create the impression that you can't take care of yourself.
5. Don't accept help from mothers' homes. That is not a relief institution, but a surveillance centre.
6. Demand an explanation in writing for all decisions you are exposed to.
7. Appeal against every decision.
8. Don't accept placements in foster homes. You won't get the child back.

9. Remember that when NCWS talks about relief measures they normally refer to taking over parental care, or surveillance.
10. If you need help, use friends or relatives – or manage yourself.

In another KKN article written in June 2017, Torp writes:[vi]

> At present, a record number of proceedings against the Kingdom of Norway concerning NCWS are ready to begin in the European Court of Human Rights (ECtHR) in Strasbourg. Twenty-one years ago, Norway was sentenced by the ECtHR in the case of Adele Johansen and her daughter Signe Malene. NCWS would not accept the sentence or listen to Carl August Fleischer, the country's leading expert on international law.
>
> "We must accept ECtHR," Fleischer said in court, where he was used as an expert witness. But NCWS always knows best.
>
> There are similarities between the former Soviet Union and today's NCWS, but its greatest influence can be found in the biological theories developed during the 1800s in Germany, which was a world leader in this field at the time. Theories such as 'behaviourism' and 'biological determinism' were developed and used to create the pseudosciences that are lumped together under the name 'psychology' today.
>
> Very few modern clinical psychologists are working on real science; the majority are carrying out personal assessments. Behaviourism was developed as a reaction against the 'biologism' of the 1800s, which was based on a flawed perception of what biology was. Behaviourism is more recent. The thread it shares with the old biologism is determinism. Leading biologists of the 1800s believed in simple determinism on the basis of biology, while behaviourists believed in simple determinism based on environment.
>
> Under the German biological determinism of the 1800s, thoughts were developed that fitted Nazism perfectly. Why were the Jews despised? One reason was that they moved

from place to place, yet the goal for Germany was a pure race. In Norway, this led to attempts to purge all travellers.

A concept that is widely used today in NCWS' assessment of parents' ability to parent is 'vagabonding': someone who moves around too much. NCWS often removes children from parents who, in the opinion of its employees, move around too much. Our church in Oslo is presently helping a family that is being harassed by NCWS for this very reason.

Out of the German ideology of the 1800s came the concept *blut und boden* ("blood and soil"), an ideological and political expression that became the slogan of German national socialistic propaganda before and after World War II. It laid the foundations for the ideology that repatriation, ethnic cleansing and purging were legitimate pursuits.

Prominent social worker and Doctor of Philosophy Kari Killén and many other Norwegian social workers have loaded the education system for NCWS workers with hostile family theories.

Among the uncontested hostile family textbooks that are ruling the ground in the education of NCWS workers are: Einar Aadland's *Etikk for helse- og sosialarbeidarar* (*Ethics for health and social workers*: Samlaget, 1998); Jan Storø's *Miljøarbeid i barnevernet: systematikk og refleksjon* (*Environmental work in child welfare*: Universitetsforlaget, 2010); and Øyvind Kvello's *Barn i risiko* (*Children at risk*: Gyldendal Akademisk, 2015). The list goes on.

These textbooks include instructions on how to take children away from their parents, and they are among the key reasons why there has been such a rapid increase in family takeovers in recent years. Inexperienced young people who are subjected to a three-year education before becoming child welfare officers have little chance of remaining objective when they face such one-sidedness and brainwashing.

The foster home industry is just that: an industry

Numerous cases have recently been presented in Norwegian media that demonstrate the existence of an extensive and well-financed foster home industry. There are some instances in which children have been given a better life with their new foster parents, but in many instances they have not, and their biological families have been ripped to pieces.

Many foster parents have been recruited to a task that occasionally gives necessary help but is quite often connected with flawed analysis on the part of immature NCWS workers who only know what they were taught by their pseudoscientific instructors. We believe many good people have been recruited as foster parents, and we need positive solutions when children are found to be victims of serious violence, genuine neglect, or extensive drug and alcohol usage.

John Alvheim and the "grand old man" of Norwegian politics, Carl I Hagen, had a fierce clash with NCWS when they presented a document challenging the agency in 1995. A debate took place before the parliamentary elections in September 1997, when another document which focused on restoring trust in child welfare during a crisis of confidence was put forward. They made their case well but were brushed aside by parliament.

It is a tragedy that twenty-three years have passed and the problems with NCWS have significantly increased. Enough is enough! NCWS must be totally reformed, and something completely new must be built from the ground up in defence of the family and children.

Norway's parental rights "down the rabbit hole"

Attorney Sorin Leahu's article, "Norway's Parental Rights Down the Rabbit Hole, America Next?", written when the Bodnariu children were still being held, reveals the dangers of Norway's destructive family ideologies, and the way these ideologies are spreading. He also suggests a better path and explains why the Church must lead in this area. Leahu writes:[vii]

> In 1865, Charles Lutwidge Dodgson, under the pseudonym Lewis Carroll, published his famous novel

Alice's Adventures in Wonderland. Readers then and now continue to be mystified by a narrative that can only be described as illogical and wholly irrational. The novel introduced readers to a world of such absurdity that it helped launch the phenomenon now known as the literary-nonsense genre.

Lately, another story has been unfolding rivalling even Carroll's work within the same genre. Our newsletter published a brief note on this case back in January. To review, in November 2015 a loving family was dragged down a legal rabbit hole and introduced to the whacky world of institutionalised kidnapping. NCWS seized Marius and Ruth Bodnariu's five children after suspicions that they were receiving "Christian indoctrination". "Christian indoctrination", of course, is a subjective term; most would recognise it simply as religious education. Not content with competing education, however, the state seized the five children and placed them with three separate foster homes where, presumably, they will receive state-sanctioned indoctrination instead. Without having committed a crime, and with no due process, two parents have lost their children. The parents must now overcome baseless charges and seek vindication in Norwegian courts, or alternatively, the European Court of Human Rights.

United States precedent

The family's prospects would be very different in the United States. Unlike Norway, the United States Supreme Court has for some time now recognised the rights of parents to raise their children as they see fit. One of the first major cases to address this issue came in 1925 when the Supreme Court decided a case called Pierce v. Society of Sisters. During this interwar period, several states become concerned with the influx of immigrants and the values they were imparting to their children. Sound familiar? As a result, citizens in Oregon passed the Compulsory Education Act, a law meant to enlist public schools in promoting American culture while simultaneously closing down parochial and private schools. All children between the ages of eight and sixteen, with some exceptions, were required to attend public school.

The Society of Sisters of the Holy Names and Hill Military Academy sued Oregon governor Walter Pierce, alleging, among other things, that the act violated the parents' rights to direct the education of their children. In a unanimous decision by Justice McReynolds, the Supreme Court agreed with the parents. The court rejected the state's arguments and held that:

> *A child is not the mere creature of the state; those who nurture him and direct his destiny have the right, coupled with the high duty, to recognise and prepare him for additional obligations.*

Among the best-known of Pierce's progeny is a case called Wisconsin v. Yoder. There, three Amish students refused to continue attending school after the eighth grade because it conflicted with their families' religious beliefs. The court again ruled against the state, holding that:

> *The history and culture of Western civilization reflect a strong tradition of parental concern for the nurture and upbringing of their children. This primary role of the parents in the upbringing of their children is now established beyond debate as an enduring American tradition.*

These cases and others like it have, for the most part, protected families in the US from what has transpired in Norway. Nevertheless, opponents continue to fight to reverse long-standing precedent.

United States precedent under attack

Legal attacks on Pierce and Yoder have come from various angles, but the most creative is the theory that the child has a right to an "open future". This right is said to trump the right of parents to raise their children. This right of autonomy, which children cannot exercise right away, is held in trust by the parents until children are old enough to make choices. It is argued that by removing children from public school, parents violate their children's right to an open future. Scandinavian countries have embraced this 'open future' to such extremes that schools in Sweden have instituted 'gender-neutral' classrooms. Teachers cannot refer to students using pronouns 'he' or 'she' because doing so would violate the child's right to an open future. After all, the child should decide for himself or herself whether he or she is a he or a she.

Other attacks come from the media. Take for instance MSNBC host Melissa-Harris Perry, who insisted that:

> *We have to break through our kind of private idea that kids belong to their parents, or kids belong to their families, and recognise that kids belong to whole communities.*

This notion that children belong to the state was specifically rejected by both Pierce and Yoder but continues to be a rallying cry for liberals in America. It stems from Karl Marx's utopian vision and must be repudiated at all cost.

The latest strategy is the state's idea of "partnership". If the state cannot claim ownership of your child, as much as it wants to, it will claim a 'partnership' interest with the parent. The Obama administration's Department of Education[5] has released its vision for education in several reports. In one report we learn that:

> *Research shows that initiatives that take on a partnership orientation – in which student achievement and school improvement are seen as a shared responsibility, relationships of trust and respect are established between home and school, and families and school staff see each other as* **equal partners** *– create the conditions for family engagement to flourish.* [emphasis added.]

5 This report was written while the Obama administration was in power.

"Equal partnership" entails equal responsibility, equal decision-making and equal authority. Needless to say, the report does not say what gives the state the right to claim such a partnership.

The path forward

The Bodnariu situation has affected all groups of people, but especially people of faith. What can people of faith do to prevent a similar happening in the US? There are several things, but I have highlighted four below:

1. Promote and defend limited government. The founders of this country envisioned a government with limited and enumerated powers. It was James Madison who said that an energetic government is always oppressive. All efforts to increase the power and size of government should be resisted.
2. Be an informed participant. Thomas Jefferson once wrote that an "educated citizenry is a vital requisite for our survival as a free people". Lack of knowledge leads to manipulation and bondage. The prophet Hosea records God's words, stating that: "My people are destroyed for lack of knowledge." More than being informed, Christians also have a responsibility to be involved. Not everyone is called to run for office, but Christians should be encouraged to attend school board meetings and town hall meetings, and to be active in local matters. At the very least, it means voting. Every election offers the opportunity to defend and promote life, family and religious liberty. Most elections also offer a choice between smaller government and bigger government.
3. Influence culture. One of the most important lessons I have learned is that "law is downstream from culture". This means that, for the most part, it is culture that influences law and not law that influences culture. Andrew Fletcher once wrote: "Let me write the songs of a nation, I care not who makes its laws." Fletcher is right to suggest that culture is a great influencer of nations. Those who influence culture influence nations and their respective laws. This means, among other things, that people of faith need to engage in the arts: film, painting, literature, music, architecture, etc. Withdrawal from society

is not only unbiblical but unwise. If the world ever needed Christian witness in culture it is now.

4. The Church must lead. The final point is the most important one. The ultimate problem is spiritual in nature. It is a problem of sin and unbelief. As important as the points above are, and they are important, the ultimate solution is one of spiritual renewal that only Christ can offer. The Church must reject false teaching within its ranks, seek the salvation of the unsaved and speak prophetically on the important issues of the day. Few people know that the American Revolution was preceded by a movement called the Great Awakening. Led by pastors such as Jonathan Edwards and George Whitefield, colonial America experienced great revival. Historians have noted that this evangelical movement contributed to the thinking of the founding fathers and led to the religious freedom we enjoy today. Churches must lead.

The present situation

Some progress has been made in the last couple weeks. Some media outlets in Norway have given attention to this case and have even expressed concern for the family. Most recently, the parents were finally allowed to meet with their five children at the same time in the same place. The three-hour visit was filled with mixed emotion, but it is a step in the right direction. The parents are to stand trial later this year.

I am still hopeful that a court, any court, will eventually vindicate the Bodnariu family. Perhaps their best chance is outside of Norway in the European Court of Human Rights. In the court of public opinion Norway is all but defeated. The large demonstrations have garnered attention from international media and Norway's reputation has been stained. Norway's image will continue to deteriorate so long as people make their voices heard. It is hard to comprehend that Norway would continue to trade its standing in the world for the ability to continue to harass families. The country prides itself as a beautiful place to live, but its totalitarian reality is becoming more lucid every day. Perhaps an excerpt from Carroll's novel best describes what Norway has become:

> *"But I don't want to go among mad people," Alice remarked.*
> *"Oh, you can't help that," said the Cat: "We're all mad here. I'm mad. You're mad."*
> *"How do you know I'm mad?" said Alice.*
> *"You must be," said the Cat, "or you wouldn't have come here."*

Echoes of communism

On April 16, 2016, as tens of thousands of people marched around the world in unity with the Bodnariu family, Dr Prunean had a very clear message for Norway. Below is a transcript of his speech:[viii]

> My name is Dr Chris Prunean. I am a Christian, a husband, a father of four children and a physician, and I am here to protest the cruel actions of NCWS and to call for the immediate reunification of the Bodnariu family and the other families whose children have been confiscated because of trivial matters.
>
> Listen to the heartbreaking testimony given by Marius and Ruth Bodnariu to the BBC:
>
> > *I was waiting for the girls to come home from school, I was waiting for the school bus... After ten to fifteen minutes when they didn't show up I started to get worried... I saw two black cars. In one of them was a child protection officer... She said I had to come to the police station for an interrogation... I was shocked and I said I was waiting for my girls... She answered that she had them... She insisted on taking the boys with her...*
> >
> > *The second day in the evening we saw two black cars again, and I remember I said: 'I think they brought the kids home...' But then I saw a policeman coming out of the car... And I told Marius: 'I think they are going to take the baby,' and there was nothing I could do..."*

Ladies and gentlemen, this sounds like a scene out of communist Romania, not modern-day Norway. This is a regular occurrence in Norway, where NCWS removes children from good families for trivial matters without a court order and without due process.

Because of this I am here to issue a challenge to the good people of Norway, especially the Christians of Norway, the majority of whom have been indifferent and silent with respect to the human rights violations perpetrated by NCWS.

Fellow Norwegian Christians who believe in God and the Bible as the Word of God, you live in a country where forty per cent of the population identifies itself as atheist, and less than five per cent attends church.

In such an arid spiritual environment you must rise up and fight injustice!

You must take a stand for the family!

Do not turn a blind eye when three-month-old Ezekiel is taken from his mum and his older siblings are secretly stolen at school in unmarked black cars!

Do not be indifferent when baby Aria is removed from her parents right after birth!

Norwegian Christians, do not remain silent when twins are confiscated from the hospital nursery after they are born under the pretext that the mum is not smart enough to care for them!

Norwegian Pentecostal leaders, why do you say that you do not want to comment on the Bodnariu case?

Why do you choose to remain silent when the Bodnariu family was harassed at school for singing Christian songs? Is it because the Church is financed by the government? Is it because Norway has a fund of $840 million allocated to churches?

Remember the words of Psalm 82:3: "Give justice to the poor and the orphan; uphold the rights of the oppressed and the destitute."

Norway, you used to be a beacon of hope in Europe. A beacon for human rights.

In 1965, a group of Norwegian Christians ransomed pastor Richard Wurmbrand when he was dying in a communist prison in Romania. They bought him for the price of $10,000 ($80,000 in today's money). This was five times the amount normally paid for the average political prisoner. Because of that, Richard Wurmbrand had the opportunity to expose the gross human rights violations happening under communism when he testified in front of the US Congress.

But now, only fifty years later, we have a reversal of roles. It is Norway that violates human rights and due process. It is Norway that destroys families based on trivial reasons.

Norwegian Christians, please hold your government accountable for what it has done to the Bodnariu family and the other families.

An NCWS psychological evaluation was conducted on the Bodnariu parents and the report gave them positive and favourable marks. Despite this, four Bodnariu children remain confiscated.

Now, after intense international protest, Norway has returned baby Ezekiel to the family. But it is not right to return just one child. **All children must be returned.**

If Norway thinks the family is safe for baby Ezekiel (and we know it has always been safe), then the other four children must be returned immediately!

To the shame of Norway, our protests will continue, and our campaign will intensify.

We will not give up, we will not tire, and we will not stop until the Bodnariu children are returned home and NCWS is reformed!

Thank you all for coming. Thank you for bringing your children. They will never forget this event. Thank you to the media that came out to cover this protest.

Evil acts

Another Christian family had all three of their children unjustly removed from them by NCWS. Samuel Svalland (now twenty-three), the eldest son of Dung and Harald Svalland, was eventually released after spending almost five years away from his family. Samuel has lived at home with his loving and caring parents for the last five years. His brother and sister have still not been returned, and may already have been brainwashed by the system.

Samuel provided the following comment for inclusion in this book:

> As long as there is money in the system it will continue with these evil acts, because people don't have any conscience as long as they get some money (or a lot of money) for lying and not really doing any work. I wish there would be no more NCWS. The state should not come and destroy families.

Trine Overå Hansen appears to agree. A journalist for *Norge Idag* (a Christian newspaper published in Bergen), and a TV host for Visjon Norge (Vision Norway, a Christian TV channel), she writes (text translated):[ix]

> When we think about asylum seekers we usually think of people from Africa and the Far East escaping to Norway and other Western countries, where peace and justice are in place. Ever since World War II, citizens have apparently been able to live safely in Norway, and the thought of refugees fleeing Norway has been unthinkable. But lately there has been a change in this situation.
>
> Several families have had to flee to other countries that are often economically inferior to Norway because they fear the greatest violation of one's rights: being deprived of their own children.
>
> Child welfare in Norway is a system that seems to have grown beyond its borders. What was originally intended as a protection for the weakest has now become the opposite, and a threat to the family's legal certainty.
>
> How could this happen? The main problem is the disproportionate power accorded to the players in this system. Poorly educated child welfare workers, often from resource-poor units with few employees, have the authority to make decisions that extend as far into their privacy as

the Court of Appeal can do in a criminal case, for example. All legal principles are threatened by such a system. It is completely arbitrary as to whether legal certainty is ensured for parents and children in each local authority.

In addition, confidentiality and shame are also employed, which allows crimes against family protection to take place in silence without most people understanding what is really happening.

The purpose of child welfare was to uncover those who could not take care of themselves, or those who abuse their children. But now child welfare has taken on the role of evaluating the quality of the parents' parenting skills. We know of many horror stories where eye contact and the thickness of bread slices have been used as an argument when child welfare services write their reports. Parents may also be accused of being too eager to interpret the child or, on the other hand, not eager enough. It is sometimes like a Kafka process. What you say and do does not matter. All you know is that you are accused, and everything you say and do can and will be used against you.

It may look like the agenda in many cases is to reveal as many errors as possible, and if they do not find anything they can construct stories, such as the mother's psychological issues, which are widely used.

NRK [a state-owned TV and radio network] recently ran a report on the child welfare office in Steigen, which had removed nineteen children from their families in this small municipality. The agency's extensive intervention has meant that children and adults alike fear it may be them the next time. Children have been picked up at school without the parents being notified and sent miles away to a foreign place. Just along a six-kilometre stretch of road in this local authority, nine children have been taken away from different families.

> *"I've heard of kids who can't get to sleep and eventually come screaming downstairs to their parents in the evening. They do not dare to sleep because they are*

> *afraid that child welfare will come and pick them up. And if they hear a strange car in the yard they throw up," says a father from Steigen.*

At this time, several families are seeking refuge overseas for protection. Natasha and Erik appeared on TV2 and told their story of how they fled to Poland to avoid their twins being taken for a second time. In addition, we know that children have been sent to other countries where families have different citizenships, so they choose a country outside Norway to avoid the child welfare system. And now the last example: Norwegian Silje Garmo has applied for asylum in Poland after she left a parent/children's centre with her daughter.

It is shameful for Norway that a Norwegian citizen feels forced to travel abroad in order to live safely with her child. Norway, which is always teaching others about democracy and state-building, cannot even give its own citizens the most fundamental rights of freedom and security. Garmo has been granted asylum in Poland after the Polish authorities concluded that Norway has committed violations against human rights, including EMC Article 6 on the right to a fair trial. It has painted Norway's reputation in a poor light in Europe, not least in conjunction with all the lawsuits against the Norwegian child welfare office from the European Court of Human Rights. It will be interesting to see the developments.

Will Norway address the problems, or will we see more Norwegians fleeing the country in the future?

Chapter 5 notes

[i] Graham, B., "A Time for Moral Courage", *Reader's Digest* Vol. 85, No. 507 (Chappaqua, NY: 1964).

[ii] "The testimony of a Norwegian [Cecilie Bedsvaag] about a case similar to the Bodnariu family": https://www.youtube.com/watch?v=xccFxaNSD_o&sns=fb

[iii] Prunean, C., "Barnevernet Terror: Romanian-Norwegian Child Abusively and Permanently Confiscated", Delight in Truth: http://delightintruth.com/2016/02/15/barnevernet-terror-romanian-norwegian-child-abusively-and-permanently-confiscated

[iv] Torp, J.-A., "Family Defense Award given to the Bodnariu family, Christian Coalition World: 1421773, Christian Coalition World: https://christiancoalition.world/news/read2/article/1421773

[v] Torp, J.-A., John Alvheim's 10 Commandments for those that are targeted by Barnevernet, Pastor Torp: https://pastortorp.wordpress.com/2016/07/27/john-alvheims-10-commandments-for-those-that-are-targeted-by-barnevernet

[vi] Torp, J.-A., "Historical celebration - but a sharp clash with 'Barnevernet'", Christian Coalition World: https://christiancoalition.world/kkn-speaks/read3/clash-barnevernet

[vii] Leahu, S., "Norway's Parental Rights Down the Rabbit Hole, America Next?", Mauck & Baker: http://mauckbaker.com/norways-parental-rights-down-the-rabbit-hole-america-next

[viii] Prunean, C., "Dr. Chris Prunean's Message to Norway on April 16th, 2016", Delight in Truth: https://delightintruth.com/2016/04/17/dr-chris-pruneans-message-to-norway-on-april-16th-2016

[ix] Hansen, T. O., "En skamplett for Norge" ("A disgrace for Norway"), *Norge Idag*: http://idag.no/index.php?page=vis_nyhet&NyhetID=28503

6

Accused

It was so strange to find myself in a cell and I just remember being so scared... The walls were coming closer and closer, and it was becoming so difficult to breathe... At one point I was thinking if I was mad; if I had in my madness been doing things I wasn't supposed to do. Had I harmed my family without really knowing it?

These words were spoken by Inez Arnesen in a BBC documentary broadcast in August 2018.[i] Inez and Knut Arnesen had eight children, four of whom were taken into 'care' by NCWS based on unsubstantiated allegations of violence on the part of the mother. The case, which involved a now-disgraced NCWS 'expert', provoked an international reaction.[6]

Victoria Holmen, the family's lawyer, highlights what many other Norwegian lawyers have also discovered in similar child welfare cases. According to Holmen, every question asked of the children was a leading question, and when the reports were analysed there was no mention of a child saying that their mother had been violent against them. Holmen claims in the documentary that:

---

6 In 2018, a specialist child psychiatrist in Norway who adopted two children from India, was convicted for having downloaded 200,000 pornographic photos of children, including videos with a total duration of 4,000 hours. He admitted to using the photos for his personal pleasure. He had practised as a child psychiatrist for twenty years, including special assignments as an 'expert' for NCWS. In this role, he was also given a leading position by the Norwegian authorities to investigate sexual abuse in children, as well as being a very influential figure when it came to supporting the confiscation of children from their parents.

> They had already formed their opinion of what this case was about. And then they questioned the children so that they would have the answer that would match their opinions.

After a long battle, which generated a significant amount of publicity, the last two boys were returned to the Arnesen family in August 2018.[ii]

Being accused of something you haven't done, or of being someone you are not, can cut very deeply at the best of times. However, when false accusations, systematic manipulation, half-truths, lies, false promises and constructed stories are put forth by NCWS with the main goal of steering a case toward a care order for a child, not only does this cut deeply, but the long-term trauma and devastation for the parents, their children and the extended family are unimaginable.

Anonymous reporting was one of the most common criticisms presented by those who opposed the Spanish Inquisition, for example at the Cortes of Castile and León in 1518. It wasn't uncommon at this time for false denunciations to be made, as envy, jealousy and rivalry were often lumped in with genuine concern.

Denunciations are anonymous in Norway, and those targeted have no legal way of uncovering the identities of their accusers. Families have been anonymously denounced for a variety of reasons including the above, along with revenge (from a bitter ex-spouse, for example), racist motives and the loathing, in some quarters, of anyone who looks as though they are getting ahead (financially, in gaining awards or through a job promotion, for example).

Helper or enemy?

Aarset's book, *Abuse of Power and the Miscarriage of Justice*, reveals how NCWS commonly builds cases and exposes its working methods, which are often very abusive toward families.[iii] The book shows how NCWS uses divide and conquer techniques in relation to a mother and her parents (the child under investigation's grandparents), and how the agency hides behind the thick fog of a confidentiality clause, using its 'best interests of the child' mantra. It also exposes the fraud, lies, pressure and betrayal used to force a mother and her child into a 'mothers' home' (parent-child centre), informally known as 'horror homes for mothers' in ever-growing circles.

According to the book, NCWS coerced one mother, eighteen-year-old Rita and her one-year-old baby into living at Trastalia Mothers' Home, telling her the purpose of the stay was for recreation and the strengthening of the mother's role; a role everyone, including NCWS, had previously claimed she was handling well. The family was also informed that a 'happy story' like that of Rita and her baby girl was needed at the mothers' home. Then came the promise: "There are a few sad stories here from time to time, but with you and your little girl things will work out fine."

After just seven days at the home, and following NCWS' discovery that Rita had appointed a lawyer, the mothers' home wrote a report that stated: "We consider that the mother's care for her baby is lacking, and in the long term we will not be able to strengthen the mother's parental skills enough to be good enough for her child." NCWS suddenly arrived and demanded that Rita participate in a meeting. Rita found herself alone with nine women aged between forty and sixty as the shocking report was read out, and the NCWS staff informed her that they were very disappointed in her. NCWS then issued an emergency decision to take over the care of the child. They told her to leave the mothers' home with the two social workers who were there. These events took place despite the fact that NCWS had said it would help Rita.

The agency took the baby away in January 2006, just a month before her one-year-old healthcare consultation. The child was placed in an emergency home, then moved to a foster home. Rita was left distraught, and was forced to live with the label of "unfit mother". This happened in spite of the fact that Rita had proven herself capable of loving and taking care of her daughter. The midwife, the nurse at the healthcare centre and the physician had found no reason to report her or her baby to NCWS. In fact, they found her to be a very capable mother, and saw a child who was developing ahead of most babies her age.

Despite this, NCWS appeared to have its own agenda. Even before the baby was born the agency seemed to have decided to create a case for this family; a case it was determined to win at any cost. The justification for this removal was its knowledge of Rita's learning difficulties and the sexual abuse she had been exposed to as a fourteen-year-old. But everyone who knew Rita was very happy about her positive emotional recovery and the stable love and care she was giving her baby.

Around a year after the baby was removed she showed signs of neglect during the check-ups she underwent while in 'care'. There were also suggestions of comprehensive mourning due to the separation from her mother and the shock of being left with strangers.

This case featured in Aarset's book is very similar to many others in Norway, where a single mother who is not highly educated is targeted. A witch hunt ensues, with NCWS and its helpers twisting everything into the most negative terms. Aarset provided the following questioning comment for inclusion in this book:

> Is it not child abuse when Barnevernet lies about the parents and their life situation just so they are able to place children in foster homes? What juridical rights do children in Norway have in all of this? What juridical rights do the parents and the children have in Norway? Is this how we want it to be?

Rita's grandmother was a Sámi[7] who had fled from the county of Finnmark during World War II and married a Tater. It should also be noted that Rita had been taken away from her biological mother for the exact same falsified reasons NCWS used to take her own baby away. On May 18, 1988, Rita's own mother had ended her life at the age of twenty-one. She had ended her life because of the brutal treatment she had received at the hands of NCWS. It is often said that "once in child welfare, always in child welfare". It is like a branding, and it often creates a cycle of misery that runs from generation to generation.

Aarset wrote her book in a desperate attempt to expose the injustice inflicted on this baby, and on her parents and grandparents, hoping that one day she would come home to her true mother. The author also hopes the book will help to prevent continued and systematic injustice toward families in Norway in the future.

---

7 The Sámi people are reindeer shepherds, a nomadic people living chiefly in Northern Scandinavia and the Kola Peninsula of Russia.

A Kafkaesque approach

Norwegian biologist Dr Åge Simonsen works in nature conservation. He has served on a local authority committee in Bergen monitoring cases prepared by NCWS, and has written a number of articles on the topic of child welfare. The following commentary serves as a stark reminder of a system that is out of control. Simonsen writes:[iv]

> In 1996, Norway was found to have violated human rights in a case concerning a child taken from her mother right after the birth in 1989. The European Court of Human Rights (ECtHR) decided that NCWS had committed a grave injustice to the mother. She then hoped that she would at least be given the right to meet her daughter and have contact with her. The foster parents, however, wished to adopt the child, and were upheld in the Norwegian court system following the ECtHR verdict in Strasbourg.
>
> Many are surprised by the violations of human rights in Norway. It is hard to understand that a country known for humanity and democracy acts in inhuman ways towards its own citizens. However, Norway is a society with a focus on equality. A welfare state has been created, which aims to eradicate differences and socially divisive lines. In the wake of this initially positive process, an ideology has developed with scant place for deviation and a demand for uniformity allowing little room for being different. The authorities tend to define as negative all circumstances departing from a defined, allegedly optimal, mean. This attitude shows clearly in the child protection system, where everything deviating from a textbook standard is counted as potentially harmful to children.
>
> Such extreme idealisation of equality often singles out newcomers to our country, who grew up and have their roots in something other than Norwegian culture. Foreigners are furthermore even less able to defend themselves against attacks from the authorities than the rest of the population. The attention of NCWS authorities is not only focused on how adults raise and treat their children, but equally

on parents' general appearance, behaviour and reactions. Such characteristics are different in foreigners from what they tend to be in Norwegian-born subjects indoctrinated through the school system and taught to fit in with more or less firm conceptions of normal and accepted conduct in Norwegian society. Research surveys show that in 75 per cent of NCWS cases, problems and behaviour which NCWS claims the parents have are given as the cause for taking small children into care. Only six per cent of the cases were based on the children's problems.

CWS investigations

If the authorities get the idea that something is not normal in a family (in the sense of 'normal' described above), NCWS starts an investigation into the family. The parents' personalities are measured relative to the norm.

The psychiatric conceptual framework utilised is of a kind that can easily consign most people to some pathological category. This is especially so if the subject is temporarily out of balance because he or she feels abused by the authorities. As the Swedish professor of psychology Lennart Sjöberg has demonstrated, people in such circumstances will often show feelings that lead psychologists to diagnose them as "borderline" or "paranoid". Such diagnoses in turn lead NCWS to conclude that the parents' ability to care for their offspring is too weak and that the children must be removed from them. Investigators for NCWS consistently look only for negative qualities in parents. Positive resources are not considered. If they are discovered at all, they are often explained away. Thus, one report about a mother said: "Because of her good intellectual functioning and good verbal skills, it is our opinion that her functioning may have been assessed as better than it really is."

Risk indicators

The method often used consists of describing parents' background, personality and relationship to their children in terms of a series of so-called strain indicators or risk indicators, such as immaturity, psychological problems, psychosis, mental retardation, alcohol and drug abuse, and other possible deficiencies and departures from the norm. The lives of the parents are analysed into categories. Along with several other factors, complications such as pelvic distortion in pregnancy and deformities in the child are counted as risk indicators for later failure to care for the child.

External risk indicators comprise housing problems, economic problems, limited social networks and problems at work. The fact that these categories are included explains why single parents, recipients of disability benefits and immigrants are parent groups in special danger of being deprived of their children. They are among those with the weakest economic means and the least energy to take part in the life of their society and to be involved in societal concerns.

Parents' alleged self-esteem as an indicator is given great importance, in spite of the lack of scientific evidence for any correlation between self-esteem and child abuse. In California, the state administration had a research group investigate how important problems could be solved by "increasing the self-esteem of the population". This task force worked through 65,000 research articles in psychology dealing with self-esteem. The result was published in the book, The Social Importance of Self-Esteem, in 1989. The chapter dealing with child abuse and care failure concludes that there is no documentation for allegations of any connection between low self-esteem and child abuse. The team found no basis for claiming that higher self-esteem would reduce abuse and neglect of children. Nor was any connection found between low self-esteem and aggression or violence… Although several hundred studies surveyed showed no such correlations, our NCWS still claims that there is a clear correlation between failure to give care and low self-esteem, which therefore counts as a risk indicator in assessing whether children are to be deprived of their parents.

Immigrants in Norway are often branded with "low self-esteem or lack of self-confidence" through the attitudes they are met with in Norwegian society. This alleged risk indicator is therefore liable to be salient in this section of the population.

Certain risk indicators are thought to offer more accurate predictions than others, and the sum total diagnosed for a parent will be a strong factor in the decision made by a social worker in whether to take the child into care.

Observation, tests and prognoses

To work out an assessment of the parents' ability to give care, they are observed by social workers in their home. Unfortunately, it is rarely possible to check what kind of methods of observation are used. Several problems follow. Since observer and observed are living individuals who influence each other, and each have attitudes and prejudices, 'observation' is no clear-cut activity and this objectivity question must be taken into account.

Such problems are standard, and have to be accounted for in any methodologically acceptable study in any social science. They do not seem to be, though, in the view of NCWS personnel. Their observations do not take place under natural conditions, but in situations where those being observed are nervous, upset or for other reasons cannot be expected to behave naturally. These barriers are not ordinarily mentioned in the NCWS reports, nor are observers' effects on the observed discussed. In many cases these deficiencies have led to misinterpretations, which have contributed to creating a case for NCWS intervention.

NCWS psychologists utilise personality tests in their work. Based on the results of these, drastic conclusions are drawn about the client. This in spite of well-known facts: such tests have been shown not to measure what they pretend to measure, and they are completely unable to predict future events and future actions.

For NCWS to trace so-called risk indicators in parents' lives back to their childhood, the parents are subjected to more or less 'clinical' interviews and observations by psychologists chosen by NCWS. The psychologists come up with prognoses for ability to give care, future care failure, relapse into psychiatric illness, etc. Such predictions based on interviews have turned out to be problematic, and in the US several studies have shown them to be largely incorrect.

That being so, the value of such pronouncements is not great. Nevertheless, the CWS draws its conclusions regarding future performance as parents on the basis of such tests and interviews.

Seeing NCWS in practice

For some years I served on a local authority committee in Bergen. The task of the committee was to go through NCWS cases before they could be taken to the county board or the courts. I have consequently read a quantity of case documents from such cases.

Around eighty per cent of NCWS' decisions to take children into care were based on claims to have diagnosed deficient parental ability to give care, so that there might be a care failure sometime in the future. In only a few cases was a present care failure documented. In no case was there any documentation of actions that could be labelled as child abuse.

There were statements and accusations from NCWS against parents which, when investigated, turned out not to be true. One example is that of a mother who had a spot on her cheek when she came to a meeting at the NCWS office. NCWS records this in its file. By the time a report arrived on the local authority committee's table, NCWS has changed it to a black eye (insinuating violence in the home). In another case, a social worker writes that the mother drank and that one should find out whether the father also has alcohol problems. Later in the same report, written on the same day and with no investigation having been carried out, the social worker claims that the father drank a lot. In yet another case from a neighbouring district the mother, being interviewed about her childhood (no doubt for the purpose of finding 'risk indicators'), had said that she had, as a girl, had a fine summer holiday at a summer camp for children at Hjellestad outside Bergen. In the report, this had been changed to a statement that she had been treated at the Hjellestad clinic (an institution that treats people with problems relating to alcoholism and drug abuse).

NCWS wants to control every aspect of the lives of a foster child to make sure that it follows the plan they have drawn up. Since NCWS considers frequent contact with biological parents to be negative for children's 'attachment' to new 'caregivers' once they are placed in foster homes, the right for parents and children to meet is cut down to a minimum and the plan is for the children to remain in foster homes until they are grown up. The need for control means that other close relatives are not considered as foster parents, except in cases where the fosterer carers are made to consider the biological parents as enemies.

In summary, there is reason to believe that NCWS' methods are more than criticisable and have a very poor scientific basis. It is abundantly clear to me from my experiences on the local authority committee and from research literature that the Norwegian child welfare service does not serve the population with welfare in the humane and competent way intended by the law and by the international conventions Norway has signed.

Checklist

The majority of child welfare offices in Norway currently use a checklist to determine whether or not they should remove a child from its home. Fifty-eight per cent of the country's local authority child welfare services use a checklist when they assess a message of concern, using the so-called Kvello model. This is a standard form that calculates the risk factors and preventive/resilience factors.

Researchers at NTNU Samfunnsforskning (NTNU Social Research) and RKBU Midt (RKBU Central Norway) interviewed child welfare workers and prosecutors from eight local authorities in Norway as part of an international project on objectivisation, measurement and standardisation in several sectors of society.

Researchers are highly critical of this standardised checklist NCWS uses. For example, the likelihood of losing your child in a child welfare case increases if you are divorced, unemployed or on social security. The experts fear that the use of checklists objectivises children and families. From starting out as different people with different needs they become comparable objects.

The child is assessed based on a variety of risk factors, such as whether he or she has developmental delays, is shy or impulsive, possesses mental or severe somatic problems, has been bullied, has been adopted or has lost siblings. The child's family members are also assessed using similar risk factors.

Based on the results of the checklist, caseworkers can fudge their way to creating a desired outcome that loosely fits the situation. If a case worker ticks six to eight risk factors, the usual outcome will be a care order. The child is then removed from the family and placed in an institution or foster home.

Journalist Frida Holsten Gullestad wrote an article titled "Counting their way to the right conclusion", which was originally published in *Klassekampen* in January 2018.[v] She suggests that the use of these checklists enables caseworkers to distance themselves further and further from the ones they are paid to help. Such an automated setup, she claims, can drastically change the threshold of a care order.

Some researchers suggest that this checklist approach does not meet the needs of the child or the parents. Furthermore, they say that it would be more beneficial to help solve the family's social and economic issues rather than tearing the family apart.

Mothers' homes

Målfrid Schartau Viken, a Norwegian mother of three children and a specialist nurse in substance abuse and psychiatry with an education in trauma care and mental health, ended up on NCWS' radar. The following extract tells the story of her stay in a mothers' home (text translated):[vi]

> I was forced to voluntarily enrol at Vilde mothers' home in

Horten when my daughter was barely two days old. NCWS arrived unannounced in the delivery room with a contract I had to sign there and then, otherwise they would have taken my newborn baby away immediately. So I signed it. In this case, NCWS and I have strongly differing views on what the term 'voluntary' means.

We arrived at the mothers' home in the evening of the second day after the birth. We were placed in a dirty room with very little furniture. It was cold, and I felt completely alone in the world. No one had told me what I would have to deal with, so it was just a coincidence that I had brought with me my own bedding and towels. Neither had anyone prepared me for a stay of thirteen weeks. I had to be there; I had no choice.

The first week you are there you are lucky enough to be in maternity. That is to say, after that you are left to yourself, full of fear, in a dirty apartment with your newborn child. There is no one serving warm soup or asking you if you need a rest after three nights in a row of crying, but at least you avoid following the compulsory scheme, which consists of a singing group, kitchen service where you cook for residents and personnel, communal washing areas and being 'investigated' by an expert.

The only thing you have to do or stand up for is when a member of staff observes you caring for, breastfeeding and bathing your child. One gets the message that they will only observe you and your baby during the first month, which means you are not given any feedback on what they think they have observed. So for a whole month you dread being labelled as having qualified as a good mum or not. Those days are very long. I cried a lot, like women who have just given birth often do, and I struggled a great deal with fear and had trouble sleeping because of how fearful I felt.

Since I was a woman and had recently given birth, on one of the first evenings we were there I asked the night watch if she could cradle my little child who was upset while I took a quick shower. The harsh and cold answer I received was a question as to why I had not showered earlier in the day. Most new mothers will understand that women who have just given birth bleed for the first few weeks. It is actually quite desirable to wash both morning and evening. I learned very quickly that one should not bother with such things in the evening at a mothers' home.

In fact, I learned quite quickly that at a mothers' home you were not meant to be yourself. Here you need to 'sell a package' that fits with the narrow mothers' home view of what a 'good-enough mum' is. There are not many mothers who are 'good-enough mums'. Around eight out of ten mothers lose their babies at Vilde. These statistics were given to us by the employees themselves.

Then comes 'the working week'. So you are finished now with your postnatal period and it's your duty to attend the singing group, the baking, the cooking, the washing, the conversations and the 'investigation' of the so-called and self-proclaimed experts on your child.

For it is they who know what your child needs and what's best for your child; not you, who has carried your baby inside you for nine months. You have to fill in each day how much time the child is asleep, when he wakes up, when he eats, gets a new nappy, cries, is quiet, is upset and the like. This was done three days in a row, twice, during our stay.

The 'assessment' consists of being examined every week about how well you know your child, and about what answer you give in every conceivable (and inconceivable) situation that could arise from the birth until the baby matures. Moreover, both you and your child have your IQ tested. It is important to have a high IQ if you are to be approved as a 'good-enough mother'. It is certainly very important to have already thought about how your child will be when he is at least twenty-five years old while the child is still four weeks old. Everything is noted by the expert and filmed so it can be used (against you) later.

Having kitchen duties means that you should learn to cook and bake like any good housewife should, for it is understood that you are not capable of doing this. Furthermore, one should learn to fill up a dishwasher and empty it, and learn to wash down benches, kitchen cabinets and the floor.

The cleaning must be done at night after supper; around the most difficult time of day for a mum with an infant. So you're cleaning because private foundations want to save what they can in terms of money to create more profit for private investors; therefore, no cleaning personnel are employed. A member of staff monitors your activity and makes a note in your journal if you wash the right or the wrong way.

It is also noted how well you safeguard your child while you clean. The room you stay in is inspected every Wednesday so they can monitor whether you clean well enough in there, too. They write down how often you wash your clothes, whether you look well-kept or not to their standard, whether you have enough eye contact with your child and the staff, and about how you feel inside.

They already know all this without having to ask you anything. Everything you do and say is questioned, and they can even make an experienced mum like me feel very insecure and afraid. Nothing is good enough, and the criticism I received was partly because I was carrying my child too much. Also, I didn't shield her enough against the noise. I kept her in a health blanket at all times and washed her bottom too much when she needed it.

Lunch and dinner are eaten together with the staff. That's when we are all a big happy family, where there are no obstacles like confidentiality, for example. The staff can do 'counselling' with some mums while the other mums are present. The 'problems' of the mother are pointed out, and then the poor mother, as a compromise, has to put up with being corrected and criticised in front of all the other mothers.

It is mandatory at 5pm to have 'observation time', where we mums need to lie on the floor with our kids and chat while the staff sit around us and watch. This is to see whether the child responds to us well enough, and whether we interact well with the child. Any suggestion of the fact that the child doesn't look at the mother enough is interpreted as the child 'consistently rejecting the mother'.

Each family admitted to the home has its own room. We're not allowed to be with others inside the room. Such interactions must be carried out in a living room with a glass wall so the staff can see what we are doing at any time and listen in to what we are talking about. There is a lot at Vilde that one is not allowed to talk about.

What were we really doing there? The experience is a negative one with childcare services; it's about how scared one can be. Outwardly, one should be grateful for being lucky enough to be allowed in there. That's what we are told during the intake meeting. It is outrageous how much money is being spent on just you and your child. The price per day for me and my baby girl at Vilde was about 4,500 kroner (around €450). Multiply that by 100 days.

Children can be taken away at almost any point in the day, from 8am until 10pm. There is no warning, but you eventually learn that when the place is suddenly flooded with child welfare people you have not seen before and are told to go into your room you know a child is being taken away from his or her mother.

Then you sit there in horror and wonder who it will be next, while your heart beats so fast and hard that it's almost impossible to breathe. The only thing you hear is a mum who cries, screams or shouts out her despair and pain. The child is taken away by the child welfare service and the mother has to stay and wash the room she stayed in with her child. It is expected of her to do this. She must stay and clean up.

Nobody talks to you afterwards about what has just happened. No one asks you if you are OK or afraid, or if you need to talk to someone about what happened. It's as though it happens in everyday life for mothers in Vilde, so you are expected to endure it.

Eventually you learn to ignore your feelings. You become colder, number and more cynical. You need to in order to survive. The only thing you need to focus on is survival and praying to the Almighty that your child might not be too traumatised by being in there. For it is not in the child's best interest that the mum is terrified and stressed every day, every hour, every minute around the clock for up to 100 days.

Most mothers there are so stressed they lose their breast milk, but the employees at Vilde don't care about that. They would rather provide you with free replacement milk and this way it's easier to take the babies away from the mothers who do not breastfeed. Do our authorities really think this is in the best interests of the child? Is this really a child's best start in life, to have a terrified mum who fights for her life and struggles with fear every day, every minute for thirteen weeks?

Or could they actually imagine that the best start would be at home, in their own homes, along with safe and older people where there is mutual trust, empathy and understanding, and where the primary focus is that the mother can manage and this child can grow up where she/he belongs from the beginning?

But by all means there was something good about Vilde. Mostly we got another dinner: a soup, leftovers from the day before or a pizza. Sometimes Tone or Kirsti, the extra guards, were at work. Then you could relax a bit and experience being spoken to like an ordinary human being with human rights and intrinsic value, and as a mum who supposedly had knowledge and intelligence enough to talk about everyday topics that were interesting.

And I met many wonderful, resourceful mums and dads, who for one reason or another had been disgraced by what we in Norway call child welfare services, and I'm very happy that I got the opportunity to meet them. We comforted, listened to and encouraged each other. Some are my friends to this day, even a year on.

> Three mums and a dad were deprived of their children while we stayed at Vilde. One mum and a single father got to travel home with their sons. The rest of us were glad about this for our children's sake, and wept for the unhappy mums and the dads who lost their children. We cried for those children who became part of the sad statistics under NCWS' care.

This mother was fortunate enough to find herself among a small minority of parents who kept custody of their children after her time at Vilde Mothers' Home. This was in spite of the 'expert' from Vilde saying the following about the mother's seven-month-old baby daughter: "It is very important that your daughter has a good relationship with child welfare services, for her children will be in childcare again one day." Is it any wonder that many of these mothers' homes in Norway are becoming known as horror homes?

Chapter 6 notes

[i] Whewell, T., *Norway's Hidden Scandal*, BBC: https://www.bbc.co.uk/news/resources/idt-sh/norways_hidden_scandal

[ii] Whewell, T., "Norway backs down in child protection scandal", BBC: https://www.bbc.com/news/world-europe-45637040

[iii] Aarset, B. *Maktovergrep og justismord* (*Abuse of power and the miscarriage of justice*): https://www.haugenbok.no

[iv] Simonsen, Å., "A Kafkaesque approach", Step up 4 Children's Rights: https://stepup4childrensrights.com/a-kafkaesque-approach-by-norways-child-welfare-system

[v] Bennett. S., "Norway's Dehumanising Strategy – Part 11", Step up 4 Children's Rights: https://stepup4childrensrights.com/norways-dehumanising-strategy-part-11

[vi] Hole, T. H., "Hun var 3 barns mor og hadde havnet i barnevernets søkelys. Dette er hennes historie" ("She was the mother of 3 and ended up in the child welfare spotlight. This is her story"), Trude Helen Hole: https://trudehelenhole.no/2017/09/07/hun-var-3-barns-mor-og-hadde-havnet-i-barnevernets-sokelys-dette-er-hennes-historie

7

Abducted

"Kaleb, when you come home from school we'll make pancakes together," said the boy's mother, Vibeke Vedvik. Kaleb smiled and made his way onto the school bus. Vibeke knew that the thought of making his favourite food when he returned would warm his heart.

Five-year-old Kaleb never returned from school. Instead, NCWS picked him up and placed him straight into foster care without even letting Kaleb say goodbye to his mummy. The first time she spoke to him on the phone after being taken, he said, "But we never got to make pancakes. I was really looking forward to that. I want to go home and eat pancakes." Vibeke promised Kaleb she would do everything she could to get him home, and that they would make those pancakes and eat them together. It became a symbol of hope for Kaleb. Even after more than two years away from home he was still holding on to that promise from his mum.

Vibeke Vedvik had all four of her children removed after she asked NCWS for help. The reason she approached the 'social care' provider was that her eldest son Tobias was struggling to finish his homework. It often starts like this in Norway. Someone asks for help, NCWS gets involved, and then a case is built on many trivial things, leading to the children losing their parents and vice versa. Court cases are long-drawn-out, and after many months of manipulating and coercing the children in care NCWS tells the parents they have become attached to their new foster carers.

It goes without saying that parenting is far from easy. Someone once said that: "Parenting is as crazy as circumnavigating the globe without a map, but oh, what a journey!" Sadly, that journey is often cut short in Norway. Vibeke is a wonderful mother facing the same challenges all parents face. It was love for her children that drove her tirelessly on through the tortuous journey toward the eventual reunification of her family.

Only her two daughters were initially returned, and Vibeke was allowed to see her two sons just four times a year, under supervision (with 'guards') and at different foster homes. NCWS wrote to Vibeke telling her that if she didn't cause any trouble she could keep her daughters and see the boys a little more often without supervision. This is a very popular tactic for NCWS. It takes all the children first, then after a while gives one or two back. The parent is half-relieved and gives child welfare some form of security, as they're effectively saying, "Play ball with us now, do what we say, and we will make life a little easier for you."

Why does NCWS keep so many children in this cycle of misery? Why can't children with functional and caring, though naturally imperfect, parents be allowed to live in their own homes with their own families?

At eleven years old, Tobias wrote to NCWS in Horten explaining how desperately he wanted to live with his mum again. Here is an extract from his letter (text translated):

> I know mum is going to a trial at the council on August 26, 2015, and in this respect I would like to say the following: I've never had any other desire than to live together with my mum and my siblings. I'm almost twelve. You don't know my siblings, but I know them insanely well. Josefine struggles during the day and is kept away from her siblings and family. This is something I find insanely annoying. She said she wants to come home to mum, like all the rest of us. And we want to have nothing to do with you. What you've done is a gigantic mistake.

This is an example of just one child among thousands who are not loved, cared for or respected enough by the child welfare system to be listened to. His mother spent 70,000 kroner (around €7,000) on an expert report, but the district court allegedly didn't take the time to read either the report or Tobias' letter. More money was drained from this family, and Vibeke even had to sell her house. NCWS uses tactics against families that resemble psychological warfare, dragging things on for years in some cases and slowly wearing people down until the family has nothing left: no energy, no money and poor health.

Manipulation

On one occasion NCWS turned up unannounced at the foster home where Tobias was staying. They purposely told him that his younger brother Kaleb, who at the time was being fostered by his own grandparents, wouldn't be able to stay there much longer. They wanted to know how Tobias felt about that.

Tobias' understanding of the conversation was that his little brother would not be allowed to stay with his grandparents any longer. But when Tobias visited his grandparents a few days later he asked why Kaleb could no longer live with them. The grandparents had no idea what was going on, as NCWS had not informed them of its destructive plan.

Kaleb was already deeply traumatised after being taken away from his mother in the first place. He continued to attend the same school, but it made him feel unsafe because that was where he had been taken from. Kaleb was a wonderful child, but he could be insecure, tired and unfocused at times, and he found school very challenging at this time. His loving grandparents spent a lot of time and effort helping to boost his confidence, and this had a very positive effect on him. He started to enjoy learning again and became one of the best pupils, particularly excelling in maths. He whistled as he left for school every morning.

NCWS planned to undo all the good that had been done, once again tearing him away from a place of security in familiar surroundings to take him to a dark and desperate place; an unknown institution. Tobias understandably felt responsible and very concerned for his little brother. The authorities had already placed a huge amount of pressure on his young shoulders simply by informing him. He lay awake at night worrying about his family, and particularly his little brother.

Vibeke's daughters also felt guilty. They had already been released and were at home with their mum again, but sadly without their brothers. Vibeke and her children felt deprived of their human rights.

In another letter to NCWS, Tobias wrote:

> I am angry and depressed! And do you know why?! Because the longer I'm kept away from my mum the more I begin to think that I don't want to live any more.
>
> I belong with my mum, but you won't listen to me. I can't take this much longer! You made my life cruel when you put me in a foster home.
>
> First I stayed with grandmother and grandad, and it was like a dream foster home. But then you put me and my sister Josefine in strange foster homes and let our brother and sister, Julie and Kaleb, stay with our grandparents.
>
> Why? It was because you said my grandmother was too old to have us! You know what? I think that was to publicly shame my grandmother!
>
> I want you to apologise to my grandmother for telling her she was too old. She has only just turned sixty and she was not even sixty when you called her too old!
>
> You chose to take me and the rest of my siblings away from our mother. So now it's my move, so I've decided this letter will be published on my mum's Facebook page so Norway and the rest of the world can see how I really am doing here!
>
> With best regards
>
> *Tobias*

Dealing with NCWS is essentially about power and control, and the phrase 'double punishment' is often used. Either you make too much effort and work too hard, or you are labelled lazy or stupid by the child welfare office. Whatever you do, you will be wrong. Vibeke believes that NCWS is set up in such a way that the real meaning of 'help' from the authorities is 'abuse of power'. Its tactics are designed to confuse and destroy the family, leaving its members in a lose-lose situation. It is utterly inhumane and heartless.

Tobias never stopped asking to be released while he was being held against his will in Horton, offering continued and desperate pleas to return to his family. On one occasion Tobias sent a message to his mum, stating that he loved her more than the whole world. He went on to say that he hoped NCWS "got what was coming to them" for taking him and his younger brother away from their family.

When it was decided that Vibeke would officially be allowed to have all her children returned to her, NCWS told her to keep quiet about it and not to tell her boys or anyone else. Vibeke was so happy to have finally won the battle that she chose to do what they asked so as not to cause any further problems. NCWS, on the other hand, appeared to have been planning something behind her back.

Its employees went to the foster home where Tobias lived and took his phone away so he could no longer contact his mother. NCWS informed Tobias that he had a decision to make, as there had been a change in plan. He was given the choice to either stay in foster care until he turned eighteen or move somewhere else. When he asked where they planned to move him they just shrugged their shoulders and said they could not tell him that yet.

Tobias was given the opportunity to stay where things were familiar or let them move him to an unknown location, or so they let him think. The truth was that the move would have taken him back home to his family, but this information was withheld. He had absolutely no idea where this new place would be, and he couldn't ask his mum for advice without his phone.

However, Tobias had no intention of playing their game, so he refused to answer and told them he wanted to speak to his mother first. This request was denied, but a little later Tobias managed to get hold of someone else's phone and was able to telephone Vibeke.

He told his mother what had happened and Vibeke suddenly understood why she had been told to keep quiet. She explained everything, so he told NCWS that he was choosing to go home. Tobias is not only a caring and loving child; he is also a very smart boy!

Kaleb and Tobias returned home on June 20, 2017, but the trauma of being separated from the rest of their family created a great deal of needless anxiety, fear and anger.

Empty shoes

In an article titled "A Christmas wish to Norway from Iraq",

Norwegian mother Ragna Heffermehl documents the tortuous process one Iraqi mother went through. The investigation eventually led to her having all five of her children taken away by NCWS in 2016. She writes:[i]

> "Forgive them, because they don't know what they do." I peek into the hallway of the woman who lost all her kids to the Norwegian child protection service, called "Barnevernet", just before our national day, 17th of May, last year. Their shoes are still there, labels with their names ironed on the inside. "She probably can't bear to remove them," I'm thinking. Silently I ask myself how much too small those shoes will be, when – or if – the children are allowed to come home.
>
> One after one, the children have stood alone in court, court case after court case, and asked to come home. This mother is the last trace of family they've got here, as she is a widow who has escaped from Iraq. All of the siblings except two were put in different locations. All the time since they were removed they have cried and pled. They have offered Barnevernet money. They have drawn faces covered with tears. Barnevernet reports that the children are "crying, but mostly when they see their mother".
>
> And the mother loves her children. That is even confirmed by Barnevernet, and by the judges in court. However, they express doubt whether she is able to give her children "emotional support". A professional term which is accepted without question by the judges, and which bends them towards their tragical conclusion: the mother is not fit. Nobody seems to think that love and emotional support are related in some way. Love is obviously not given much credit.
>
> **Norwegian Standard, abbreviated NS**
>
> There's a new documentary about Barnevernet in the making, called Norwegian Standard. The abbreviation is NS – which was also the name that the Norwegian Nazi party during the war, "Nasjonal Samling", went under. So I'm tempted to search for similarities between the Norwegian system and the Nazi

regime. What I find is the lack of love. Love means nothing. Intellectual and professional constructions legitimise brutal violations by the bureaucrats, who are merely "doing their job". Is it unpleasant to remove children from their families? Sure. At least until you get used to it.

"I understand that you miss your children," the employee from Barnevernet purrs to the devastated mother, "but the children are very well taken care of. Two of them are living together in a huge, modern house. They are successful at school. Their new parents are not working, so they can take care of the children all the time."

What scant relief for the mother that the new parents don't need to work for a living, and that they have such a nice big house.

Barnevernet seems to have a preference for people with high socio-economic status when it comes to choosing who are suitable as parents for the children of the Norwegian state. This mother, like so many others, has been accused of being too poor.

Another alternative favoured by Barnevernet is to select foster parents for whom they create good economic conditions by paying them rather generously. To aspiring foster parents, Barnevernet is a most lucrative opportunity. In several cases foster parents have been paid for their new "needs" such as an extra car, or renovation of their house, with the new child as leverage. They're also granted the use of extra temporary step-in foster parents who take care of the child during holidays.

More tempting still is the offer of the equivalent of a full salary, so that one foster parent can stay home and ensure good care of the child.

The economic advantages of being a foster parent are heavily advertised by the state, regardless of the fact that it may attract people with other motives than to love a child like their own. The state is in desperate need of foster homes. On average, the state removes five children from their parents every day – in one of the smallest countries in the world.

Norwegian professor Tove Stang-Dahl has done research on the history of Barnevernet. Her conclusion is this:

> *In an uninterrupted line from the end of the 18th century and right until this day, the explicit goal of Barnevernet has been to weaken the power and freedom of the family. The premise has been the same the whole time: to exert social control over the groups in society who are, at any point in time, seen as a threat against social order.*

The dark depths of the human mind

Last year the mother had hoped to celebrate Christmas with her children. Barnevernet refused and told her to deliver her gifts at their office for professional distribution to each child. This Christmas she has lost any hope of seeing her children. Barnevernet won't give her more than what the judges said: four times a year, one-and-a-half hours each time, supervised. That means there has to be an observer from Barnevernet who can't leave the mother and child alone at any moment – not even in the bathroom. An interpreter is also there to translate everything they say to each other.

To the victims, it may seem like Barnevernet, with its unlimited power to destroy the lives of individuals, experiences a subtle joy in doing exactly that. Unfortunately, I believe it's a human trait.

The famous Stanford experiment illustrates this. Twenty-one mentally healthy persons were randomly given roles as 'prisoners' or 'guards', and placed in a prison-like locale. The guards were instructed to keep order, nothing else, and psychologists were to observe what happened. The experiment was meant to last two weeks, but had to be stopped after six days because of the way the guards abused the prisoners, harassing them psychologically and forcing them to do humiliating things. By the end of the six days a third of the guards were believed to have developed sadistic traits.

In our human minds, the same psychological mechanisms are latent. And they will flourish if the power structure allows them to.

Norwegian law on children – a breeding ground for abuse

It is heading the wrong way. Before, the law said that children should live with their biological parents, if possible. In 2012 this law was reformulated. Now they have the "right" to grow up with people who can provide the best conditions materially and mentally. The children are to be "good and productive citizens, for the good of the nation", the law says.

This sentence reminds me of Nazi perfectionism. It can justify almost any abduction from parents with a lower socio-economic status. We have to ask which values are the most important: the love of the parents or the development of "productive citizens"?

A Christmas wish

"Forgive them, for they don't know what they do." I'm writing Christmas cards. Thinking of my friends and my enemies, and of the ones it might be time to forgive.

And I think of my new friend from abroad, who's sticking to me as if clutching at a straw. Because I'm Norwegian, probably. But who am I against Barnevernet? The people there have developed a very thick skin. In a system where cruel decisions are part of their everyday job, they will not bend to any appeal for empathy. They don't listen to anybody – not even doctors, nurses, or psychologists, who sometimes very openly disagree with their decisions to separate a family based on their own observations of that family. I'm really nothing more than a straw in this field; a field ravaged by storms of prejudices and by a past most of us are ignorant of.

Can one really forgive without the other party admitting and changing anything? It seems that for politicians and for Barnevernet it is difficult to admit that something has gone wrong. They seldom talk about the pain inflicted upon children and parents. I've rarely seen anything coming close to a real debate without all the justifications for Barnevernet being brought up again and again. In reality, no one disagrees that in some serious cases children should be taken away and given another home.

This is being used to overshadow all those children who maybe needed some help, but absolutely not of that kind. Now, they're being traumatised for life for absolutely no other good reason than to protect the one who made the wrong decision in the first place. What about all their calls and crying for their true home and parents, without anybody paying attention? The brutality of these acts – and the numbers of them – are rarely mentioned. Some lawyers have estimated that these cases to represent around eighty per cent of all the children being forcibly displaced.

So I'm not ready to forgive Barnevernet yet. The snow that fell last year is still falling, and nothing seems to change things, as long as we have a trust-based system where the employees from Barnevernet can do what they want. They can command the police to take a child at any time. Even if they make a wrong decision it can still take months and years before the children are returned to their family – if ever.

Instead of forgiveness, I have a Christmas wish. I wish that people would open their eyes to what is happening. The actions of the Norwegian Barnevernet will forever be remembered by the rest of the world as our acts, as my acts. Every Norwegian should understand how easily one can lose a child to the Norwegian state, and try to care a little bit about how they want this country to be.

This is my Christmas wish, so that I might regain some pride in my country. All the time since the 17th of May celebration last year I have only been ashamed. During the celebration at our school, my daughter told me the news about the girl in her class being removed. I went to look for the mother in the crowd while two girls talked into the

> microphone about how lucky we are in Norway. "Not many countries have as fair and humane laws as Norway", they said. But I know of no country where the mother has less of a right to express love and to care for what comes from her own womb.
>
> I have a life which the immigrant woman would have done anything to get: I'll celebrate Christmas, happy to be with my children. As is the case for any other parent, there have been incidents or errors that could have separated us forever had they been judged by the wrong person.
>
> But my red-coloured tablecloth, delicious food, my decorations and Christmas-red curtains can't match the memory of the pale red shoes in the home of a woman who is not taking part in our celebration. The red shoes will always be lying there, in my consciousness, empty of children's feet.

At the time of writing this book, the Iraqi mother had persevered through the whole court system in Norway but the case had been refused in the high courts, as so often happens with NCWS cases. Her children have still not been released, and the mother now lives alone and is quite isolated from Norwegian society. She has tried hard to find a job, but positions that require no training are scarce in Norway. She wants to open a new case as soon as possible, but this may take another year as the process is painfully slow.

Every time Ragna meets her, the mother speaks about her children and her concerns for them. Her oldest daughter, who is now fourteen, is still saying that she wants to come home to her mother. She has expressed a great deal of sorrow and depression since she was taken away, and continues to do so. The younger girls are more impressionable, so it is difficult to find out how they are really doing.

What has happened to human compassion?

In an article titled "Where is humanity?", Norwegian clinical psychologist Einar C. Salvesen expresses his concern about the lack of assurance that justice will be served by the legal system when it comes to NCWS.

Salvesen has extensive experience as an expert witness in numerous legal cases that involved the removal of children from their parents' care. He highlights significant flaws in the process, and describes how NCWS assumes control over, and imposes care arrangements on, children and their families.

His views have garnered interest among academics, in the media and at ministerial level, but from those on the receiving end of his sharp criticism – those who are personally responsible as experts in the field – his criticism has provoked nothing but silence.

Under the subheading "A crisis of confidence is said to exist between the child welfare services in Norway and minority groups in this country. Is this lack of trust justified?" Salvesen writes (text translated):[ii]

> On April 8, 2014, the television program *Brennpunkt*[iii] introduced viewers to some highly unconventional methods employed by Polish parents for the purpose of being reunited with their children, who had been taken into care and placed in foster homes or institutions by NCWS. Krystof Rudowsky, one of the main protagonists and a former Polish MP, likened the manner and methods used by NCWS to those perpetrated by the *Hitlerjugend* [Hitler youth] and dog catchers. On this basis he justified the "kidnapping" of these children [from NCWS] so they could be reunited with their parents.
>
> My own experience of the processes and methods by which some children have been taken into care by statutory services is that they have appeared to be unnecessary, excessive and occasionally without rational foundation. Consequently, I have observed that those most directly affected react with desperation and despair. In direct consequence of the perceived injustice, some are prepared to go to extreme lengths in order to be reunited with their children. Otherwise law-abiding parents lose all trust in the process of law, which they no longer believe will deliver fair and just outcomes. With no other perceived option to pursue, they resort to all or any possible means to "save" their children.
>
> Any action taken may amount to civil disobedience in response to a system which, to a much greater extent than

we might wish to believe, fails to deliver outcomes that can be considered to be "in the child's best interests". As long as NCWS maintains what in many instances amounts to poor standards of communication, arrogance and undemocratic dialogue with individuals from other cultures, we only have ourselves to thank when confronted with the recent diplomatic crises that have disrupted Norway's relationship with other nations, as well as the total crisis of confidence and trust in our relationship with immigrant populations now settled in this country.

The situation also arises in part from what appears to be an intolerant and dismissive attitude toward those who come to Norway from societies with a tradition of child-rearing practices that differ from those commonly practised in this country. Creating trust between children and adults in different education methods and relationships requires time, dialogue, respect and, not least, empathy. This is often absent from NCWS. In this regard I wish to make it perfectly clear that I do not in any way accept or condone violence or assault perpetrated against children, whatever the context may be. However, in instances where parents have resorted to disciplinary actions involving hitting, slapping or locking children behind closed doors, it is known that focused and empathic guidance and advice to parents typically puts an end to the use of these methods.

The nature of the problems I encounter in these cases (a problem that is also highly relevant to relationships within Norwegian families who, by their own standards, find themselves at odds with the narrow framework of acceptability used by NCWS) can be illustrated by a case study taken from legal hearings I was involved in as an expert witness, which involved a Kurdish father and his son. When the child was seven years old he once disclosed to staff at his school that his father had hit him. The school failed to take the natural step of calling the father in for an interview. The allegations were immediately reported to NCWS.

Without further consultation, the statutory service

jumped to the conclusion that the boy had been subjected to a violent assault, whereupon he was urgently admitted to a children's institution (he was later transferred to a foster family). All of this was actioned by NCWS without a prior interview with either the father or his son. No attempt was made to give advice or enter into dialogue involving all parties with a view to keeping the small family unit together (the boy's mother suffered from a psychiatric disorder, which had left the father as the sole responsible adult).

At no point was the father informed about what had happened until the urgent and sudden action had been enforced. He was granted visiting rights under supervision, but when he handed his son slips of paper with messages detailing everything he was doing with a view to getting him home again, the time allocated for visits was reduced to a minimum.

The father started the long and expensive process of getting his son back, which took two-and-a-half years before it took effect. Only the decision of a sensible judge made it possible to bring the true nature of the case into the public domain. I maintained contact with the family and at follow-up established how hard the struggle had been to overcome the damage caused by the enforced and prolonged separation. In my opinion, the boy bears clear signs of having been traumatised as a direct consequence of being taken away from his family and into care.

In summary, it should be added that NCWS had notified the police about the father allegedly hitting his son on a couple of occasions. It did so in line with standard practice in this type of case. Prosecution services charged the father, who was sentenced to community service and had to pay a large fine. The father, who was already heavily burdened by debt from covering the costs of the legal case to get his son back, had to pay out even more money to the state. The community service order of sixty hours had to be worked at weekends due to the fact that he was in full-time employment. The family only had a small support network in Norway, which meant the little boy had to be on his own while his father did his hours of service for the Norwegian community rather than his own family. In this instance, when NCWS could have been of invaluable assistance to the family, it remained conspicuously and totally absent.

Where, we may ask, is the humanitarian compassion in NCWS? Given that the question has arisen at all, it is not surprising that there is a crisis of confidence and trust between large sections of our immigrant population and the official Norwegian child welfare system.

Documented

Norwegian film-maker Kathrine Haugen writes here about the moment she received the shocking news that turned her world upside down (text translated):[iv]

> I was in Cyprus for a week to plan the recording of the feature film *Skvis* [*Squeeze*]. I was in the hotel room when one of my best friends called and told me that NCWS and the police had taken their children away.
>
> Of course, I did not understand what my friend had told me – this had to be some kind of misunderstanding. I refused to believe that what my best friend was telling me had taken place in Norway. But the rug had been pulled out from beneath my feet, and in fact I now feel constantly insecure whenever I'm on Norwegian soil. Unfortunately, I don't think it will ever be safe again in Norway – not as long as there are children in my life that I care about.
>
> What I eventually realised was that I could use my knowledge and experience as a film-maker to make a film that showed off this hidden universe known as NCWS in Norway. I did not know how to do it, but I knew that the identities of my friend and her children would be exposed and made known. At that time, I was not aware of how many people in Norway were affected by this system, but slowly and surely it became apparent to me just how extensive the 'child council' of the Norwegian state was, and what it was really doing. I realised relatively early in the process that

this movie was going to take up many years of my life, and I'm sorry for that.

My first idea was to make a fictional movie with a little girl in the lead role. But as I started researching – filming the people I interviewed – it became clear that a documentary would be more appropriate.

I then decided to take a master's at NTNU [the Norwegian University of Science and Technology] to make sure that I could receive help from the best people in the country, which actually happened.

I started filming in November 2011, and I have followed several families since then. Others have met me along the way. As meeting with NCWS has such a fundamental impact on human life, it was important for me to do a thorough job. I wanted to explain how and why the system works the way it does today. And then I had to go back to the starting point before the first Child Welfare Act came into force in 1900.

The saying, "If you are going through hell, keep going", describes the last six years of my life. And it's not much comfort to know that the families exposed to NCWS are far worse off than me. That just makes the job even harder. There is nothing about this system I find attractive. There is no point to it. It's just destructive.

Having said that, I'm very grateful for all the people I've made friends with through the making of this film. I'm also glad that I have been able to change myself as a person. I believe that at one point or another in life everyone is forced along the wide path and into the forest, where the opening to the underworld is located. You go down into the darkness to see what is happening where the daylight does not reach, and then getting out the other side helps you grow up.

Seeing the world through a veil of naivety is comfortable as long as you can live in peace, but when you suddenly face a conflict with a massive power system like the Norwegian state it is desirable to understand and recognise the realities as quickly as possible. I think it is important to make known the ideology and methodology used by the state of

Norway against families and children. Then you can be on guard and take some precautions. Unfortunately, many of the families I have come to know have, like me, had too much trust in the system, and therefore were not prepared for what came the day that society turned on them.

Like Dante, I managed to go down into the dark alone. I became familiar with a lawyer who for more than twenty years worked on child welfare cases. She had been down into the darkness before and was able to tell me what was happening, both inside and outside the judicial system, in these cases. I have gained many experiences, which have been affirmed through a thorough review of many things. Through this lawyer I also became familiar with a group of researchers at the University of Bergen, who investigate words relating to justice from a literary point of view. By being an observer of this group under Professor Arild Linneberg, the content of this film has become far better than I had hoped when I started out in 2011.

Chapter 7 notes

[i] Heffermehl, R., "A Christmas wish – To Norway from Iraq. Here, her 5 children are taken away", Mariana Gurza: http://www.marianagurza.ro/blog/2016/12/03/ragna-heffermehl-a-christmas-wish-to-norway-from-iraq-here-her-5-children-are-taken-away

[ii] Salvesen, E. C., "Hvor er humaniteten?" ("Where is Humanity?"), *Da Nye Meninger*: https://www.dagsavisen.no/nyemeninger/hvor-er-humaniteten-1.456070

[iii] *Brennpunkt*, "Child welfare diplomacy" ("Barnediplomatiet"), NRK TV: https://tv.nrk.no/serie/brennpunkt/MDUP11000714/08-04-2014

[iv] Haugen, K., "Into the dark alone", Step Up 4 Children's Rights: https://stepup4childrensrights.com/into-the-dark-alone

8

Confidential

Czech MEP Tomáš Zdechovský believes NCWS is very proficient in the area of destroying parents' reputations. In Eva Michaláková's case, records from the meetings between the mother and her children showed that the foster parents had repeatedly told the children their mother was mean. "If a person is constantly exposed to a character assassination by lies and filth, where is such a person to get justice?" Zdechovský commented.[i]

Confidentiality is one of the tools used by NCWS to assassinate the characters of biological parents. The term *taushetsplikt* is translated to mean 'confidentiality' in English, but it cannot be translated with complete accuracy. It is a bit like a non-disclosure agreement, only more sinister and involving a greater threat. Anything that is protected by taushetsplikt is automatically off-limits. Taushetsplikt is upheld by doctors to protect patients and by the police to withhold the identities of criminals or their victims.

NCWS claims to use taushetsplikt to protect families and children, but in reality it protects the agency from having to explain its actions or from responding to anyone who challenges its authority. It gives NCWS the opportunity to tell half-truths and decide which part of the 'truth' best suits their aims. For instance, the foster parents are not told straight away why the child has been relocated. The child is allowed to 'adjust' for a while first. NCWS sets up a meeting with the foster parents a couple of weeks later and starts by asking how things are going. The foster parents are encouraged to talk about the difficulties they are facing with the new child, then NCWS starts to insinuate things, leaving the foster parents to fill in the gaps.

If the foster parents see things that could be interpreted as negative about the biological parents, NCWS will back that story up and make it part of the 'truth'. The agency then works to substantiate the story using stories from other segments of its work, and eventually, when the biological parents try to defend themselves against these lies, both in the community and in court, they are faced with massive resistance from a united group of people who are now dealing with their child. And of course NCWS can neither confirm nor deny any of the stories told due to its confidentiality (taushetsplikt) rules.

One of the statements it uses most frequently with anyone who has contact with the biological parents is: "For the sake of the child and our confidentiality obligation there are things we cannot talk about. Nevertheless, we strongly urge you to let us know if there is anything you experience or observe about the child that could help us with this case." NCWS uses this statement when it contacts schools, kindergartens, neighbours and other people who encounter the family in everyday life.

In this way, NCWS poisons the biological family's surroundings until people start to think something really must be wrong, which leads some to create their own version of the truth. It's enough for many people to know that NCWS is concerned; no one feels the need to know the truth or hear the biological parents' side of the story. The few who choose not to believe the NCWS narrative are also attacked and ostracised, and their reputations are destroyed using the same tactics.

The following saying is also used as a mantra in NCWS circles: "You won't see it until you believe it." It's a play on words, similar to something you might find in a Bible passage, albeit with a very different agenda. NCWS encourages people to see things that are not really there. It reaches for confirmations to support the last piece of 'truth' it created. Confirmation bias – searching for, interpreting and communicating information in a way that confirms pre-existing suspicions – is used to build up a foolproof case, starting with a creatively put-together rumour. Many people are frightened by these allegations and assertions. They would rather support the claims just in case the child grows up neglected or abused with its biological parents.

Secrets and lies

Zdechovský presented his observations about NCWS in the following open letter to Solveig Horne:[ii]

> Dear Madame Minister,
>
> In the European Parliament I have been dealing with the topic of children being removed from their parents in Norway for some time now, not only in response to the widely publicised case of the Czech family of Eva Michaláková. Since the number of complaints about the dealings of NCWS addressed to the European Parliament increased, I continue to take this matter very seriously.
>
> In June 2015 I organised a round-table meeting on this topic in the European Parliament, which many MEPs and a Norwegian ambassador attended. This topic also became the subject of meetings held by the European Parliament's Committee on Petitions (PETI).
>
> I have encountered Norwegian diplomats many times, and I have met families from Norway who have had their children removed by NCWS and have been prohibited from seeing their children with no reasons given. These families were offered no help and had no opportunity to prove their parental abilities or love for their children. I am aware of a few hundred cases like this in Norway, and I am sure this is just the tip of the iceberg.

In an article entitled "Norway's Orwellian system of child protection and care", Zdechovský writes: [iii]

> NCWS is an institution vested with unlimited powers that enable it to carry out forced confiscations and frame innocent parents.
>
> If I have to talk about NCWS, I admit that I have exchanged my favourite quote: "Believe in victory, and victory will believe in you" for a different one: "A blind person is not the one who cannot see, but the one who does not want to see."
>
> The case foremost in my mind is that of Czech mother Eva Michaláková, whose two sons were taken by NCWS.

This was the first case of state-sponsored child-snatching I got involved in. Before this I was mostly fighting for the rights of fathers to have access to their children after divorce. These fathers had been unfairly prevented from having a full relationship with their children, but Eva's case was far worse. Her boys had been taken away based on allegations of child abuse that had been proven false, yet the children were not returned. Even three years after the allegations were found to be false, NCWS refused to return the children.

The unfortunate brothers are still being brought up separately in two different foster families. NCWS claims they are allowed to see each other once a month for a short time. Eva was initially permitted to see them individually for two hours twice a year. Such visits took place were under strict supervision and very harsh rules. No physical contact was allowed and use of the boys' mother tongue, Czech, was prohibited. If she reminded the boys of special moments they had spent together in the past the visitation would immediately be terminated.

Even this meagre visitation was later cancelled on the grounds that the mother had 'harmed' the children by going public with the story of their removal. The boys' grandfather was deprived, even on his deathbed, of the chance to speak to them one last time before he died. He was not even permitted to contact them via Skype on the grounds that he had shared one of the boys' illustrations on Facebook, which NCWS claimed had been 'uncomfortable' for the boy. It turned out that even this silly claim was false, as the grandfather had no Facebook account, and he had no way of getting an illustration from the boy.

The case of Eva's children shows us that the current system of 'child protection' in Norway is dysfunctional. Under the mask of the protection of children's rights, we are in fact violating their rights and the rights of their parents, while also eliminating grandparents from the lives of the children. Instead of protecting the real victims of child abuse, NCWS artificially constructs cases against innocent parents.

When I personally met Eva Michaláková for the first time in January 2015 I was impressed by her persistence and strength. An ordinary and modest woman, she was fighting valiantly against a hostile and non-transparent system where everything you say is used against you and no parent is given a second chance to fix even small mistakes.

After learning of Eva's case I began investigating further, and found that many others had accused NCWS of wrongly snatching children. Immigrant families were often targeted, even when they came from the neighbouring country of Sweden. In Sweden there are dozens of reports and articles, and thousands of blogs, warning 'poorer' Swedes against working in Norway for fear of being targeted by NCWS.

Even native Norwegians complain of abuse on the part of NCWS. One parent who is not afraid to speak openly about the situation in Norway is Monika. Her daughter was repeatedly beaten up and raped in an institution she was placed in because she reported that her stepfather had molested her. All evident signs of violence were denied by the institution and described as 'self-harm' in response to the 'bad influence' of her family. The institution and NCWS even threatened to bar the mother from seeing her daughter if she persisted with these allegations.

Another mother secretly took photos of her teenage daughter, who had been institutionalised, to prove that she had been brutally strangled while there. The daughter said she had been repeatedly physically punished and even molested by a sixteen-year-old fellow inmate. NCWS dismissed the allegations, saying the bruises on the daughter's neck were from an allergic reaction and that she had made up the claim about the sexual assault.

When I first heard about these cases of beaten and raped children in Norwegian institutions and foster homes I did not want to believe them. I set out to verify all claims and spent many hours reading the case files and looking at the photos. I met with the abused children and their parents.

At the end of my investigations I was convinced that many of these cases were genuine.

When I asked Norwegian politicians about them they mostly kept silent or said that nothing like this could be possibly true. Some claimed that it was all 'Russian propaganda' against Norway because Norwegian crude oil and gas meant that Europe was not dependent on Russia. These assertions usually faded away when I presented them with photos of the victims and records from their cases. Then they would fall silent or say that this had to be an isolated case of malpractice.

Some time ago, Norwegian politicians made strong commitments to stop NCWS stealing children. This was after a series of scandals of unjustified child confiscations broke, from the case of the Bhattacharya children to Eva's case, which I have already mentioned, and the case of a Romanian-Norwegian family, the Bodnarius, whose children were taken away based on allegations of 'Christian indoctrination'.

But nothing seems to have changed. Recently, another horrifying case of child abduction involving an African family has emerged. The parents had come to Norway as refugees. On various occasions they encountered hostility from Norwegian social workers, facing prejudice owing to their ethnicity. In 2013, their two children were removed based on the findings of an inexperienced social worker who claimed that one of them, a little girl of three, had been playing with her doll in a 'sexually suggestive way'.

The father was detained and both parents were accused of abuse. But the suspicion was proven to be completely unjustified. The father was released after a few days and both children were returned from foster care after two months. Two years later, in December 2015, the children were removed again, this time on suspicion of violence being used against them. Again, the suspicions were found to be unjustified and the children were returned.

But in January 2016, while the case was still ongoing, the mother, who was pregnant with their third child, gave birth, and the baby was removed just an hour after delivery. The older children were returned in March 2017, but the baby was not returned on the grounds that he had bonded with his foster carers! This was despite the courts having found, in the case of the older children (the ongoing nature of which was the only reason for the baby's removal in the first place), that there was no evidence of any circumstances that would justify the removal of the children, and that NCWS had failed to conform to the basic requirements of a proper hearing of the case.

Norway is gaining an increasingly bad reputation in Europe for child-snatching. In recent years, eight child removal cases have been filed against Norway with the European Court of Human Rights. My colleague, Polish MEP Julia Pitera, was able to raise this issue ~~last~~ in February [2017] during the inter-parliamentary meeting between the European Parliament and its Norwegian representatives. We even have a case of a native Norwegian, Silje Garmo, whose father was a long-serving MP in Norway, who fled to Poland with her baby and officially applied for asylum there. Her father, who had once been a defender of NCWS, has changed his opinion after seeing the persecution of his own family.

The Norwegian image of having the best child protection system in the world is breaking down because the real behaviour of NCWS officials is totally different from what they are theoretically supposed to be doing. The difficulty primarily lies in the unlimited power of NCWS. Virtually nobody has effective control over this state organisation. Another great hindrance to reform is that Norwegian society is typically uncritical of the state. People consider the state to be a 'friend' who wants the best for them, and any criticism is viewed with suspicion.

Evidence that there is something seriously wrong with NCWS is mounting. The question is, when will it change? In the meantime, countries like the Czech Republic and India should beware of attempts on the part of child protection lobbies to bring this Orwellian system into force in our countries.

Harassment that knows no boundaries

The foster parents of Eva's children openly published pictures of themselves with Eva's sons on Facebook. This would be nothing out of the ordinary had it not been for the fact that the children's own mother would have ended up in serious trouble with NCWS had she done so. The agency would have quickly moved against her. She is not even allowed to take pictures of her children during the very rare contact NCWS allows her to have with them. My question is, why is there such a prohibition for the mother when it comes to taking photos of her children for her own personal use? Isn't this another glaring example of NCWS' tyrannical harassment?

It would have been far better for Eva and her extended family if the foster family had never posted pictures of Denis and David publicly. However, the real responsibility has to lie with NCWS. Had the children not been taken away from their mother the family would not have had to deal with this issue, and the children's pictures would not be appearing on social media platforms every day.

NCWS claims these rules are in place to protect children and their privacy. This is the mantra it uses to justify its often-unjustifiable conduct. The greatest infraction against the children's safety and privacy was, however, their removal, which was entirely unjustified and not based on 'independent expert evaluations' as it claimed. The experts in question were two Norwegian psychologists who were not only alleged to be lovers, but were also on NCWS' payroll. This does not bear the hallmarks of an independent evaluation.

Eva's children's interests have clearly been violated by NCWS' dubious actions. The agency's name and job description imply that its aim is to protect children, but in reality it achieves the exact opposite time and time again. What could be worse in the life of a small child than the destruction of a functioning family? The family may not be entirely perfect, but what is truly perfect in this world?

On Saturday May 30, 2015, demonstrations were held in Prague, Brno, London, Oslo, Moscow, Warsaw, Vilnius, Dublin,

Bratislava and Edinburgh to protest against NCWS' practices. This new wave of demonstrations was triggered by the possibility that Eva's children might be legally adopted. On June 2, 2015, a round-table conference took place in the European Parliament to focus on the cases of Eva and several other parents.

What happened to Eva could happen to anybody who lives in Norway. Parents are often falsely accused, and instead of receiving an apology the child is taken away. Such injustice has not been perpetrated against Czech citizens since the time of World War II. Although the Norwegian authorities repeatedly claimed that Eva's children would not be adopted, and promised to improve the way they communicate, the news that adoption was on the table suddenly resurfaced.

The harsh reality

Norway likes to lecture other countries about human rights, yet at the same time it has absolutely no interest in finding a solution to its own serious problems. In 2015, the Council of Europe sharply criticised Norway with regard to its frequent use of foster care for children within its small Roma community. According to the Council of Europe, 120 Oslo-based Roma children between the ages of six and fifteen are already in foster care or threats have been made to that effect. This accounts for around half of all Roma children living in Oslo.

The Council of Europe's report states that many Roma women in Norway no longer have the courage to give birth in hospital because they fear their children will be taken away.[iv] There have been cases where mothers (and not only those from the Roma community) have tried to commit suicide after their children were taken away immediately after giving birth. Is the plight of Roma families living in Oslo so terrible that no better solution can be offered than simply taking away their children?

From a Czech point of view, the abusive practices of NCWS have been known since the end of 2014, but public criticism began much earlier than this. Back in 2005 the UN observed with concern the increasing number of children being placed in foster care. Since then the situation has worsened. Furthermore, the report claims that many children see their biological parents only twice a year, and that they lack knowledge about their own culture and language. Eva's case clearly supports this claim.

NCWS pretends that everything it does is in accordance with the recommendations of the Council of Europe's Commissioner for Human Rights, Nils Muižnieks. For example, it appears to agree that removing children from their parents must be a last resort, employed only when all other solutions have failed. According to Muižnieks, the Norwegian authorities must also offer alternative care to support Roma parents in accordance with human rights laws. Sadly, the reality is very different.

The main reason for taking the children away is the families' inferior social status. But as Muižnieks confirms, poverty in itself is not sufficient reason to impose such harsh measures. The European Council has also called on the Norwegian authorities to find out why so many children have been taken from their families, and to investigate whether such confiscations are in accordance with international law.

The Norwegian government stated in its response that its people are not registered by ethnicity, and therefore it cannot comment on reports that nearly half of all Roma children in Oslo have been placed in foster care. There are certainly no statistics relating to the removal of children according to their ethnic origin. On paper, child protection laws must be applied to all children, regardless of their ethnic origin.

Two possible conclusions can be drawn from this information. Either NCWS comes out as a racist organisation with a terrifying image, or, in the interests of political correctness, Norwegians are simply unable to solve problems relating specifically to the Roma community. Whichever is the case, a very serious failure has occurred here. Given its stubborn refusal to accept criticism, Norway is harming its own reputation and the reputations of many parents across the country.

Norwegian fairy tales

In an article entitled "A new Norwegian empire of happy people and fairy tales", Zdechovský writes:[v]

> The problem with children being taken away from able

> and caring families in Norway is finally beginning to move society, which is a good thing. However, other problems foreigners face are also appearing on the horizon. A change in the law in 2015 has allowed the authorities to force children to go to kindergarten. If parents refuse, the authorities can take their children away. This new law makes the situation even worse for foreigners.

According to Kjetil Odin Johnsen, CEO of Whatif AS, which provides software relating to risk and data protection, families will soon be forced to send children to preschool, watch Norwegian television and have a set number of Norwegian friends. In an article titled, "With coercion we will build the country", he asks two very important questions:[vi]

- Has any research been carried out with regard to whether the new amendment to the Children's Act is lawful in relation to human rights?
- Secondly, as stated in the media, the new change is specially aimed at immigrant children. Is the government allowed to create laws that are designed only for a few? Isn't this a form of discrimination?

Johnsen finishes his article by reminding readers of the Sámi people, and how Sámi children were denied the opportunity to learn their mother tongue. Instead, they were forced to understand everything that was foreign to them. Although the King of Norway apologised to the Sámi people for what happened to them, we appear to be doing the very same thing to children from ethnic minorities today.

There is a difference between taking a child away from drug addicts or alcoholics who are systematically abusing their children and taking a child away from a completely 'normal' family that is just a bit 'different'. Added to this, the most prominent parenting moralists often turn out to be the worst parents!

For example, Peter Newell was a leading children's rights campaigner who worked for UNICEF and led the UK's anti-smacking campaign in London. In fact, Newell also helped prepare

UNICEF's Implementation Handbook for the Convention on the Rights of the Child. In 2018 he was convicted at Blackfriars Crown Court of several horrific sexual assaults, including the rape of a thirteen-year-old boy.[vii]

Children of the state

In an article entitled "Everything you wanted to know about Norwegian CPS Barnevernet and you were afraid to ask", Zdechovský writes about a new documentary about NCWS called *Children of the State*,[viii] which was shown on Czech television. He writes:[ix]

> The director, Ivana Pauerova-Miloševič, does not press her views on the viewer. In fact, she makes a concerted effort to keep her distance, also drawing attention to comparable failures in the Czech child protection service (CPS), particularly in its excessive use of institutional care for toddlers. But she leaves viewers in no doubt that there is something fundamentally wrong with the Norwegian child welfare system, and makes it clear that it would be a mistake to overlook these problems.
>
> In spite of the many frightening abduction cases, the documentary attempts to explain Norway's approach to the Czech public. The road to hell is often paved with good intentions, and the documentary clearly shows how this statement fully applies to NCWS. The whole film confirms virtually everything I have been saying for the last five years.
>
> Certain significant numbers should be mentioned whenever NCWS is discussed, and these figures are stated in the documentary. According to sources featured in the documentary, 3,000 cases of removal are reported in Norway each year. Czech figures are slightly higher, but the country is twice the size of Norway. NCWS receives up to 70,000 anonymous reports annually, and eighty per cent of these are investigated. Around 53,000 children receive some form of 'assistance', such as a 'weekend foster-man who cuts wood with children'. This is one method used

in cases where NCWS considers that a child being raised by a single mother is missing out on a male role model, as Margaret Hruza, the documentary's co-author, reveals in one of the interviews.

Indeed, the key reasons behind the removal of children are very different for each country. In the Czech Republic the most common reason for removing children is the families' inferior social status, while the most common reason in Norway is a lack of parental ability. This is where problem begins, because this is such a vague reason, under which anything can be hidden; even a badly prepared breakfast.

I have mentioned many times that the difficulty primarily lies in the fact that NCWS has unlimited power. Virtually nobody has effective control over the state organisation. This fact is particularly well known by the family of a woman named Charlotte, whose two children were removed on the basis of her stepmother's report, which claimed that Charlotte was failing to give her children sufficient care.

The children were returned to Charlotte after seventeen months. It was only after this prolonged period that the Norwegian courts declared that the removal had been completely unjustified. During the proceedings, however, the mother had become pregnant again. The newborn was preventively taken away just fourteen hours after the birth! This third child was not returned as NCWS stated that the six-month-old girl had become used to the foster parents. The family has been fighting for return of the daughter for more than five years now. At the very least they want to see her more than four times a year.

Charlotte's partner, who was also interviewed for the documentary, believes NCWS goes way too far when it takes children into care. Its actions seem to come down to the fact that it can, not because they are needed. "Where abusive power can be abused, it will be abused," as Hruza says. If they don't like you they will take your child and find some reason for doing so. NCWS can explain everything it does. For example, when Charlotte and her partner tidied the house, as they usually did before each official visit,

NCWS reported that it looked as though no children were living in their home.

The words of Charlotte's partner were also (unintentionally) confirmed by staff at one NCWS office, which allowed a televised interview to take place. The staff member admitted that sometimes they went too far in trying to provide the best care for the children under their supervision. According to Pauerová-Miloševič, NCWS no longer deals with genuinely problematic cases, but solely examines whether parents are good enough to keep their children.

Anyone who wants to know more about the child protection philosophy in Norway should read Norwegian social worker Kari Killén's book *Sveket*, which is translated as *Betrayal.*[8] This is the Barnevernet Bible, and, as the title indicates, betrayed children are blamed for the way society is today.

The following points are therefore listed in the book: the state is supposed to protect the child from every act of violence committed by parents and foster parents; protecting children from any negative stimulus has to be an absolute priority; the child must not be exposed to any stress or stimulus that could cause depression; and showing sadness in front of a child is unacceptable.

According to the book, the state does everything it can to ensure that children are brought up to achieve their potential. To this end, NCWS holds free 'parent management' courses for parents. It advocates that the child should receive more recognition for what it does (for example washing dishes), although this sort of chore should be considered normal.

The documentary also points out, indirectly, that in NCWS' view a child's upbringing is only a technical matter, and that the biological parents' emotional bond with the child plays virtually no role. If a child is taken away and

8 The subtitle, "Omsorgssvikt er alles ansvar", means "Neglect is everyone's responsibility", and the book encourages people from all walks of life to report even the slightest concern they might have about a child, even if it is nothing more than a rumour or a lie, with no evidence needed to substantiate the claim.

entrusted to another person for a long period of time, the principle is that they must be kept away from their original home to consolidate the newly created bond.

Watching the documentary, you can sense the struggle people face in talking publicly about NCWS. This particularly applies to those who are willing to voice their criticism. As Hruza says at the beginning, people can lose their jobs if they publicly criticise Norwegian social workers.

The truth is, being under the 'care' of Barnevernet means social stigma, and therefore people refuse to talk about it. Other members of the public think something really must have happened if NCWS has turned up. Why? Because they cannot admit that it could be a mistake. Even Hruza's Norwegian partner was unwilling to speak on this subject because he was unwilling to accept any criticism against the Norwegian system.

Those who have observed the situation over a long period are not surprised that NCWS showed little willingness to speak in the film. The secrecy it employs when it comes to acting in the 'best interests of the child' is a long-standing problem. Its reluctance to speak openly was explained by the aforementioned NCWS employee. She explained that it was because Czech media sources do not write positive things about the institution.

Norwegian society is typically uncritical of the state, and has a close and trusting relationship with it. The state is considered to be a 'friend' who only wants the best for its people. The same applies when it comes to following unwritten social conventions that everyone knows are to be observed. Even though they are unwritten, failure to comply may rouse suspicion in others, and the people in question are soon likely to find themselves in NCWS' viewfinder or facing other social issues.

This reminded me of the almost 200-year-old words of French political thinker Alexis de Tocqueville who, in his famous work *De La Démocratie en Amérique* ("*Democracy in America*"), warned against the tyranny of the majority manifesting exactly as described above.[x] He argued that society is expected to comply with a number of social norms, and that no one should stray too far from them. Those who do face the likelihood of becoming ostracised from the rest of society.

The same applies in today's Norway. Every parent must keep an eye on one another. The pressure to adhere to these unwritten societal rules is enormous. For example, Sofie, Hruza's young daughter, told her mother at the beginning of the documentary that she would like to invite her friends, or even just some girls, to her birthday party, but that she was unable to do so. Why? Because other children would be sad if they were not also invited. To save their feelings they would have to invite the entire class, and this was not possible, so there could be no party.

The fact that societal pressure in Norway can be very unpleasant, especially for foreigners, is eloquently demonstrated through the story of journalist Andrej Ruščák. Ruščák lived in Norway for several years but recently decided to return to the Czech Republic. He did not feel comfortable in Norway precisely because of this ubiquitous watchfulness. The way children were controlled at preschool reminded him of an interrogation, while the general social pressure around compliance and the enforcement of informal rules was hard for Ruščák and his family to bear. The thought of NCWS was the last straw, and he described his move back to the Czech Republic as a 'statement': an open expression of disagreement with what was happening in Norway.

The *Children of the State* documentary makes a very strong statement, indicating that there is something seriously wrong in Norway, and that all the talk of unjust kidnappings is not just an elaborate rumour. I wonder how many documentaries like this must be filmed before all the uncritical NCWS supporters finally understand that there is something fundamentally wrong, and that they should stop downplaying the situation and holding Norway up as an example for change in relation to overseas child protection systems.

Chapter 8 notes

[i] Zdechovský, T., "Barnevernet's Harassment of Czech Mother Knows No Boundaries in Norway" Tumblr: https://tomaszdechovskymep.tumblr.com/post/112615247607/barnevernets-harassment-of-czech-mother-knows-no

[ii] Zdechovský, T., "Baby Aria and her family", Justice for baby Aria and her family: https://baby-aria-and-the-fight-for-justice.webnode.com/tomas-zdechovskys-letters-to-solveig-horne

[iii] Zdechovský, T., "Norway's Orwellian system of child protection and care", *The Sunday Guardian Live*: https://www.sundayguardianlive.com/culture/norways-orwellian-system-child-protection-care

[iv] Muižnieks, N., "Council of Europe report on the Human Rights of people with disabilities": https://rm.coe.int/ref/CommDH(2015)9

[v] Zdechovský, T., "New Norwegian Empire of Happy People and Fairy Tales", Tumblr: https://tomaszdechovskymep.tumblr.com/post/130680728872/new-norwegian-empire-of-happy-people-and-fairy

[vi] Johnsen, K. O., "Med tvang skal vi bygge landet" ("With coercion we will build the country"), Nordnorsk Debatt: http://nordnorskdebatt.no/article/tvang-skal-vi-bygge-landet

[vii] Fielding, J., "Top UNICEF children's rights campaigner – who led UK's anti-smacking campaign – is jailed for rape of boy, 13, in latest charity sex scandal", MailOnline: http://www.dailymail.co.uk/news/article-5399247/UNICEF-kids-rights-campaigner-jailed-rape-boy-13.html#ixzz5BmwQvTuO

[viii] *Children of the State*, Česká: https://www.ceskatelevize.cz/ivysilani/10408111009-cesky-zurnal/216562262600004-deti-statu

[ix] Zdechovský, T., "Everything you wanted to know about Norwegian CPS Barnevernet and you were afraid to ask", Tumblr: https://tomaszdechovskymep.tumblr.com/post/167871848652/everything-you-wanted-to-know-about-norwegian-cps

[x] Henary, S., "What Would Tocqueville Do?" *The American Conservative*: https://www.theamericanconservative.com/articles/what-would-tocqueville-do

9

Dehumanised

Our culture divides people into two classes: civilized men, a title bestowed on the persons who do the classifying; and others, who have only the human form, who may perish or go to the dogs for all the "civilized men" care.

Oh, this "noble" culture of ours! It speaks so piously of human dignity and human rights and then disregards this dignity and these rights of countless millions and treads them underfoot... This culture has no right to speak of personal dignity and human rights.

French-German theologian Albert Schweitzer in his book, Reverence for Life.[i]

The teaching materials NCWS employees are exposed to are a significant driving force behind the agency's abusive attitude and actions toward Norwegian families and their children. The recommendations offered in the teaching material do not only lack professional input but are also unsupported from a scientific viewpoint. Weak claims and 'investigations' support the weakening of the family unit, forcing children away from their parents and into the arms of NCWS. These warped ideologies have a disastrous impact on children and their parents. Few books have caused as much pain as *Sveket* by Kari Killén.

Margaret Hennum lifted the lid on NCWS by exploring its inhumane ideology and foundations, which have created inferior and superior people groups in Norway, disregarding the most basic human rights and personal dignity, especially of the most vulnerable in society: children. She writes (text translated):[ii]

I am a paediatric nurse with forty years of work experience in the healthcare sector. With increasing knowledge of

> NCWS' working methods it has struck me that they have a different view of people from the one I have, based on my own professional life.
>
> Frustrated and heavily tested parents describe a child welfare system that does not create any dialogue, but only observes, commands and reports. Frustrated health workers, teachers, day care workers and child welfare workers also describe a child welfare system that does not create dialogue but only requires them to file reports.
>
> *Sveket* by Kari Killén is the main book about childcare failure that is used in the education of NCWS workers. This book was written based on her opinion of a mother who did not want her child, as she herself stated at a seminar in Molde in 2009.

Hennum cites p. 505 of Killén's book, which urges NCWS employees to cut all emotional bonds with the parents they are investigating. The parents are told to admit to things that are not true, for example that their grief is selfish and not related to the child's suffering. According to Killén, this demonstrates an immature need for the parents to keep the child in order to make themselves feel safe, cared for and complete, which constitutes a 'primitive' emotional need.

Hennum continues:

> Killén also claimed at this seminar in Molde that parents who do not give good care to their children are rarely able to learn how to do so.
>
> NCWS dehumanises parents, and I think these statements from Killén explain why. They are purely based on her own ideas, and are not anchored in research. Killén's book provides a long list of references to research reports, but where she relies on research in the text it would have been helpful to reference which pieces of research she is basing her statements and conclusions on! The lack of such information makes it impossible to test her claims in relation to the reference material.
>
> NCWS produces a large number of child welfare cases based on statistics. The methods are described in a

book called *Rettferdiggjøring av omsorgsovertakelse* (*The Justification of Care Orders*) by Elisabeth Backe-Hansen.[iii]

The dehumanisation strategies social workers are taught through their studies make them treat people as Untermensch ["subhuman"], a familiar term used in Europe during the 1930s and 1940s.

Joar Tranøy, a psychologist who shone a significant spotlight on the dysfunctional Norwegian child welfare system, claims that such treatment of parents by NCWS is copied by the rest of society over time (stigmatisation).

Dehumanisation in child welfare threatens the legal security of the parents and violates the human rights of children and their families (for example Norwegian TV2 news reports in 2016-17 that show parents with allegedly low IQ scores have been deprived of their children for that reason).

In the book he co-wrote with Nina Langfeldt, *Kampen om barnets beste* (*The fight for the child's best interest*), Tranøy writes the following about the way human opinion is expressed in NCWS' work [text translated]:[iv]

- NCWS consistently considers the child's best interests as contradictory to the interests of the parents.
- There is a mistrust of parents' explanations, competence, knowledge, descriptions and perceptions of reality.
- Parents' arguments are not discussed or considered.
- Good cooperation is defined by NCWS as the parents doing as NCWS says, agreeing to accept NCWS staff as the experts and acknowledging that NCWS knows better than them in every respect.
- Conflicts between NCWS and parents or foster parents are always considered to be the parents' fault.

German-American psychologist Wolf Wolfensberger stated:[v]

> The most serious devaluation happens when we collectively or as an entire community devalue others collectively (as a group or class). This devaluation on a 'higher level' is the most drastic, because it creates a society that devalues others

through class status, which results in the systematic ill-treatment of citizens and of the social structure, including the community's help.

The trump card and puzzle cases

It has been said in NCWS circles that a good case worker can take any child at any time from any parent. But how can a case worker take children away from their parents unless it is an extreme and exceptional situation in which they could come to serious harm as a result of a parent's behaviour?

A trump card is one strategy NCWS uses to take children away from functional and able parents. When the agency has a specific reason to get involved in a family's life, for instance it may discover that one or both parents have health issues or are receiving medical treatment (prescription drugs), or that the parents were beaten when they were growing up (violence toward children is as inheritable as the colour of one's skin, according to NCWS) or that they experimented with recreational drugs as teenagers. It takes nothing more than a parent being prescribed the 'wrong' medication or a child saying that the mother has done something she hasn't for drastic action to be taken.

One recent example involves a child who told kindergarten workers her mum had thrown a towel at her. It was a complete accident, but NCWS typically pulled it out as a trump card. All it takes is for NCWS to receive a report from a 'concerned' citizen. It will then start an investigation and look for pieces that fit into the false puzzle it is creating.

If a trump card cannot be used, 'puzzle cases' are created by finding normal things in the parenting process and turning them into what NCWS considers to be a form of abuse. In a nutshell, it builds cases based on menial issues.

NCWS will routinely enter the family home and observe its members. These observations may be carried out unexpectedly or as planned events, the former usually being more stressful than the latter. The puzzle pieces are usually constructed from tiny things, such as the tone of a mother's voice, a lack of eye contact or the parents' IQ level, which NCWS sometimes tests.

Its employees use every possible tactic to stress the parents out in order to observe their reactions under pressure. If a parent becomes angry NCWS suspects violent behaviour in front of, or toward, the children. If the parents do not react strongly they are considered to lack the ability to see themselves objectively or to understand life. 'Apathy' is a word commonly used to describe a shocked parent. In this case, NCWS suspects that the parents lack the ability to take care of the child, so its staff take the child away. These puzzle-style cases usually consist of piles of documents designed to convey a parent's lack of parenting skills. This is what NCWS employees are trained to do. If they are able to present numerous puzzle pieces this takes the place of a trump card, and these fragments are put together to justify taking innocent children away from perfectly able and caring parents. The ideology that underpins NCWS' work gives it the power to turn a perfectly normal parent into what appears to be a terrible caregiver.

Berit Aarset reveals the dark and distorted ideology that justifies the destruction of perfectly normal families in Norway:[vi]

> When I became aware of Elisabeth Backe-Hansen's dissertation and her book *Justification of Care Orders* I was deeply shocked. As Elisabeth Backe-Hansen is a psychologist she should, in my opinion, be more critical of the methods described here, especially in connection with the so-called puzzle cases.
>
> My encounter with this thesis was a driving force behind my decision to write the Abuse of Power and the Miscarriage of Justice, a book in which I present my experiences as a foster mother/grandmother, and in which all the papers in our case are published.
>
> Puzzle cases are what we see in most of our work at Human Rights Alert – Norway (HRA-N). Our organisation often encounters negative and frequently untrue statements from NCWS.
>
> This puzzle method can be used to frame anyone, and the result is often the wrongful removal of children. NCWS speaks publicly about violence and abuse cases. The widespread notion of NCWS' cases is largely based on this.

The Backe-Hansen dissertation refers to sixteen cases (twenty-one children aged under seven living with care measures in their homes, with suggestions being made by NCWS about future foster home placements), which are most likely based on Kari Killén's theories.

Killén's child welfare theories have consistently been used for the education of social workers, and are employed as an expert foundation for most of the work that takes place within NCWS. There is no reason to believe that these sixteen cases are any different. For many years, Backe-Hansen and Killén have been colleagues at the Norwegian Social Research's (NOVA's) child protection research department. One may therefore ask whether the research has been executed in a critical light.

The title *Justification of Care Orders* can be seen as a returning boomerang for Backe-Hansen. She indirectly justifies these methods, while refusing to admit to the possibility of NCWS committing errors. Backe-Hansen must be considered a very important person when it comes to the development of Norwegian child welfare services, as she has been part of NOVA since its inception in 1996.

For anyone who is in contact with child welfare services – those with an ongoing case, relatives of children who have been taken, civic-minded people and politicians – my book will provide insight into a typical puzzle case described in the summary above.

Trump cards are vague and often relate to things that are no longer a real issue by the time NCWS involves itself in a family's life. Take, for example, parents with substance abuse issues. Parents who are part of the LAR [methadone] project and are not scrutinised by NCWS will most likely be allowed to keep their children. But investigated parents who have somehow been involved with drugs – perhaps during their teenage years, having since managed to get away from them – often lose their children as it is assumed they will 'crack' in the future.

Ten trump cards

The following summary of reasons for early intervention in 'troubled families' is found in the book *Child Abuse* written by German authors Ruth S. Kempe and C. Henry Kempe.[vii] (Interestingly, the book has the same name as a very similar manual written by Killén, which was published several years later.[viii]) The Kempes claim to be able to foresee the risk of child abuse, and support the practice of taking children away from their biological families before any trouble should arise. The ten 'commandments' featured in the book function as a list of reasons repeatedly used by NCWS to create a case against a family. These reasons will be familiar to the Norwegian parents who have to fight to win their children back, and to achieve justice.

Some of the reasons used to justify creating a case against a family include the parents (or even just one of them) being beaten repeatedly or grossly neglected as children. Other reasons include one or both of the parents having a criminal record, or having been hospitalised for a psychiatric disorder. Other reasons that could trigger a case against a family include a child being perceived as provocative and difficult, or an assumption that the parents having difficulty establishing emotional bonds with the child.

Projected failure

Rune Fardal hosts The Family Channel, a live-stream service in Norway that focuses on children, the family and human rights. Fardal studies psychology and personality disorders with an emphasis on narcissism. He shared serious concerns about Kari Killén with the author of this book:

> Kari Killén has been given goddess status in textbooks, lectures and lessons for future child welfare social workers. For several decades, serious abuses and lack of knowledge in child welfare services have been revealed. Who is this Killén, this person who has been dominating this field for so long without anyone asking serious and critical questions of her methods and her knowledge?
>
> Killén has based her knowledge on her own research of seventeen children in 1988. In her book, *Omsorgssvikt*

> *og barnemishandling – en kasusstudie og etterundersøkelse av barn I omsorgssviktsituasjoner* (*Caregiving and child abuse: a case study and follow-up study of children in neglect situations*), she developed her own method for determining and predicting neglect on the part of parents. The study is based on the parents of these seventeen children without the use of any kind of control group!

Fardal recognises that Killén is very concerned about parents neglecting their children, so it's worth asking the following questions: what actually happened in Killén's childhood? And how did Killén treat her own children?

He refers to the technique Killén describes as 'projective identification' and goes on to explain that this is a kind of primitive psychological defence mechanism that has prompted Killén to pass on her experience and infiltrate NCWS with it. Fardal claims projective identification projects a parent's frustration and negative traits onto others, making them appear to be the frustrated ones. This perceived frustration can then be used to take children away from their parents.

Killén's doctoral thesis on the study of seventeen children has in some way shaped today's NCWS. She suggested that social workers should evaluate which parents can help children survive, and NCWS took her theories very seriously. The result of this has been tragic for many families.

Killén presents the idea that 45 per cent of Norwegian children suffer from emotional neglect due to uncertain bonding, meaning that 45 per cent of children will be traumatised by their own parents. This gives NCWS a reason to 'assist' families it considers to be incapable of raising children so that the parents do not damage their children. Killén insists that understanding what she calls "the emotional neglect in the middle classes" demands a higher education than professionals such as doctors and nurses gain through their studies. She insists that her students are educated to the highest level.

One thing is certain: government support for these theories has led to the creation of many jobs for professionals and people associated with them and, power and influence has increased for a select few.[ix]

Weak foundations

Lawyer Mette Jacobsen Heap is Kari Killén's daughter. Here is an extract from Heap's forthcoming book:[x]

> About twelve years ago I said yes to a project in a small West Jutland community, where my task was simply to clean up the region's family cases. In short, the council placed the children in care, then afterwards I had to find out whether the law had been followed. If the law had not been followed these shortcomings had to be repaired. Without exaggeration, a great deal of issues were in need of repair.
>
> Even after a short while I became very worried about what I had witnessed. I saw that in many of these cases the rights of the parents and the children had been completely ignored. I often wondered how, without any attempt to help the families, they chose removal from the family and placement elsewhere as the first and only solution.
>
> During the first couple of weeks in the region, several people commented on my middle name [Heap was using Killén as her middle name at the time]. Among others, a health worker came to my office one day and told me she had heard I was the daughter of her great role model and guru, and that they made great use of Killén's theories in their local authority.
>
> This idolisation of my mother and her books shocked me. I grew up in a home where both my parents were writing, but I had not read their books and had never paid attention to their content. During my time working on this project I read Killén's books, and I was stunned. Her usual logic, which I had grown up with, pervaded her work: "First, we decide what the conclusion is and then we can always find some conditions that fit afterwards." I was already wondering why professionals were not more critical. I was sitting there with piles of cases that were completely unimaginable; where professionalism, law, empathy and compassion were absolutely non-existent in the decisions. And it sent shivers down my spine when I realised that what I had really been employed to do was clean up after my mother's disciples.

> My book is an attempt to understand how, using such a sparsely theoretical basis, a woman can gain so much recognition throughout the world without any of the many counter arguments being heard. The most vulnerable group I work with includes parents who are at risk of having their children confiscated and placed in foster care. They, more than anyone, need to be treated with respect, attentiveness and confidence. It is often a difficult job to establish this trust because they are traumatised by the system and are terribly afraid of losing what matters most to them. In addition, they are ashamed that their ability to be good parents is being questioned. When I meet them – let alone when the system meets them – they feel afraid, powerless and ashamed.
>
> This brings me back to Killén and her theories and methods. In one of her books she wrote that it may be necessary to intentionally stress the parents out in observation situations to investigate how they handle pressure. I would like to classify this method as evil. In addition to classifying this method as evil, it is also cynical and cold. Evil, cynicism and coldness do not belong in social work, or in legal work within social work situations.
>
> As I was right in the middle of it all and saw the horrified look in one particular mother's eyes, I could only feel a deep powerlessness and anger. The anger was caused by how sick and manipulative this system, which was supposedly put there to help and protect children, has become. At the same time, I felt an indescribable sense of disgrace that the founder of this idea to stress parents out on purpose within observation situations was my own mother!
>
> At that moment I decided that I would no longer avoid family cases. I would rather take on the fight and use my professionalism to ensure that children and parents in vulnerable situations are treated with decency and sober judgement.

Heap concedes that her mother failed her miserably as a parent. In fact, she explains in detail how Kari Killén never met the expectations of the parenting skills checklist she compiled for parents living in Norway and other Nordic states, including Denmark.

Killén's book is poorly researched and unscientific, with a distorted anti-family ideology intertwined throughout. It works backwards, starting with defining a very scary reality that a child finds him or herself in, which only exists, it would seem, in the author's imagination. The result of this type of ideology leads to the justification that it is necessary in the 'best interests of the child', to abuse families and their children, as we are witnessing in Norway today.

The abuse carried out by the Norwegian authorities against the Sámi, Kven, Tater and Romani people was not supported by any literature; however, in the last few decades this abuse has been supported by 'expert' research. This research has given NCWS the green light to target any family it chooses wherever these theories are put into practice.

The abuse of power in the name of doing good

Based on almost forty years of close contact with NCWS, Gro Hillestad Thune claims in her article, "The abuse of power in the name of doing good", that human rights violations are a huge problem. She writes:[xi]

> The ground beneath the feet of NCWS is burning. Children are exposed to serious maltreatment and abuses of power every day.
>
> NCWS employees also describe the heartbreaking harassment of their own children [usually by frustrated and heartbroken family members who are connected in some way to a child that was removed by NCWS]. The turnover of jobs is rapid, and new employees quickly replace those who leave, most likely with the initial intention of helping the children they meet.
>
> Families who are in contact with local child welfare services are, if it is possible, even more despairing and angry about having their lives torn apart than those who have experienced the dark side of NCWS from working within the agency. The rage is often well-founded, and it is shared by those of us who are seeing at close hand how

the supposed children's safety net often causes children irreparable harm and trauma for life.

Solveig Horne and her department are making stubborn attempts to overcome these challenges. However, it is usually a case of covering up the holes in a system that almost nobody trusts any more.

If we try to take a bird's-eye perspective, it's easy to see that the fundamental problem is something neither the many investigations nor the meaningless debates between child welfare critics and defenders have pointed out: that the child welfare crisis is based on something as unpleasant as the abuse of power in the name of doing good, managed by people who have the task of helping children, and who probably even think that's what they are doing.

Norway has been voted the world's happiest country. Many believe that we have the world's best welfare services. If anyone dares to claim that our health workers and social workers have power, and that some of them abuse this power in a way that affects innocent people, the defenders quickly surface with their arrogant arguments.

As a human rights lawyer, I have, for a long time now, documented the fact that in Norway we are much less cautious than other countries when it comes to giving health workers and social workers the right to use their power as they see fit, almost without any control. The Norwegian parliament adopts laws and measures that give NCWS great freedom of action, with almost unlimited confidence in its widely used laws and measures.

The freedom of action given to those fronting our welfare state may not be seen as power that can be used and abused. Elected MPs and local councillors are strikingly indifferent to our public prosecutors' abuse of power. The same goes for our media and research communities. Little attention is given to the security of those the welfare services were established to help.

An unreasonable force

It is striking how disinterested people are in investigating how the established complaints and control systems actually work. This applies to politicians, research communities, trade unions, the media and society in general. When there are individual cases that reveal how employees have exceeded their legitimate power they are seen as the exception to the rule.

When Norway was sentenced [by the European Court of Human Rights] in Strasbourg in the Adele Johansen child welfare case, the response was that the old men who had passed the sentence must not have had an adequate comprehension of the safe and well-functioning Norwegian child welfare system.

I think we can expect the same reaction if Norway is convicted again in one or more of the eight cases that are currently under scrutiny in Strasbourg. If [Norwegian writers and social critics] Jens Bjørneboe or Arnulf Øverland were alive today, they would be pleading with us to wake up.

Many believe that abuse of power, physical abuse and human rights violations directed toward children and adults by NCWS employees cannot be a widespread problem. Based on almost forty years of close contact with the child welfare sector in Norway I can confirm that the opposite is true.

Children are exposed, every day, and in many areas of this country, to serious foolishness and abuses of power, often in contravention of the fundamental rights they have been given by the Norwegian parliament, and by the Human Rights Act and section 104 of the constitution.

Even parents who haven't done anything wrong will constantly feel the unreasonable force of NCWS; a force the vast majority of us still fear coming into contact with. This is not the way a society should function. What children really need is a child welfare system they can trust.

The community closes its eyes

Many years have gone by while we have spent time tricking

ourselves into believing that everything was going well and that NCWS' work is always carried out with wisdom, respect and responsibility. Along with the Norwegian prime minister and the minister in charge of child welfare, the Norwegian people have been encouraged to report even the slightest concern about a child's situation.

In my opinion, this encouragement is based on a naive, life-threatening trust that the child will end up in safe hands. Police, healthcare centres, psychiatrists, principals, NAV employees[9] and the rest of us are obliged to trust that NCWS prosecutors always know what these children need.

The system currently works in such a way that all other public servants have been pushed into the role of minions beneath the NCWS officers who, because of their child welfare experience, have been given the status of experts and an exclusive right to determine the 'best interests of the child'.

The opinions of neighbours, preschool employees, grandparents, police officers, parents of the child's friends and others who know the child well do not count if they happen to contradict NCWS' opinion on what is best for the child. There are countless examples where children's statutory rights to be heard and involved in their own cases were not worth the paper they were written on.

The present crisis in the Norwegian child welfare system is a glittering example of how wrong things can go when society closes its eyes to the fact that power – regardless of the good intentions it is based on – can be abused. It is high time to acknowledge how risky it is to provide a closed auxiliary system, populated by young people with three years of college education, the right and duty to enter into people's private spheres with extensive authorisation to use these coercion tactics at their own discretion.

9 The Norwegian Labour and Welfare Administration (NAV) is responsible for administering unemployment benefit, child benefit, pensions and so on.

Where is parliament?

To me, it is impossible to comprehend that our parliament has not responded to the many warning lights that are now shining all over the world. Foreign journalists are swarming in. They are curious about the silence and are calling for an open debate around a system in which errors are not recorded, in which basic principles of quality assurance are absent and in which basic legal principles are not observed.

We have a local welfare system that is beyond the control of the politicians who are releasing government funds to support it, and a Bufdir[10] which, for incomprehensible reasons, has been empowered with overall responsibility for the quality of NCWS' work. NCWS has also been given a wide berth by the media and the public spotlight because of its dubious use of confidentiality.

Foreign journalists quickly discovered the same thing I did: that many innocent children and adults are subjected to abuses of power in child welfare cases. In reality, they are defenceless. In the 'National Report of Concern about NCWS', 250 professionals announced their great alarm, but apparently parliament is not responding. This is happening as we speak in Norway: the country of human rights.

Margaret Hennum responded to Thune's article with the following comment:[xii]

> Norwegians are concerned about human rights violations: but only the ones that happen far away from here, where those responsible are people we do not know. Amnesty Norway was shocked when the prime minister refused to confront and address human rights violations in China while she was there for political reasons. What is it that makes us Norwegians, Amnesty included, so ignorant of our history that we honestly believe crimes against our own people do not occur here at home?

10 The Norwegian Directorate for Children, Youth and Family Affairs, Bufdir, is the government body responsible for child welfare.

Chapter 9 notes

[i] Schweitzer, A., *Reverence for Life* (Ardent Media, 1979), p.53.

[ii] Hennum, M., "Noreg Sin Dehumaniserande Strategi, Del 1" ("Norway's Dehumanising Strategy: Part 1"), Human Rights Alert – Norway: http://www.hra-n.no/noreg-sin-dehumaniserande-strategi-del-1

[iii] Backe-Hansen, E., *Rettferdiggjøring av omsorgsovertakelse* ("*The Justification of Care Orders*"), NOVA Report 2/01, 2001: http://www.hioa.no/Om-OsloMet/Senter-for-velferds-og-arbeidslivsforskning/NOVA/Publikasjonar/Rapporter/2001/Rettferdiggjoering-av-omsorgsovertakelse

[iv] Tranøy, J. and Langfeldt, N., Kampen om barnets beste ("The fight for the child's best interest"), (Lanser, 2012).

[v] Wolfensberger, W., *A brief introduction to social valorization as a higher order concept for structuring human services* (Valor Press, 2013).

[vi] Aarset, B., cited by Bennett, S. in "Norges Dehumaniserende Strategi Del 2" ("Norway's Dehumanisation Strategy: Part 2), Facebook: https://www.facebook.com/notes/margaret-hennum/norges-dehumaniserende-strategi-del-2/1873481582900606

[vii] Kempe, R. S. and Kempe, C. H., *Child Abuse* (Harvard University Press, 1977).

[viii] Killén, K. *Barnemishandling: behandlerens dilemma* (*Child abuse: the therapist's dilemma*) (Tanum-Norli, 1981).

i[x] Christensen, E. [pseudonym], "The rise and fall (?) of the Norwegian CPS", Wings of the Wind: https://chrisreimersblog.com/tag/kari-killen

[x] Heap, M. J., *Svigtet: af hvem?* (*Let Down: by whom?*), not yet published at the time of writing this book.

[xi] Thune, G. H., "Maktmisbruk i det godes navn" ("Abuse of power in the name of doing good"), NRK: https://www.nrk.no/ytring/makt-utenfor-kontroll-1.13448919

[xii] Hennum, M., "Ignorance Isn't bliss - It's terrifying", Step Up 4 Children's Rights: https://stepup4childrensrights.com/ignorance-isnt-bliss-its-terrifying.

10

Attached

UK-born psychiatrist John Bowlby is renowned for creating the Attachment Theory that has been widely adopted by international NGOs and is also being used by NCWS to justify removing children from capable and caring parents. Keep in mind the following as you read through this chapter:

- John Bowlby's grandfather died in a tragic accident when John's father was five years old.
- A nanny raised John Bowlby, and he and his siblings only saw his mother for around an hour each day for most of the year.
- John Bowlby's nanny was cold and sarcastic toward him and his siblings, and the early loss of Bowlby's mother figure (his nursemaid Minnie), led to him creating the Attachment Theory.[i]

NCWS often removes babies and toddlers from their homes, claiming that the attachment they have with a parent (usually the mother) is lacking based on vague observations, such as whether a baby seeks eye contact with other people, which is perceived as evidence of it having an unloving mother. Parents are often analysed like guinea pigs in a social experiment. Child-and-parent interaction, personality traits, education level and so on can all be used to justify care orders.

Diversity

Dr Nandita Chaudhary, who taught at the University of Delhi for more than three decades, and Dr Heidi Keller, professor emeritus at Osnabrück University in Germany and director of research unit Nevet at the Hebrew University of Jerusalem, investigated the reliability of the Attachment Theory. They pointed out various settings in which the universal methods and practices would not apply and could easily lead to an incorrect evaluation of the attachment bond between a parent and child. While the need for parental love and care is universally recognised, the expression of this love and care varies, and the Attachment Theory fails to account for this variation.

Chaudhary and Keller write:[ii]

> Among several African communities, the expression 'It takes a village' is used to exemplify the number of people required to successfully raise a child. However, the Western study of childhood has focused largely on mothers, and recently, also on fathers… According to Attachment Theory an early, exclusive, sensitive and mutual bond between a baby and a caregiver (mother) is best for the child worldwide. From this early experience with the caregiver, a long-term model of relationships is said to be formed in the child's psyche, which determines its ability to form future relationships.
>
> Attachment Theory has gained much popularity in the 'scientific' study of childhood and has impacted child policy, parenting and education the world over. We argue that it is a major flaw of Attachment Theory not to take into account the historical and cultural diversity in beliefs and practices related to children's care.
>
> Families all over the world value children and try to do their best for them, yet the expression of care and love is different in different cultures. This is necessary, because care practices are delicately adapted to the ecological conditions and social history of any given community. For instance, the practice of separating a young baby from the mother to sleep in another room is considered necessary in some cultures, and seriously neglectful in others. Some parents promote the use of pacifiers for young infants, whereas others consider it harmful. Although these practices may have other reasons for their

prevalence, such as susceptibility to infections or space available in a home, they are taken as having serious and moral consequences.

Children for their part display an innate ability to adjust to different conditions and thrive under very diverse settings. Attachment Theory fails to accept this variability. It promotes the normative view that a baby must form an attachment with the constant presence of the mother, who is advised to dedicate her full attention and time to loving and caring for her baby in order for it to develop well.

Every community, every family, and, in fact, every parent has the right to bring up its children within the range of normative practices available to and valued by them. This is not an argument for 'anything goes', but to present a case against a narrow vision of Western childcare popularised by Attachment Theory that does not adequately represent variation even in the West. Such a view pathologises a majority of the world's populations and promotes a culturally specific, historically limited pattern of bringing up children, with a hint of moral superiority.

In many languages, (such as Hindi and German), there is no equivalent word for 'parenting'. It may come as a surprise that the word 'parenting' is a relatively new expression even in the English language, emerging in the 1970s. Its usage can be attributed to a shift in focus from affectionate care to purposeful stimulation. Whereas earlier children used to 'grow up', the focus has shifted to them being "brought up".

The human baby is by far the most dependent of all animal species at birth. However, along with modernisation, technological advancement and other changes in society, the period of vulnerability of young children seems to have been extended into later years.

The vulnerability of the child and belief in long-term consequences of early experiences has fed into an industry of stimulation for brain development (such as the animation series: *Little Einstein*). This is also a time when extended family bonds are weakened and adults hardly experience

> children before they have their own. The advent of birth control, higher education, work opportunities and increased individualism is accompanied by a significant slowing down of population growth and an 'inward turn', with greater importance on individual identity and self-presentation. Rather than promoting close relationships with a large social circle, there is a preference for promoting autonomy and independence. Children are encouraged from a very early age to do things on their own rather than depending on others. Culturally, the separation from other people is encouraged in contrast to the relational, interdependent and socially adapted notion of a person in the global South.

As intergenerational ties weakened and parents were left to their own means for childcare, the scientist entered the home. The first entry was made by paediatricians (like Dr Benjamin Spock), followed by psychologists and neurologists. 'Expert' advice was given priority over 'old wives' tales', and childhood became a science project. Early childhood education gained popularity and children gained special status, in need of strategic investment for a productive future. Discourse about parenting became a worldwide reality for educated parents and 'parenting' was established as a purposeful profession.

The care networks of children in non-Western lifestyles are, more often than not, extensive, with childcare and other responsibilities distributed among adults and children, kin and kith alike. One person may be the child's primary caregiver, but this caregiver may spend less time caring for the child than the combined collective input of all other caregivers.

As observed among the Efe foragers of the Democratic Republic of Congo, children are cared for by a range of people. Research among Senegalese villagers describes their belief that an adult is 'crazy' if she talks to a baby who obviously does not understand what is being said, "No one is there", it is said.

Being sensitive and conversational with babies is not a universal practice, although affection and care is. This love is expressed in many different ways. Communities differ in how much a child is believed to understand, and what the early reactions of babies mean. For instance, a child's early dreams may be attributed to neurological signals by some, but are believed by others to be echoes of a past life.

Some cultures follow and respond to children more often, while others tend to direct and instruct children from a very early age. Thus there is a wide-ranging variety in childcare settings and strategies.

Within multigenerational joint families in India, the typical form of care for children is several caregivers with many children. Grandparents, aunts, uncles, cousins and siblings are all roped into the care of a young child.

In such a setting, importance is given to a child's willingness and ability to get along with many adults, and several social games are arranged to promote this skill from a very young age. It is common to playfully tease a baby who is clinging to one person by pretending to briefly take her away. People around watch closely for a baby's reaction and then discuss these in the child's presence to provide feedback about temperament and relationships. A clingy child may experience more such social challenges. There is a constant encouragement of children to learn to get along with others. Large families and many relationships are also considered beneficial for others in the family. They provide valuable occupation for the elderly and are an important training ground for future caregiving among younger people. In such a setting, the notion of a self-contained autonomous individual as an outcome of development is subordinated to connectedness with others, relationality, sensitivity and obligation toward others from a very early age.

The roles and responsibilities of children's caregivers, including the mother, are likely to vary across people groups and time. In rural Madagascar, for example, role expectations of mothers are largely confined to caring for their children's physical needs. It is children who play and talk with other children. In fact, anthropological research has shown that there is very little evidence to suggest that mother-infant play is universal, let alone common.

Among Indian multigenerational joint families, mothers are urged to be "judiciously neglectful" so that others can step in to care for the baby. When this fails to happen and the mother-child bond appears too close, social pressure is placed on the mother to follow this practice.

In such settings, Attachment Theory and its methods would not apply. The expressions of sensitive care and warm responsiveness would not be discernible the way they are in a nuclear family system. If these relationships and children's adaptations are seen from the perspective and procedures of Attachment Theory, one can easily – but wrongly – conclude that there is a problem with the attachment bond when a young child does not react to a mother's departure from the room (because she may be used to being with others, and without the mother).

Many other practices are at odds with a relational and social orientation of childcare. For instance, the focus on always praising your child in order to promote self-esteem is another practice that would be considered inappropriate because is believed to be counterproductive to group living. Furthermore, public praise is also believed to make a child vulnerable to envy from others, something that is termed colloquially in some countries as *nazar* or 'the evil eye'. The focus on articulating feelings toward children by saying things like "I love you" or "you are the best" or "great job" all emerge from the project of building self-esteem that comes from the ideology of individualism in contrast to an orientation toward others.

Although Attachment Theory obviously promotes ideas about parenting and child development that are in stark contrast to what the majority of the world's population thinks and believes, it has become extremely powerful on account of the moral and cultural claims it makes of being the best way to bring up children. Once it was adopted by international NGOs the theory became the basis of intervention programmes worldwide.

Children's development is considered to be isolated from social context in documents such the United Nations Convention on the Rights of the Child. This is predicated on the notion of the individual as separate from society, and human or child development as separate from culture. When we accept these as 'universal principles', there is an overestimation of the role of science based on a Western philosophy of individualism. When such rules are accepted as binding, local cultural practices are undermined. Global policy presents a globalised view of childhood without acknowledging that it is conceptualised only in Euro-American ideology. We need to keep a critical vigilance on any policy that impacts the cultural lives of others to ensure that ethical boundaries are not crossed.

Caregiving in every community, every family, is directed toward goals that are related to cultural models that are valuable to a community. Variety and diversity in styles of caregiver-infant behaviour across cultures is the human condition. In the care of children, we have to accept that children are valued and cared for universally, but this universalism does not imply uniformity. When we are confronted with cultural diversity, for both ethical and scientific reasons, we must accept that the care of children is diverse and adapted to ecological settings. No one culture can have all the answers to the care of children.

Upside down

While the Bodnariu children were still being held by the Norwegian authorities, Dr Daniela Mariş wrote an article titled "Barnevernet or Upside-Down Psychiatry for Dummies" after researching the practices of NCWS. Mariş observed:[iii]

> From the moment information began to appear on social media I have followed the unfolding drama of the Bodnariu family. Like many of you, I went through several stages of processing the reality of this situation. The first stage was denial. The picture of an idyllic Nordic country, namely Norway, which is highly developed and very civilised, somehow didn't line up with the unbelievable act of confiscating five children, the youngest of whom was still being breastfed.
>
> I then moved to the next stage: I wanted information. I researched the practices of NCWS, the already infamous structure of the Norwegian child protection service. As the weeks progressed, curious aspects started to emerge. More and more documented situations that were surprisingly similar to the case of the Bodnariu family began to appear in the public eye...

A litany of questions emerged. What does the way one makes an omelette or how thick one slices the bread have to do with the confiscation of children? Why is the child not allowed to smile at strangers on the street? Why does the parent have to be punished because the baby is turning his or her head in the opposite direction when its face is being washed?

Every experiment, be it medical, social or otherwise, is motivated by a particular theory. And no matter how genius or ridiculous that theory might be, I have tried to unearth the one governing NCWS' activities. Because of my early interest in psychiatry, which began when I studied at the Iuliu Hațieganu University of Medicine and Pharmacy, and was sparked by the research of people like Dr Mariana Goron and Mr Steven Bennett, I have been drawn, on one hand, to the Attachment Theory and, on the other hand, to the Norwegian laws regarding the protection of children. So, can sense be made of this situation?

Let's discuss these problems in order. The Attachment Theory was launched by Mr John Bowbly, a British psychiatrist, and completed by the Canadian Mrs Mary Ainsworth. Based on the evolutionist model, the theory argues that, at the heart of the relational behaviour of every person there lies a relationship of fundamental attachment to a single individual, which is genetically determined and formed right after birth. Initially, this was considered to be the mother. This person was generically referred to as 'the person of reference' or 'the caregiver'. This attachment is of a great importance for the child in as much as he or she will formulate his or her behaviour and thinking to perpetuate this relationship. This continuity becomes essential to the survival of the individual. The attachment to the caregiver is so important for the child that he will prioritise it over his own well-being,

This child-caregiver attachment relationship is so strong that its impairment, destruction or disappearance leads to emotional and cognitive distresses in childhood as well as into adulthood. These distresses appear through passiveness, apathy, failure to thrive, agitation, lack of attention, the inability to form significant long-term relationships, emotional instability, depression, etc. It is important to emphasise here that there are several types of attachment, which are considered 'normal', even though not all of them are ideal: the secure (optimal), anxious-ambivalent, anxious-avoiding, disorganised and unclassified attachment. There are also pathological types of attachment disorder.

According to the Diagnosis and Statistics Manual of Mental Disorder (DSM),[iv] these are diagnosed by a psychologist or a psychiatrist following an in-depth evaluation and thorough standardised tests, as well as by verifying the qualifying criteria for psychiatric pathology(s). It is treated only under the direction of a psychiatrist. The most serious causes leading to these pathological attachment disorders are negligence, abuse or the violence of the caregiver inflicted upon the child.

This information is all well and good. The problems begin, however, with the way the NCWS agents are putting this theory in practice. In Romania we have a saying: *Teoria ca teoria, dar practica ne omoară*. Essentially, this means that an idea may be difficult in theory, but in practice it will be far more so. I have read about multiple families that are suffering greatly under this system. Without exception, I have identified a few of the major problems at the root of each case:

1. The most condemning problem is that this 'practice' launches from the presumption that the parent is guilty. From the very beginning the process starts off with the unshakeable conviction that these children (who will ultimately be taken away from their families) are, in fact, suffering from a pathological attachment disorder. This automatically means that they have either been abused, neglected or beaten in some way, and must therefore be immediately removed from this aggressive environment. The natural result of this presumption is to look for (or create, when actual incriminating evidence is lacking) proofs to justify this purpose.

2. The presumption of guilt originates when 'concerns' or 'assumptions' are expressed by people who have no psychiatric qualifications to evaluate or assess the given situation but are given the instructions and authority to do exactly that: evaluate and assess. This opens wide the doors that have led to abuses throughout the system. Observe the Bodnariu girls' situation. They were taken from their parents after a denouncement in which the director of their school expressed her 'concern' that the girls 'might be' being disciplined at home.

3. Another glaring problem is that the diagnosis of pathological attachment disorder has been given by individuals who are not psychiatrists! In the majority of cases the diagnosis is false. If, in the best-case scenario, those assessing the situation actually were psychologists, it has been revealed that they did not apply standardised testing nor repeated evaluation in giving a diagnosis according to all the criteria found in the DSM. This has been the case in all the situations presented thus far. They would not have had the time to follow this protocol because everything was done so quickly. It has been justified that 'this is how things are', without proof. And then the children are removed as an emergency. According to the declarations given by Norwegian activist Marius Reikerås, even the psychologists who tried to point out the discordance between the family's situation and the severity of the measures taken became undesirable to those in charge of the system. Lecturer Gunn Astrid Baugerud from Oslo and Akershus University College of Applied Sciences [HiOA, now Oslo Metropolitan University] noted in a study of criminalistic psychology that this discrepancy between the problems of the family and the extreme measures of urgently taking children away has appeared in an unjustified number of cases.

4. The way the evidence is fabricated is an insult to civilised psychology and medicine, and most especially to psychiatry.

Here are a few examples:

- The child turning his or her face away when it is being washed by the father. For NCWS this means the child is afraid that the father would hit him or her, not a normal reaction of a child when a wet hand is placed on his or her face.
- The child is intently watching people passing by on the street. For NCWS, this means that the A2 criteria from DSM-IV-TR shows that the child has an under-reactive attachment disorder or undiscriminating sociability, rather than, as is actually the case, a normal interest in other human beings, which demonstrates the standard psychological development of the child.
- The mother cries when the baby is ripped from her arms by NCWS. This supposedly means that she suffers from depression, a decision made without an evaluation, without any diagnostic criteria and without any differential diagnosis.
- The mother is suffering from a profound ambivalence in her interpersonal relations. An ambivalence or inconsistency, which is, of course, denied by the father. For NCWS, this suggests that the mother has a pathological attachment disorder herself, which will be reflected in the attachment of the child to the mother; an aspect sustained by the Attachment Theory but unconfirmed by those who know the mother personally.
- The child is eating too quickly. Surely this child was the victim of incest.
- The child is eating too slowly. Surely the child was the victim of incest.
- The child does not like caviar. Surely the child was the victim of incest. (In the last three cases I could not find a corresponding theory in present-day psychiatry).
- The child is obsessively taken to the family doctor or the emergency room for fictitious reasons, only to demonstrate the inability of the mother to care for her own child. And so on.

5. The way the children are treated afterwards is again an upside-down approach to the attachment theory. The obvious intention is to break all stable attachments formed

within the biological family, and to recreate an attachment to a different family. NCWS calls this 'the best interests of the child'. It is like peeling a stamp from one place to relocate it to another.

Let's take the Bodnariu children as an example. Why were the five children separated? Because you can 'populate' three new families with them; five stamps on three different envelopes, right? Why were the older children grouped by twos with the sibling of the closest age? Why were the parents given different visitation schedules for each set of children? Because their attachment to the biological family is in different stages of development, based on their ages. Eliana and Naomi already have a stable attachment, having developed from the ages of five and six, so they had to be completely separated from their parents without visitation rights, presents or phone calls. As a result, the ten-minute phone call that was granted to the parents for each of the girls was an enormous concession, made possible only because of the actions of the Romanian authorities.

This thing should have never happened, according to NCWS. But it did, as did the recent one-hour meeting with the parents, thanks to the involvement of all who came out onto the streets to protest. As a result, it was also discovered that there was a letter to the parents from the girls that had never been delivered. One of the girls declared: "I thought you were going to die." They were never supposed to have found out that their parents were still alive. They should have already begun to work through the reattachment mechanisms to the new family in conformity with NCWS' plans.

With the two boys, Matei and Ioan, aged five and two, the situation is even more inhumane. According to the Attachment Theory, this is the age when repeated separations will have an effect similar to that of mourning after a person has died. As a result, Ruth was permitted to see her sons periodically so they could develop aggression toward her. The end goal for NCWS? In the end they won't want to see her any more. This is what the theory tells us should happen. This is why one of the boys asked, "Did Daddy truly say he misses me?"

The authorities didn't bother too much with the youngest. They 'generously' allowed the mother to visit him twice a week. It didn't matter that they had risked failure-to-thrive syndrome by pulling him away from his mother's breast. It didn't matter that they had irradiated him for no reason by exposing him to a head-to-toe CT scan, even though they could have done non-invasive ultrasound on different parts of the body to see whether or not he had been abused.

Going back to the second point of my argument – the one regarding the Norwegian child protection legislation – a few facts need to be mentioned. The primary reason for taking a child away from its biological family and placing him or her in a foster family are exactly the ones described in the Attachment Theory: negligence, abuse or violence toward the child. This would not be a problem in itself, but the statistics published by the National Bureau of Norwegian Statistics reveal that, of the total number of reasons given for the removal of children from their biological homes, only twenty per cent of the cases refer to negligence, violence, abuse of any nature and/or the consumption of drugs. The other eighty per cent provide unjustified reasons ('other reasons').

The law articles that govern NCWS' activity, and are the most frowned upon, are those found under number 4.12, sections A-D. For example, section A allows the state to take the children if the physical and psychological conditions of the child's lifestyle are not up to its standards. This is why, if the agent doesn't like the way the mother is cooking an omelette, or if he or she considers that the bread slices are too thick, the child is taken away. If the child's clothes are not folded the way the agent likes, the child is taken away. Very logical, right? Also, section D of the same law indicates that the state is free to take the child away if it suspects the child will be neglected or abused at some point in the future.

As a result, the parent who is a product of the NCWS system is branded with a hot iron stamp and is automatically considered at risk, which means they will never be allowed to keep their own children. Any parent who has requested NCWS' help in the past is also blacklisted and will be followed up on. For the parents who have already had children removed, it is clear that any future children they have in Norway will be removed in the same way: without assistance, suitable treatment, help, counselling or correct diagnosis; with unprofessional activity that is forced upon people by agents who lack proper training or credentials; disguised as being in 'the best interests of the child' and glazed over with a bit of an upside-down psychiatry. This is child protection in Norway.

I cannot end this article without briefly shining the spotlight on another kind of psychiatric care in Norway. This is the kind that Ruth Johanne Bodnariu, as a nurse who specialised in child psychiatry, understood and practised. She counselled teenagers to help them avoid acts of self-aggression through the emergency phone line Kirken SOS. For this, and for her activity with street children in Romania, she was mentioned in the most prestigious psychiatric journal from the Nordic countries, the International Journal of Mental Health Nursing, in 2012. NCWS repays her contribution to society by taking her children away. If somehow in all of this there is any personal vendetta at the hands of an NCWS agent it is even more heinous. The end result is humiliating for the entire medical profession.

I am now at the final stage of my NCWS diagnosis. I did not rush to declare it because I wanted time to carry out some research. These life and death situations cannot and should not be evaluated in just a few short days. But as long as the Norwegian state continues to endorse the flagrant abuses against human rights and against all principles of good medical practice introduced by NCWS, I firmly declare that I do not want to see the fiords in the next fifty years.

Connected

NCWS uses a number of unproven and unscientific theories on a regular basis. The psychological approach of behaviourism is used to justify the very extreme action of taking newborn babies away from their mothers not long after the birth, for instance. The behaviourism approach assumes that we come into this world without any instincts, and that behaviours are learned through contact with the individual's environment. Therefore, NCWS does not believe that a baby should form an attachment to its mother.

Attachment Theory is one of the most studied theories in psychology, but many academics do not support it. NCWS does, however, and it allows the agency to effectively say that parents are of little importance to their children because a child can learn from anyone.

There is a very special attachment between a biological parent and child. This is often demonstrated when adopted children seek out their biological parents later in life. This need for adopted children to contact their biological parents never leaves them, even in adulthood.

When children are desperately crying out to return home, NCWS often refuses to allow them to do so, stating that they have already become attached to the foster carers, and therefore it wouldn't be in the child's best interests. But it is always in the child's best interests to return home, apart from in extreme and exceptional cases when the child might come to serious harm should he or she be returned to the biological parents.

Attachment Theory should not be considered valid by any serious scholar. The long-term trauma and illness caused by the separation of children from their families has been scientifically proven. As long as attachment and behaviourism theories form the foundation of NCWS philosophy, children will continue to be exposed to a form of systemic violence that constitutes child abuse.

Chapter 10 notes

[i] Van Dijken, S., *John Bowlby: His Early Life* (Free Association Books, 1998).

[ii] Chaudhary, N. and Keller. H., "Is Attachment Theory always reliable as a measure of child welfare?", Save Your Children: http://saveyourchildren.in/is-attachment-theory-always-reliable-as-a-measure-of-child-welfare-by-nandita-chaudhary-and-heidi-keller

[iii] Mariş, D., "Barnevernet or Upside-Down Psychiatry for Dummies", Bodnariu Family website: http://bodnariufamily.org/4825

[iv] American Psychiatric Association, Diagnostic and Statistical Manual of Mental Disorders: Fourth Edition: DSM-IV-TR (American Psychiatric Press, 1994).

11

Stripped

Jewish author and rabbi Chaim Potok wrote: "Everything has a past. Everything – a person, an object, a word, everything. If you don't know the past, you can't understand the present and plan properly for the future."[i]

A distinctive feature of Norway's current child welfare system is the striking similarity in many areas to past child welfare systems that were responsible for stolen generations.

On April 2, 2016, a documentary titled *Mot en av mine minste* (*To one of the least of these*) was shown on Norwegian news channel NRK.[ii] Put together by film-maker Marius Loland, and project initiator and co-producer Kai Erland, it documented the way the state confiscated children of the Tater people and placed them in orphanages. The title is a reference to a Bible verse found in Matthew 25:45 (NKJV):

> Then He will answer them, saying, "Assuredly, I say to you, inasmuch as you did not do it to one of the least of these, you did not do it to Me."

Between 1897 and 1989 an organisation called Norwegian Missionary Among the Homeless (NMAH) took around 1,500 Tater children away from their families. Many experienced rape in the orphanages, as well as hard physical and psychological punishments, and some were completely cut off from their siblings and parents. The documentary focuses on a Tater boy called Martin Larsen and a Tater girl called Solveig Imeland, both of whom were separated from their families. They were sent to Sørland's Orphanage in Songdalen and eventually placed with foster families.

Martin was sent to the orphanage at the age of eight. He was later housed with a foster family in Østfold, where he was largely used as free labour on their farm. Aged eighty-seven when the documentary was filmed, he speaks out about the state's removal of him and his six siblings. Martin describes what everyday life was like at the orphanage and the tough treatment meted out to him at a foster home in eastern Norway, which he describes as "slavery". He gives a unique insight into the way Tater children were treated in Norway.

Solveig was taken to the orphanage as a two-year-old and sent on to a foster home in Sørlandet when she was six. She did not experience the same level of brutality as Martin, but her story still helps to confirm the harsh treatment of defenceless children. Solveig shares in the film how she was treated when she ended up in foster care.

The state's treatment of these people has greatly challenged their ability to function in society, and the film offers a valuable reminder of what happens when a state identifies a particular people group as a 'problem'.

A report featured in the film entitled "Examination of schools and orphanages in East and West Agder", which discusses Sørland's Orphanage, contains interviews with ten children, all of whom allude to the harsh discipline they experienced there.[iii] Many are still struggling with the after-effects today.

Film-maker Loland commented:

> We went to the orphanage in Songdalen to make a film, and this building is completely preserved as it was when it was in full operation. Among other things, the basement and the small closets where the children were locked up were completely untouched, as well as a bathroom with a variety of small bathtubs and sinks. These rooms and the orphanage itself make it possible to take viewers back in time and let them experience what the everyday life of the children must have been like.
>
> The local authority gave the children from the orphanages financial compensation based on the aforementioned report, but they did not get help in finding family members

> or with other challenges they have faced as a result of the abuse. Still today many Romani-Tater people experience closed doors when they approach the public authorities to try to find their family members.

Perhaps the key reason behind the abuse of Tater children was that the state gave NMAH the authority to enforce the Vagabond Act in 1914. This meant that the mission had unrestricted leeway to deprive travellers of their children without notice or interference from the government.

The mission was given state funding each year to carry out this work. The Tater-Romani people were highly stigmatised at this time, and a huge amount of racism was directed toward them across Norway.

Below are excerpts from the documentary (speech translated):

Narrator: Martin is eighty-seven years old and lives in the small village of Laudal. His life bears witness to a major disgrace in Norwegian history… In his home town Martin is perceived as eccentric. He talks a lot about religious experiences, visions and prophecies. He has not lost his faith in God, even though the people of the Church were responsible for giving him a traumatic childhood.

Martin: I received a tremendous message, which should be spread all over the world: they need to put their trust in God now. It's not long now, I think... before Jerusalem is done and before something happens. Then Jesus will come with all his angels and gather them…

Narrator: Martin likes to talk about his faith, but when he starts to talk about his childhood he cannot be stopped. He cannot ignore the great injustice that has changed his life. Martin is a Romani; a Tater. At the age of eight he was forcibly removed from his family.

Martin: I remember how it happened. It was cruel. They just came and took us. Destroyed the house, everything. They ruined the houses, took us kids and drove us away in a car. We were not allowed to mention our parents once. If we did we got a smack in the face. Can you imagine such terrible people?

Narrator Nobody knows for sure where the Romani, or Tater, people come from. One theory is that they came to Norway from India 500 years ago. They were often called 'the travellers' because they travelled around with horses and wagons for most of the year. When they started moving up the valley to the villages it was a sure sign of spring in Norway.

Ann-Katrine Svang (Martin's former neighbour): I remember the wagons that were placed in a semicircle in the square there: caravans, a dining tent... Then they would set up a place for the bonfire, placing long logs in a square around it. And there we were invited to sit. Grandpa used to talk a lot with these people about where they had been… There was a little girl who wanted me to play with her. I didn't know if I wanted to right away, but we ended up playing and it was fun. I saw the horses too. They were standing in the grove eating.

Narrator: It was Johan, Martin's father, who was Romani or Tater. He was a travelling tinsmith and earned extra money by playing the fiddle at dances. But this travelling lifestyle was highly undesirable to the Norwegian authorities. The solution was to take the children from the travellers and place them in orphanages. This was carried out by the organisation Norwegian Mission Among the Homeless.

Karen Sofie Pettersen (researcher at HiOA): The organisation consisted of highly respected citizens. It received some support from strong personalities in society. Among other people, it received support from the king. The Svanvik Labour Colony was given as a gift from the Astrup family [of well-known businessmen] to the mission.

Narrator: Martin and his family were sent to a labour colony in Nordmøre. This is where travellers were expected to learn to live in a residence, have a permanent job and become good Christian citizens. They were not allowed to have visitors or to speak their own language, Romani. Martin's father had to stop playing his fiddle because 'Tater music' was forbidden. All letters were opened and read before they received them. There was a daily inspection of the houses and they were not allowed to leave or go outside the camp.

One boy had all his hair cut off with a knife for a trivial reason and was subsequently ridiculed by the manager and the other staff. The priest and manager, Knut Myhre, once grabbed a girl and screamed so cruelly at her that she wet herself. Martin's family eventually had enough of this treatment and wanted to leave. They were told they could go but the children had to stay behind. In spite of this, they left with all the children and settled in a house in Mandal. Not long afterwards the mission came and took the children away from their parents.

Martin: What a brutal thing to do! Pure evil! How can people do something like that – Huh? – split up the families? Their parents are the best thing they have on this earth. Then there was Mum, you know… "Remember," she said to all the children, "keep holding on to Jesus and ask Jesus for help, and he will be there to take care of it all."

Narrator: This is Solveig. She also ended up in the custody of the mission as a small child.

Solveig: [She shows some pictures.] This is me with 'Mother' at the orphanage... And then here I am in the bedroom at Birkelid. This was probably in the evening when I was going to bed.

Narrator: In Solveig's case it was her biological mother who brought her to the orphanage on her own initiative.

Solveig: You know, my home in Arendal was destroyed by alcohol and my mother was very sick. She had three children, and the other two grew up with our grandfather and grandmother. I was in the middle but was ripped out; my brother is older, my sister is younger. But I had rickets and was born a couple of months premature. Apparently, I was sent to Kristiansand, to the hospital. And from there to Birkelid, or so we think...

Narrator: Both Martin and Solveig came to the Sørlandet orphanage at Birkelid. This is among the last of the mission's homes that are still standing today. The time they experienced here was good, more or less. That was not the case for everyone. In 2009, the county governor of West Agder ordered a review of the children's homes in Sørlandet.

In the review, ten former Birkelid children shared about their time at the home.

Out of the ten children interviewed by the committee, nine claimed it was common to be pulled by the hair, spanked and pulled by the ears, but all the children claimed that confinement was a common and widely used punishment.

Solveig: The trauma surfaced after I left there. I have always been nervous of many things. I could not go up or down an escalator. And having curtains covering the window at night, I just can't. I have never been able to. I need to have a light on or something like that.

Narrator: The cause of the trauma is unknown. She was between one and two years old when she arrived at the orphanage.

Solveig: I was probably exposed to things at Birkelid with all the others who were there. I have an inkling about something in the loft, with such horror... I don't know how to explain it, but I feel that there was something scary in a way.

Narrator: Martin also experienced children being punished. One method was to hit all the children's fingers with a stick until the one who had done something wrong admitted to it. Once, when Martin was out in the garden, he heard a three- or four-year-old boy screaming from the basement.

Martin: "They're killing me! They're killing me!" the boy shouted… I went to the window. A little boy was holding on to her white skirt and was terrified. She was about to spank him. But I... It was quiet. I regret it. I should have gone down there, you know.

Narrator: The brother of one of the children was subjected to abuse by a female employee. A girl was subjected to extensive sexual abuse at the hands of a man connected to the orphanage. The abuse occurred regularly from when she was three until she was seven or eight years old. The assaults are described as "brutal rapes" and there were "threats of punishment" if she told anyone. This was well known to the manager, without her intervening.

A former employee explains that as a result of all the practical work assignments there was far too little time to spend with the children, who were often left to fend for themselves, or in the care of the older children. Due to the difference in treatment, some developed a close relationship with the managerial person while others perceived care to be absent.

Karen Sofie Pettersen: In my opinion, abuse was made possible as a result of the institutions being so closed. From very early on the mission had its own supervisors for the foster homes and institutions. We know now that this supervision system did not work. There was no culture in place to ask children how they were doing. When working with children it is very important to have openness; a transparent system and insight into what is happening. Some systems were not in place, and it gave the mission the room to commit abuse.

Narrator: Between 1900 and 1987, 1,500 Tater children were taken from their parents in Norway. During the same period, somewhere between 3,000 and 5,000 Tater people were registered in the country.

Solveig: Not only in the time when you were there, but afterwards, when you were adopted... Oh my! Then they came and picked me up in Kristiansand. I was supposed to go and live with some strange people that I had never seen before in my life. Today you would get to know them for a few months first. Back then you just took a small suitcase with something in it and travelled to Kristiansand.

There I met the woman I was being adopted by. And then they asked what I wanted to be named. Named? “Can I not keep the name I was given at birth: Kitty?” I was not allowed. I had to change my name. “Isn’t Solveig a nice name?” they asked. How should a six-year-old answer that? Then my name was Solveig. I did not have a clue about anything, and I did not know anyone there. It is one thing to have lived at Birkelid and another to be adopted without knowing those people at all.

And let me tell you, every year someone came and visited me. A little girl and a boy. And an elderly lady visited twice a year or something like that. Then when I was twelve years old I asked the girl, who was eight years old, “Why are you coming to visit me once or twice a year? Are we family?” Because it was always in me:

what if I have a family? Then she says, “Yes, we are family.” I started asking, “Are we second cousins?” “No.” “Are we cousins, then?” “No.” “Then we must be siblings,” I said. “Yes, we are, but I’m not allowed by my mother to tell you that.”

My adoptive parents did not tell me where I came from. They were as good as they could be. They did not know what was best for me, but they said nothing. Therefore, I never really confided in them either.

Narrator: In Martin’s case, the road from the orphanage led to a farm in eastern Norway.

Martin: It looks a lot like that farm there. The stables, the basement. It really looks a lot like it. The bridge to the barn. The washhouse there... They have done a lot of repairs to it, though.

Journalist: Do you have any good memories from here?

Martin: I will need to think carefully... Where should I look for them? No, I don’t have any. I don’t have one good memory of this place. Not one good memory. All of that field, I had to pick potatoes alone and fertilise it. The one-hundred kilo bags... We had to carry them up a narrow staircase that went there, right up to the little window you see there: oats and wheat. We did not have time to do homework. We had to get in the barn or outside and work, digging ditches. Now they have filled the whole ditch again that they used me to dig. They were also digging. But I got so many blisters on my hands that at school my hands burned all the time. I did not manage to do my homework because the ditches had to be cleaned. Think about the size of it. Far down there, all the way to that neighbour.

Narrator: A former neighbour clearly remembers how Martin worked on the land.

Martin: Do you recognise me?

Arne Gunnar Brenne (a neighbour of Martin’s foster family): Yes, Martin, I remember you well…

Martin: It has been many years… Things have really changed around here.

Arne Gunnar Brenne: Yes, things have changed. Do you remember when you ran after those cows down in the swamp only wearing slippers on your feet? Then you lost the slippers. No wonder! It was not the right equipment for running like that. No... You really did work for your food. Sevesen must have been very strict. You were sharpening fence poles and he stood there, ready with the next pole. Once you were done with one, then came the next one. I remember you digging up potatoes in the small field next to the forest. I was on my way to Moen with the horse and you were digging for those potatoes. "Are you picking potatoes?" I asked. "Yes, they must be picked before they get too big," you said.

Martin: Yes, I think I can remember that.

Narrator: Martin handled his new duties with pride, but gradually life became even harder for the orphanage boy.

Martin: I'll tell you how they got to me in the worst way. Not with the working; from that I grew strong, and I knew that. I grew bigger and bigger, stronger and stronger! But they figured that out. When I really did get big they made plans. We were going to repair a wall around the back. Then the old man said [to another guy], "You go top, him in the middle and I'm staying down here." They had made plans, you know... I realised this. Then we got up and put up those boards… And suddenly I got a saw in my head, a jigsaw. I took that saw and threw it to the ground where I was standing. The next time I got a hammer straight onto my head. Then I fell down and just ran inside. When I got in there I fell to the ground and fainted… He was even a KrF [Kristelig Folkeparti, or Christian Democratic Party] member…

Narrator: Aspects of Romani and Tater culture are still alive, despite the state persecution. Bussi is one of those who travels around reviving the fire from the old sparks.

Hilmar "Bussi" Karlsen-Rosenborg (musician and a mediator for Romani and Tater culture): There were two different pathways. You had the painful one, with persecutions and all that terror. I can barely talk about it; I get so filled with anger. But the good path...

We could travel from Trønderlag, through eastern Norway, down to Sørlandet... Stop and rest, sleep over in a home somewhere. We were known. Dad would sit there and trade clocks with the old man in the house, and we, the children, calmed down. Dad took down the clock and brushed it a little while he sang:

Two girls are walking in the rosy grove
and picking fair petals.
One of these girls
is oh so happy,
The other sorrowful and sad.

Narrator: Martin never experienced this culture, and throughout his adult life his painful memories and experiences have presented him with many challenges. In recent times there have been various compensation funds for Tater and Romani people. Martin is one of those who has received compensation.

Martin: I got 150,000 kroner [around €15,000]. But what is that in comparison to a completely ruined life? Because they really did ruin everything. When your family is destroyed you become a fugitive in this world. You really do.

Solveig: I have read about that. A few years ago, some people got compensation. I have not thought about it because it does nothing for me. Money is of no help; far from it. So I have never thought and will never think about it.

Journalist: But do you think they owe you an apology?

Solveig: No... I really don't. No, far from it. I do not think that... No...

[The scene shifts to parliament, where the following comments are made.]

Jan Tore Sanner, former Local MP: We sincerely apologise for the violations committed against the Romani and Tater groups, and the suffering that the group and individuals have suffered.

Helga Haugland Byfuglien, 'Preses' of the bishops' committee

for the Norwegian Church: The Norwegian Church asks the Tater people and the Romani people for forgiveness for the injustice, abuse and neglect committed by the Church against their people.

Helmut M Liessem, general secretary of Kirkens Sosialtjeneste (the Social Service of the Church, SSC): On behalf of the SSC, I strongly apologise for the assaults and offences that the Tater and Romani people were exposed to by the Norwegian Mission Among the Homeless.

Narrator: The SSC took over all employees and buildings when NMAH was abolished in 1989. In 2015, a report was made on the situation of the Tater people in Norway over the last 100 years. The committee's chairman believes the authorities should now focus on the future.

Knut Vollebæk, leader of the Tater and Romani Commission: We actually have quite a few specific suggestions for follow-up: among other things, information about who the Tater and Romani people are, what rights they have as a national minority and their culture. Because that will have a significant impact on wider society's attitude toward them. I think we all need dignity and pride. Until now, these people have been deprived of their dignity and pride. Then you do not become a good and constructive citizen. So that's one of the most important things.

Narrator: Nevertheless, Martin does not trust the government's decisions…

Martin: There is a song that says something like, "No book is as dear to me as my mother's Bible." And that is for sure. Her prayers have been heard; it has been proven now. I got to see Jesus. Not only that, but I've had help in many difficult situations, which neither king nor government can repeat. I appreciate that very much. That's why I keep Jesus as my number one leader. I will continue to respect him and keep his promises.

Social Darwinists rejected the idea of inherent dignity in all human beings, believing instead that the survival of the fittest theory prevailed. This widespread acceptance led to a view that some people were less worthy than others, resulting in the bloodiest century to come known to mankind.

The behaviour perpetrated against the Tater people by NMAH is very much a blueprint for today's NCWS. All dignity is stripped away from families in a step-by-step approach, resulting in the destruction of an individual's sense of value and worth. Just like NMAH, NCWS is a closed system without any legal obligations or an independent body to oversee it.

The NMAH barged straight into people's lives with full authority, giving families commands about what they could and couldn't do. If families refused to obey they were stigmatised and their children were taken away. The children suffered in confinement and their names were sometimes changed. The children had to reject their own language, culture and heritage.

No one stood up for the victims, and all these abuses against families were supported by those in power, financed by taxpayers' money. NMAH's employees were absolved of any responsibility. The government trusted NMAH, giving it the freedom to work without interference or supervision, and with the help of the police, hospitals, the school system and so on. NCWS' behaviour bears all the hallmarks of this former system. Sadly, old habits die hard.

Chapter 11 notes

[i] Potok, C., *Davita's Harp* (Ballantine Books, 1996).

[ii] "Mot en av mine minste" ("To one of the least of these"), NRK: https://mariusloland.no/2017/03/30/mot-en-av-mine-minste-pa-nrk

[iii] Staff writer, "Barnehjem og barnevernsinstitusjoner i Vest-Agder" ("Examination of schools and orphanages in East and West Agder") Examination Committee II, Statsarkivet i Kristiansand: https://www.arkivverket.no/dokumentasjon/barnevern-og-spesialskoler/barnevern-og-barnehjem/_/attachment/download/492f2442-899a-4151-9827-c26b1a304b14:b4a147dbea62e62dee0120b780461196b59e65af/Barnehjem%20i%20VA%20-%20oversikt.pdf

12

Cycle

The abuses carried out against the Tater and Romani people were not isolated events in Norwegian history. Stolen generations came in other forms as well. The Sámi and Kven people were forced to become Norwegians, the 'Bastøy boys' were locked up on 'Devil's Island' and the 'Lebensborn' children went from being the venerated to the despised.

Sámi and Kven people

Between 1850 and 1980, the Sámi (the indigenous population in the north of Norway, originally believed to have come from Asia) and Kven (originally of Finnish origin) people were forced to become Norwegians as part of a policy to wipe out an entire culture. The trauma and wounds from this still exist within the Sámi and Kven communities, and according to professor of history at the University of Tromsø, Henry Minde, it may take more than 100 years to re-establish Sámi culture.[i]

Some of the similarities between the tactics used by those responsible for the Norwegianisation of the Kven and Sámi people, and by those working for NCWS today, are striking. For instance, as more money was added to the malfunctioning Norwegianisation programme this only resulted in feeding an abusive and dysfunctional system, making it more efficient, but at the same time ignoring the real issues. Teachers and schools benefitted financially from keeping the system going, just as we see from the foster industry and other institutions in Norway today.

Propaganda twisted the way the majority of people in Norway felt by creating, or at least exposing, a situation that painted the Sámi and Kven people in a bad light. Once the majority supported this 'cleansing' idea that would supposedly help to 'fix the problem', the authorities let the people become the lynch mob, encouraging them to report anything and everything.

Many Sámi and Kven children were taken away and forced to attend boarding schools, which were not dissimilar to NCWS institutions. There they experienced what can only be described as a living hell. They learned that they came from a race that had less value, and that their place in society was beneath that of a 'real Norwegian'. Children had to face this discrimination all alone from the age of seven. They were regularly beaten and starved, and were given little time to sleep. Some were sexually abused. There was no pretence of pursuing the child's best interests; it purely came down to financial gain. Children had to disown their families and reject their heritage. They were never allowed to use their native languages, their knowledge of which had pretty much been beaten out of them. Sámi and Kven children were not allowed to be children.

Some of the methods used to Norwegianise these minority groups are the same ones NCWS uses today. The Sámi and Kven people lived in hiding and were always on the move, just like the Tater-Romani people. This constant moving about was not only part of their blood and tradition, but also a means of evading capture by the authorities. Children were often ripped from their parents' arms and placed in boarding schools whenever the police or authorities caught up with them.

To prove that they had become Norwegians the wanderers had to settle down and build fixed homes. If they didn't, they would lose their children to the state forever. In order to keep their children or try to get them back, many travelling communities did their best to meet the government requirements. The Sámi and Kven people lived in tents, so building a home became an expensive business, but, the Tater-Romani people found a solution to that problem. They built a rock foundation on the property they managed to buy, then took the wheels off their wagons and placed the wagons on top of the rock foundations. They kept the wheels as 'garden ornaments', but more often than not they were looking for the first opportunity to put those wheels back on and get their families out of the country. These types of wheelless wagon shacks can still be found in some parts of Norway.

In 1997, King Harald V publicly apologised to the Sámi people for the abuse that was inflicted on them by the Norwegian authorities. He said:[ii]

> The state of Norway was founded on the territory of two peoples: the Sámi people and the Norwegians. Sámi history is closely intertwined with Norwegian history. Today, we express our regret on behalf of the state for the injustice committed against the Sámi people through its harsh policy of Norwegianisation.

Devil's Island

Tove Stang Dahl, a legal scholar, criminologist and law professor, claimed that Norwegian child welfare law had been implemented based on the ruling classes' need to exercise control rather than a desire to protect children from abuse and neglect within the family.

The Norwegian government set up an 'education centre' – a juvenile detention centre – on Bastøy Island (which became known as 'Devil's Island') in 1900, just after the first 'child protection' law in the world came into force. The children who were sent to Devil's Island hadn't actually broken the law, but they were deprived of their freedom for many years, nonetheless. The child protection law was used to maintain social order, and to this day the Norwegian authorities continue to introduce more new laws to make it even easier for those in authority to control and shape those who don't quite meet up with the Norwegian standard. The inhumane treatment they were subjected to also included compulsory sterilisation in some cases; a tactic frequently used against travellers.

Kongen av Bastøy (*King of Devil's Island*) is a French-Norwegian film based on real-life events.[iii] It shows how, on the evening of May 20, 1915, four young boys called Karl, Oskar, Alf and Norman snuck out of their dormitory and ran into the forest. They had spent a long time at the juvenile centre. Like the other boys, they had been deprived of their names, had their hair shaved off, and been given blue uniforms with numbers on. At dawn they crossed over to the boathouse and escaped from their living hell.

The public version of events has been rewritten by the Norwegian authorities from this point onwards. The information available on subjects such as Norwegianisation and the Bastøy Boys' home only gives an overview of 'significant' facts. There are no individual stories or testimonies; only cold and distant facts.

"What one could read between the lines made me curious," commented the film's director, Marius Holst (text translated).[iv] Holst dug deep into old archives to find out what had actually taken place at the juvenile centre. "I came across things so bad that people would not believe me if I told them," he added.

One very telling detail that appeared in a related documentary called *Bastøy Boys: Sentenced to Correctional Education*[v] was revealed when the film crew started looking for amateur actors for the roles, deliberately searching for boys who could relate to the Bastøy boys' situation. Guess where many of these boys came from? Inside NCWS institutions. As the film director says: "These boys would have been at Bastøy today if it still existed." Despite knowing little about the current child welfare setup, the film crew easily made this link. It should come as no surprise that this documentary was taken down by NRK, Norway's government-owned public broadcasting company, given that it revealed that many truths have been swept under the carpet.

One of the young actors says in the documentary:

> This is a shameful aspect of recent Norwegian history. The government supported this place. It paid to maintain a corrupt system, and it let the people in it do whatever they wanted to the children.

It sounds as though this actor discovered something of his country's history that he had never imagined existed, and the camera caught the truth in the faces of more people in that film than just those of the young actors. The director appears pretty upset and choked when he is being interviewed or simply thinking out loud. He looks as though he wants to take the children away from their lives and fix everything but realises how powerless he really is.

Well-known Scandinavian actor Stellan Skarsgaard is also interviewed about what happened on Bastøy Island and whether *King of Devil's Island* manages to communicate it well. He says in the interview that the camera captures the truth in these boys from troubled backgrounds – a truth they would never be able to articulate – and that the film tells the stories of these troubled young actors in a way words never could, bringing real credibility to the story encapsulated in the film.

The *Bastøy Boys* documentary finishes with the poignant words: "Dedicated to those who have been living at Bastøy, and to all the young people living in today's institutions."

Interestingly, many stories about growing up in social services were supported by the Norwegian media between 2011-2014, but after this the coverage stopped abruptly. Since then, Norwegian laws have been changed to prevent these stories from being told; not in one giant leap that forbids it, but by making it possible to strike down anyone who tries to present the truth in such a way. Tactics such as violation of confidentiality rules and harassment of public employees are used as a form of suppression.

Lebensborn children

The Nazi SS *Lebensborn* ("Fount of life") programme, which ran from 1941 to 1945 in Norway, was set up to create a 'superior race' for the German Reich. Nazi soldiers were encouraged to have children with Norwegian women, who were considered to be part of the 'pure Aryan race'. Around 8,000 Lebensborn children were born in institutions in Germany, while up to 12,000 were born in Norway, alongside countless others across Europe.

Selected Nordic women were given incentives for bearing children with Nazi soldiers, and during this time they were treated like royalty. They were offered financial support and privileged treatment in maternity homes.[11] As Norway was one of the poorest countries during the war, many Norwegian women strategically seized this opportunity as a means of survival. ABBA's Frida Lyngstad is a well-known example of a Lebensborn child. Born in Norway to a Norwegian mother and German father, she grew up in Sweden.

But everything changed at the end of World War II, when a new war was declared against Lebensborn children and their mothers. Lebensborn children in Norway were exposed to the most horrifying physical, sexual and psychological abuse in

11 Similar to the maternity wards in hospitals we have today, where mothers go to give birth but are not observed in the same way as in the mothers' homes.

children's homes, 'special institutions' and mental asylums. Many Lebensborn children in other countries were also institutionalised, but reports suggest that the suffering experienced elsewhere was negligible in comparison.

Lebensborn mothers in Norway were ostracised, shamed and beaten, and were sometimes forced to carry out unpaid hard labour at internment camps. Some left Norway and quite a few ended up in Germany, losing their Norwegian citizenship at the same time. A number of women returned after a few years and some of those who had been members of the Nazi party were sentenced to prison and had to work at Grini prison camp for women. Lebensborn children were persistently bullied, abused and rejected, and time and again they found themselves placed in mental institutions. The Norwegian authorities even tried to banish Lebensborn children to Germany, Brazil and Australia, but to no avail.

According to a BBC News article, many Lebensborn children, who are now in their sixties and seventies, tell horrifying stories of how they were tied to their beds, unable to play outside, and had to relieve themselves in the same place where they ate their food.[vi] The mothers who had their children confiscated never saw them again.

Concentration camp cruelty

What happens when young, impressionable adults choose to follow a destructive ideology? The Norwegian Nazi guards, known for their cruelty, paint a disturbing picture. There are claims that some tied starving rats to prisoners in concentration camps for their own amusement to watch them eat away at their bodies. The conditions at the prison caused the prisoners to become sick and emaciated. The German SS soldiers supervising the Norwegian guards were so shocked they confiscated weapons from them, gave them disciplinary warnings and temporarily jailed some of them, according to an article entitled "Norwegian camp guards shocked SS with brutality".[vii] To this day, justice has never been served for the families who suffered so dreadfully at the hands of Norwegian Nazi collaborators.

In 1959, world-renowned professor of criminology Nils Christie wrote his first academic work called "Prisoners in concentration camps".[viii] His task was to find out why some guards abused prisoners at the German concentration camps in Norway. Similar experiments, such as the Stanford Prison Experiment and the Milgram Experiment, have been carried out elsewhere, but Christie's investigation went deeper, and his findings and knowledge are crucial in helping us understand NCWS today. The guards who only had the information the Germans had given them about the prisoners viewed them as subhuman. On the other hand, guards who made the effort to get to know the prisoners, talking with them and sharing family photos, treated them relatively well.

Christie warned of the dangers of setting up a justice system that viewed part of the population as subhuman, but this has fallen on deaf ears as segments of the population are still considered inferior and superior in today's Norway. Time and time again we witness the same degrading, dehumanising and destructive behaviours inflicted upon families by NCWS. Christie remarked that it is very easy to create a monster in the form of a stranger, and this is exactly what is happening today.

Life in an institution

IT consultant and former politician Øyvind Michelsen spent the first eighteen years of his life in a Norwegian institution. Michelsen is a tenor soloist and has a keen interest in music. He has regular contact with his two brothers, and believes it is only because of them that he survived his tough upbringing at the orphanage. "What made us feel good was that we had each other. We held each other and helped each other. What makes children in orphanages feel bad is that they are often completely alone," he is reported to have said in a *Nordlys* article titled "Finally, the child's son, Øyvind, finds his father's grave after 45 years of exploration".[ix]

Michelsen states that he is not alive today *because of* NCWS, but *in spite of* it. Most of the other children at the institution are now either dead or in jail serving life sentences. It grieves Michelsen to hear that child welfare institutions are in no better shape today.

Michelsen did not see much of his father – a Nazi sympathiser – during his childhood, and he and his brothers were not even informed about his father's funeral when he died. After four decades of searching, Michelsen finally found his father's grave. "I kissed the gravestone, and then I sat down and talked an hour with him. I know that he cannot hear me and that sounds a bit dull, but it was very good for me to get those feelings out," he says (text translated).

"I do not support any of his political points of view and disagree completely with what happened during the war, but children should not be held responsible for the actions of their parents. I had to find the man I had been forbidden to contact," said Michelsen.

His father had ten siblings and Michelsen is now in touch with many of his cousins in Tromsø. At the graveside, Michelsen told his father about the family and what they have all achieved. "I hope no one sees me, or they'll think there's a madman up there on the burial ground talking to thin air," he says, laughing.

When child welfare becomes an enemy

Prejudice in Norway is by no means limited to those who perhaps look Norwegian but have 'questionable' roots (such as the Kven people or the Lebensborn). Those who have migrated from other countries are also considered suspicious by many, particularly if they continue to observe certain cultural traditions or ways of life observed in their home countries. Elvis Chi Nwosu, councillor and project leader for African Cultural Awareness and project manager for a child welfare link project, has observed that NCWS lacks a fundamental understanding of other cultures, which has resulted in a mistrust of many immigrant parents. He writes (text translated):[x]

> We see that more countries have recently focused on Norway because of what they believe is a lack of legal protection for their citizens in child welfare cases… Something is wrong if immigrant parents live in constant fear of being deprived of the care of their own children by NCWS. We must not forget that Norway previously deprived the Tater people of their children because they thought it was in the children's best interests…
>
> Immigrants are overrepresented within child welfare circles and their children are 'laundered' through Norwegian foster homes, where they lose their native languages and

> cultural identities. In many cases they could have been placed in foster homes with their own relatives. In my job of improving contact between immigrants and NCWS I see that NCWS lacks cultural competence.

One family who fled from Syria were given asylum in Norway. This same family are now seeking asylum for a second time in Poland. The youngest daughter Leen, went to school one day and didn't come home. Leen's sister Hiba, with the help of the rest of the family, franticly went looking for Leen, but they couldn't find her.

Allegedly Leen had told the nurse that she had been physically abused, but after she was in care for a year, she ran away with her mother to Poland. Leen said that the original allegation of abuse was made by another child at her school, the school where she was being bullied.

While in care, Leen was being pumped with many different types of drugs, which made her physically ill. Medical tests that were carried out in Poland confirmed that Leen was physically fit, but still suffering from stress from her harrowing experience in Norway.

> When we came to Norway, we thought that this was where we would live in peace and we would forget all the traumatic and sad events," Hiba says, referring to the family's escape from Syria. "But we have all lived this trauma again."[xi]

Professional with the Australian Red Cross Blood Service, Cristina Nicoli, wrote an article titled "Norway's Barnevernet and its parallels in human history". She writes:[xii]

> Growing up in Australia, I learnt about its recent past. I discovered its dark aspects, such as the 'Stolen Generation' of part-Aboriginal children, which occurred throughout most of the 20th century. This knowledge hit a nerve when I first heard of NCWS.
>
> Like most Romanians around the world, I saw news of a young Romanian-Norwegian family, the Bodnarius, who were caught up in a surreal drama in Norway. Their five children, including a three-month-old suckling infant, had been removed.

There were various reasons given for the separation of the Bodnariu family, such as "Christian radicalism and indoctrination". The family were practising Romanian Pentecostal Christians, a religious minority in Norway.

None of the reasons given by NCWS justified the treatment of the family. One would think the immediate removal was a result of neglect, abuse, violence, or an unsafe environment, such as drugs or alcohol. However, not only did no such factors exist in this family, even NCWS made no such allegation.

The ease with which NCWS swooped in was also shocking. There was no forewarning, no court proceeding, no thorough investigation or assistance given to the family prior to the taking of the children. The entourage of police, staff and resources used to collect the children was heavy-handed, and caused immediate and long-term trauma to the children.

The silence and bureaucratic jungle which the parents faced in order to regain their children proved to be a living nightmare. It soon became evident that this family was being mindlessly destroyed.

Romanians around the world protested, taking to the streets in their thousands. After months of demonstrations, the Bodnariu family was reunited, but the episode revealed, once again, the systemic dysfunction in Norway's child protection system.

It raises the question: is this an acceptable trait for the most developed nation in the world?

It was an abuse of power and it was impossible for me to ignore the similarities between NCWS and Australia's own stolen generation.

Australia was "discovered" in 1770, and soon after was declared "Terra Nullius", which means "uninhabited" or "no one's land". Captain James Cook took possession of the entire east coast in the name of King George III. The boats moored into harbour and slowly the people began inhabiting the coast.

However, this ignorant claim led to multiple levels

of abuse on the part of the Europeans. They completely overlooked an established population with culture, beliefs, traditions, languages, legal system and well-functioning family structures; they were the Aboriginal people.

Tragically, the 'integration' of Europeans meant oppression with violence and forced labour inflicted on the indigenous population.

One other such crime, and yet not the least, was the rape of many women. When they gave birth, the Europeans decided, due to the part breed, that the children should receive some form of education, and thus began the 'Stolen Generation'.

Children were taken out of the arms of their mothers, sent interstate or a great distance from their families, and kept in 'mission camps' where the education was actually 're-education'. Most of these children never saw their families again.

The children cried and screamed but were met with extreme force. Their wild outbursts were not viewed as trauma, but rather the part that was 'Aboriginal'. This happened legally between 1910 to 1970.

Despite the different geography, nationality or belief system, no matter what Norway wants to call it, their child welfare system is fundamentally similar to the one deployed in Australia and, technically, Norway is creating a stolen generation right now.

NCWS claims to be guided by the "best interests of the child"; however, this is a guise for inferior standards for assessing families. Among other judgements, NCWS tends to profile large or impoverished families as a risk.

While the Bodnariu family were being victimised in Norway, I considered my own family history. My parents married young and had six daughters when they fled communist Romania for Australia. They struggled as immigrants, and as the family grew to eleven children, there were times of poverty. Despite all of that, my parents managed to raise us to become caring, socially active and aware people who are responsible and grounded.

I shudder at the thought that NCWS could easily have targeted my family had it existed during my childhood. Looking back, I delight in the fact that my parents provided a safe environment for all of us children to prosper, and NCWS would have made a huge mistake had it intervened.

To be fair, every continent has some history of abuse against children. Spain abducted up to 300,000 children during the Spanish Civil War and Francoist Spain during 1944-1954, and these are known as the 'Lost Children of Francoism'. Argentina stole children from parents fighting against the regime during 1976-1983, and unfortunately up to 30,000 were killed. Part of the Generalplan Ost (*General Plan East*), Germany took Aryan-looking children from around Europe – an estimated 400,000 during 1939-1944 – and moved them to Germany for "Germanisation"; a form of indoctrination to help them become culturally German. This "Eugenics-Forced Sterilisation" occurred during 1934-1975 in Sweden, where approximately 21,000 people were either forced or coerced into sterilisation. Since the 1850s, and well into the 20th century, Swiss children were taken from their parents to work on farms and the era between 1850-1980is known as "Contract Children".

The list goes on, and while these events are now in the past, they are stains that should not be ignored because without genuine reflection history can repeat itself.

A society that can look back and acknowledge ancestral mistakes takes the first step toward proper healing.

In February 2008, the then Prime Minister of Australia, Kevin Rudd, publicly apologised to the Stolen Generation. But the emotional distress of lost families, lost culture, lost memories and lost choice can never be replaced or compensated. Unfortunately, the Aboriginal people are now considered to be a "Lost Generation".

Another form of child removal in Australia was "Forced Adoptions". This was legal from the 1950s to the 1970s, and young mothers from poor families were targeted. In 2013, the first female Prime Minister, Julia Gillard, officially apologised. She started her apology with, "Today, this parliament, on behalf of the Australian people, takes responsibility and apologises for the policies and practices that forced the separation of mothers from their babies which created a lifelong legacy of pain and suffering."

The Opposition Leader at the time, Tony Abbott, added his own views on the issue, claiming, "I cannot imagine a grief greater than that of a parent and a child parted from each other… This is a tragedy for them and for our nation, and we must atone for it."

This gives me hope that, while a nation's history may be dark, a future government can see the devastation and apologise.

If a 'less developed' nation like Australia can recognise its shame, could Norway one day be as bold?

This is why I am committed to the cause of exposing the unjust confiscation of children from their families by NCWS. Because I would like to see a Norwegian government apologise, on behalf of itself and the nation, for the inhumane practices of today. My journey protesting NCWS atrocities began with the Bodnariu family, but it did not end there. For me, that was just the beginning.

Similarities

Many countries around the world have attempted to suppress segments of society, and particularly those who are considered racially 'inferior'. Like NCWS, the countries listed below removed many children from their family homes as a form of ethnic cleansing. The pattern of children being renamed and having their native languages banned, and of subsequently being neglected and abused within the care system, appears to be one that has repeated itself throughout history and across the world. The aim to improve the lives of these children by absorbing them into mainstream culture is failing in Norway, just as it failed for the stolen generations of Australia and many other nations:

Australia

The exact number of children removed in Australia is unknown, but estimates suggest that at least 100,000 were taken.[xiii]

Poland

Approximately 200,000 Polish children were stolen by the Nazis between 1939 and 1944 to be 'Germanised' in Germany. Only around 20 per cent were returned to their families. Thousands grew up completely unaware of their true identity and heritage.[xiv]

Spain

Around 300,000 babies are believed to have been taken during Spain's Franco years and up to 1990.[xv] Many are believed to have been taken from 'undesirable' families and rehomed with 'approved' families.

Argentina

Around 500 Argentinean children are believed to have been stolen during the 1970s and brought up in families that were loyal to the regime and its 'right' ideology.[xvi]

Canada

Between 1960 and 1990s an estimated 20,000 aboriginal children in Canada were taken from their families and placed in foster homes or put up for adoption. This era is known as the "Sixties Scoop", which refers to the scooping away of children from their families.

In 1985, the Kimelman Report, which delivered a scathing attack on child welfare policies in Canada stated that:[xvii]

> The native people of Manitoba had charged that the interpretation of the term "best interest of the child' had been wrought with cultural bias in a system dominated by white, middle class workers, boards of directors, administrators, lawyers and judges. They also alleged that in application of the legislation, there were many factors which were crucially important to the native people which had been ignored, misinterpreted, or simply not recognized by the child welfare system.

Kimelman considered the loss of Canada's children to be a 'cultural genocide'. As we see from this list, child welfare workers around the world, and across many generations, have often be dangerously free of accountability or responsibility for their actions. This should act as a powerful wake-up call to those who continue to deny that the Norwegian government might be capable of carrying out such cruel and questionable actions.

Escape to freedom

In 2017, TV2 reported the story of a Norwegian mother, Tonje, who had fled from Norway to Sweden to give birth.[xviii] She was diagnosed as having slight learning difficulties in Norway, where she felt persecuted by the authorities, but in Sweden she is considered to be a good mother and very capable in her parenting.

TV2 has confirmed that the Habilitetcenter (Centre for Rehabilitation and Competence, or CRC) at Innlandet Hospital in Norway recommends that everyone with the diagnosis Tonje received should not have children. The CRC carries out studies and diagnoses patients, then provides advice and guidance to those who have physical or other disabilities.

When Tonje became pregnant her mother Sissel called the CRC. They told her Tonje had learning disabilities, and the soon-to-be grandmother sought advice as the daughter was about to become a single mum. According to Sissel, the CRC advised those with this particular diagnosis to be sterilised. Sissel was shocked and stunned that they should say such a thing about her daughter.

TV2 drew attention in the documentary to a web article from 2015 that had been written by the CRC's leader, Wenche Røkke. Former CRC employees had written what they would normally say to young people with developmental disabilities or learning difficulties, and the word 'sterilisation' was used. Here is an extract:

> This surgery is called sterilisation, and it is cost-free for those with learning disabilities in Norway… We know of no one with a learning disability that has been permitted to keep their baby after it was born. Children's services have a separate law that takes care of the child's rights, and it becomes too difficult for those with learning disabilities

> to take care of their children. Therefore, NCWS helps the children, so they are able to live with someone who can take good care of them…

Røkke reportedly apologised to the mother. She agreed that the report could be interpreted as discriminatory but said that employees had to adhere to its content. The CRC does not recommend that people with learning disabilities of this kind have children. NCWS was made aware of the human rights violation, but no action was taken in response. The CRC leader again confirmed the advice that people it considers to have minor learning difficulties should not have children.

TV2 also recently revealed that an IQ test inflicted upon several thousand young people in Norway between 2003 and 2009 contained flaws that may have resulted in many incorrect diagnoses.

TV2 also filmed in Sweden, where expert opinions are very different. Its child welfare services suggest those with learning difficulties simply need support if they choose to become parents, though they are clear on the fact that a significant number may be unable to handle the task.

As a result, government agencies in Sweden give people like Tonje customised help. TV2 met with several mothers with learning disabilities who consider themselves to be great parents. "Absolutely, of course. Why wouldn't we be? With the right kind of help everything is possible," says one mother, who has a seventeen-year-old son.

Røkke refused to comment on the TV2 report from Sweden and would only provide answers on the Norwegian side in the show. "We cannot decide anything or force anyone to do anything. We give our advice based on our professional stance," she says.

According to the Human Rights Act, people with learning disabilities have every right to start a family and have children. This right is also included in the conventions Norway has signed, including the Convention on the Rights of Persons with Disabilities.

"Do you admit that your advice contravenes human rights?" the TV2 reporter asks Røkke.

"The way you ask the question, I will have to say that it does," she replies, adding that CRC is only concerned with the best interests of the child.

"So you think no disabled person should have children?" Røkke is asked.

"Yes, I think I have given you a very clear answer to that now," she replies.

Sissel reacted strongly to CRC's statements: "It's so discriminatory that I don't have any words for it, really."

After Tonje had given birth, Norway sent a message of concern to child welfare services in Sweden (Socialstyrelsen). As a result, home visits and observations were set up with the mother and her baby. TV2 was present when the mother and her lawyer received the results of Socialstyrelsen's findings.

"The agency had no concerns at all about the mother's parental ability. It recognised that the baby and mother got on well together, and has followed up on this over the last four months," says the mother's lawyer.

After hearing that Tonje is a great mother, Sissel faces her daughter on-screen and says: "You know what, you're the best mum. That was so great to hear."

And of course it was fantastic news for Tonje, who says: "I was completely shocked, and so very happy."

Sissel feels that the CRC has shown a total lack of respect for the family: "None; either to my daughter, to the expected baby or to us as parents," she says.

Barnevernet accused of human trafficking

Oddvar Espegard, a Norwegian entrepreneur and father of five sons, carried out his own extensive investigation into NCWS. He provided the following observations for inclusion in this book:

> NCWS has nothing to do with keeping children safe. NCWS is a peculiar agency. The average citizen in this country always thinks the best when it comes to NCWS. People think there is a need to take care of all these poor children who are suffering in thousands of Norwegian homes. This is how NCWS and the authorities access their unlimited playground. They are still sailing with the wind, keeping this up year after year without hesitation. But the

reality is completely different. The reality is gruesome, ugly, and so cruel and criminal that I have trouble finding words to describe it.

I have studied and followed this madness almost every night and day for more than three years, and the truth has started to dawn on me. Again and again we read about legal violations within child welfare in the newspapers. That happens when the county governor visits a municipality and looks into the conditions, and the result is a report that is usually printed in the newspapers. What is usually pointed out are formality errors, deadline overruns and the like.

However, in the report from the Norwegian Institute for Urban and Regional Research (NIBR) written by Lars B Kristofersen, which deals with child welfare between 1990 and 2002, much is said about how unsuccessful NCWS is in its work.[xix] It points to high suicide rates among children, adolescents and parents, and to children and parents who die younger than normal, and youth who do not manage to lead normal lives involving education and work. It suggests that child welfare produces four times as many addicted children as the number of children who grow up with addicted parents in their own homes. These are sobering numbers and statistics, and it is strange that no one is reacting to them.

Another thing we often read is that NCWS forces fathers and mothers to divorce. The agency drives a wedge between couples and says that if the parents split up one will get to keep the children. This is just a lie of course; it doesn't happen. These children are often thrown from one foster home into another, and are exposed to such devastating trauma and stress that they are damaged in their minds and souls. They are often completely broken and have to struggle with these issues for the rest of their lives.

Then we have the cases where the Supreme Court decides that the children should be returned to the parents. However, NCWS refuses to comply as they are of a different opinion. They often don't return the children as the Supreme Court has ruled. The Supreme Court has, of course, examined the

> reality and the evidence of the case. What is the value of the children's minister when she excuses herself from taking any responsibility, but rather passes all power to the courts? The fact that the parents raise their cases at the district courts has no value! In most cases NCWS plays a rough game. Often it has built up its case over a long period and has spent a lot of money breaking the family. The family rarely has enough money to stand up against this abuse of power.
>
> NCWS has this mantra: "in the child's best interests". It's just a cover-up and a phrase that is a 100 per cent lie. In almost all cases NCWS puts the children through the worst possible distress: being taken away from their homes. So what if everything is not entirely tidy, or if the home is missing one thing or another? That is nothing compared with children losing their parents. That is the biggest tragedy any child can experience.
>
> Then you wonder how such a monster of an agency has been able to stay in power and acquire more investment. The answer is probably complicated, but the socialist dogma regarding the perfect ideology is most certainly a contributing factor here. It's the wickedness of men, where people get so angry with each other that they say, "It's only right that those parents lose their children." It has become human trafficking, in which money plays the biggest role. The foster homes are receiving high incomes, trade is maintained and the tax money flows into the municipal treasury.

Perhaps one of the best remarks about history repeating itself was made by Winston Churchill:[xx]

> When the situation was manageable it was neglected, and now that it is thoroughly out of hand we apply too late the remedies which then might have effected a cure. There is nothing new in the story… It falls into that long, dismal catalogue of the fruitlessness of experience and the confirmed unteachability of mankind. Want of foresight, unwillingness to act when action would be simple and effective, lack of clear thinking, confusion of counsel until the emergency comes, until self-preservation strikes its jarring gong – these are the features which constitute the endless repetition of history.

Chapter 12 notes

[i] Jensen, B. H., cited by Minde, H. in "Assimilation of the Sami – Implementation and Consequences", Western University: https://ir.lib.uwo.ca/cgi/viewcontent.cgi?article=1248&context=aprci

[ii] Strømsnes, K., "Multicultural Citizenship as Sami in Norway", Topology Atlas: http://at.yorku.ca/c/a/m/m/60.htm

[iii] Staff writer, *King of Devil's Island* review, IMDB: https://www.imdb.com/title/tt1332134

[iv] Færden, S., "Bastøy - historien om Djeveløya" ("Bastøy - the story of Djeveløya"), *Aftenposten*: https://www.aftenposten.no/osloby/byliv/i/K3V1X/Bastoy---historien-om-Djeveloya

[v] Magnitoman, "Bastøygutter - Dømt Til Oppdragelse" ("Bastøy Boys: Sentenced to Education"), YouTube: https://www.youtube.com/watch?v=4jkub-j0d88

[vi] Rosenberg, S., "Living hell of Norway's 'Nazi' children", BBC News: http://news.bbc.co.uk/2/hi/europe/6432157.stm

[vii] Orange, R., "Norwegian camp guards shocked SS with brutality", *The Local*: https://www.thelocal.no/20131106/norwegian-camps-guards-shocked-ss-with-brutality

[viii] Pedersen, W., "Fangevoktere i konsentrasjonsleire" ("Prisoners in Concentration Camps"), Sosiologen: https://sosiologen.no/hva-er-sosiologi/sosiologisk-kanon/fangevoktere-konsentrasjonsleire

[ix] Bjørkly, M. and Bjørklund, E., "Her finner endelig barnehjemsgutten Øyvind sin fars grav etter 45 års leting" ("Finally, the child's son, Øyvind, finds his father's grave after 45 years of exploration"), *Nordlys*: https://www.nordlys.no/nyheter/her-finner-endelig-barnehjemsgutten-oyvind-sin-fars-grav-etter-45-ars-leting/s/1-79-6800067

[x] Nwosu, E. C., "Når barnevernet blir en fiende" ("When child welfare becomes an enemy"), NRK: https://www.nrk.no/ytring/nar-barnevernet-blir-en-fiende-1.11654527

[xi] Whewell, T., *Norway's Hidden Scandal*, BBC: https://www.bbc.co.uk/news/resources/idt-sh/norways_hidden_scandal

[xii] Nicoli, C., "Norway's Barnevernet and its parallels in human history", *The Sunday Guardian Live*: https://www.sundayguardianlive.com/lifestyle/11573-norway-s-barnevernet-and-its-parallels-human-history

[xiii] McSmith, A. and Finn, C., "Australia's stolen generation: 'To the mothers and the fathers, the brothers and the sisters, we say sorry'", *The Independent*: https://www.independent.co.uk/news/world/australasia/australias-stolen-generation-to-the-mothers-and-the-fathers-the-brothers-and-the-sisters-we-say-781543.html

[xiv] Dyck, B. D., "Hitler's Stolen Children", Warfare History Network: http://warfarehistorynetwork.com/daily/wwii/hitlers-stolen-children

[xv] Adler, K., "Spain's stolen babies and the families who lived a lie", BBC: https://www.bbc.co.uk/news/magazine-15335899

[xvi] Staff writer, "Argentina's stolen children: Decades after junta, people deal with their stolen identities", RT News: https://www.rt.com/news/227635-argentina-stolen-children-documentary

[xvii] Staff writer, "Sixties Scoop – Modern Residential Schools and Genocide in Canada", Stop Racism and Hate Canada: http://www.stopracism.ca/content/sixties-scoop-modern-residential-schools-and-genocide-canada

[xviii] Øyhovden, A., "Tonjes mor: Hun sa de pleide å anbefale sterilisering" ("Tonje's mother: She said they used to recommend sterilisation"), TV2: http://www.tv2.no/a/9010508

[xix] "Høy dødelighet hos barnevernsbarn", ("High mortality rate among child welfare children"), *Aftenposten*: https://www.aftenposten.no/norge/i/LljMV/Hoy-dodelighet-hos-barnevernsbarn

[xx] Churchill, W. cited by winstonchurchill.org (speech given at the House of Commons on 2 May 1935, after the Stresa Conference in which Britain, France and Italy agreed to cooperate to maintain the independence of Austria): https://winstonchurchill.org/publications/finest-hour/finest-hour-156/wit-and-wisdom-2

13

Branded

Often when a parent has at some point been linked with NCWS the whole family becomes stigmatised. The chances of children from 'child welfare families' eventually losing their own children when they start a family are worryingly high. Once NCWS has branded a child, and that child has grown into an adult, this individual is rarely expected to have the caring ability or parenting skills to raise his or her own children. Therefore, many parents lose their children, sometimes just after birth, because of their foster care history.

Maxine's story

MEP Tomáš Zdechovský tells the tragic story of a baby who was ripped from her parents' loving arms. To their pure delight, Maxine was born to the Ladická family in January 2015, but sadly their joy did not last long, as Zdechovský explains:[i]

> I have received several letters from people seeking my help in cases involving children being taken away from their parents abroad. A Slovakian citizen and a Norwegian citizen naively asked NCWS for help and, like many others, became victims of the system. In March 2015, at two-and-a-half months old, Maxine, a fully breastfed baby, was torn from her mother's arms.
>
> I was shocked by this case, but not surprised by its absurdity or by the nonsensical process used by NCWS to take children away for no good reason and without any prior warning. It is necessary to mention that the mother of the child, Sara, is deaf, which can in no way be a reason for taking a child away from her. The mother's

hearing impairment does not mean the child will have a worse upbringing, especially when the other parent has full hearing and is able to help with the upbringing, as in this case. It's also worth noting that the mother was in the foster care system during her childhood.

Under surveillance

This tragic story began after the birth, when Maxine developed hepatitis. After she was released from the hospital everything seemed to be fine until NCWS entered the picture and offered its 'help'. The parents made the terrible mistake of accepting this so-called help. NCWS started to visit their household regularly, which, to cut a long story short, resulted in the eventual removal of their child.

The mother texted her partner, Andrej, that two women from NCWS had arrived unannounced. She had to wake up her ten-day-old baby. If it had happened once, it would not have mattered that much. It would be understandable if the social worker had come to check that everything was fine and then left. But later that evening, after Andrej had finished work, he received a phone call from an NCWS case worker. The intrusive woman asked why Sara had not opened the door for them. Andrej explained that Sara was deaf and could not hear the door, so the two women from NCWS waited for Andrej to come back from work at 11pm and visited the family again.

The day after that, a Saturday, more people from Barnevernet came to visit the family, first at around lunchtime and then again in the evening. This continued for the next few days. NCWS eventually concluded that late-night visits were not necessary. However, its staff showed up very frequently and unexpectedly from then on.

I guess everyone understands that these regular visits were not at all pleasant because the family's everyday life was being turned upside down with no serious issues uncovered. They never knew the day or the hour of the next visit from the social workers. But the worst was yet to come.

How NCWS wanted to 'help'

One day at a meeting with NCWS, social workers came up with the idea to offer the Ladická family further 'help'. This meant transporting the family to a special house for families in Gjøvik, which is approximately a one-hour drive from Lillehammer, where the family lived, and approximately one-and-a-half hours from where the father worked. They were to be observed by cameras for three months under the supervision of a special team, while living among other families.

NCWS gave the family an ultimatum: either choose Gjøvik or lose their baby. There was a brief mention of a third option, which involved taking a special parenting course. However, they were not given the chance to take the course and were blackmailed into choosing to go to Gjøvik or lose Maxine. The social worker finally mentioned a fourth option: home visits.

A debate lasting two-and-a-half hours followed. After this, the parents flatly refused to go to Gjøvik. The father said that his mum (Maxine's grandmother Janka) had handed in her resignation at work and intended to help the young family. Sara informed NCWS of their decision, and later that day NCWS texted to say that its staff wanted to video the mother and her baby together.

Minimal eye contact

At first, Sara and Andrej were recorded during a ten-minute video. Filming took place in a very small and claustrophobic room, which was very uncomfortable, particularly for little Maxine. Andrej was supposed to change Maxine's nappy during this time. Apparently, Maxine maintained "minimal eye contact" with her parents during those ten minutes.

After being filmed the parents waited a couple of days for feedback from the social worker. A message came from NCWS stating that the parents and their baby had to go back for another meeting. The parents went with their daughter, as always, but this time there were two plain-clothes policemen at the entrance wearing name tags and badges. At that moment Andrej realised the situation was serious, and this was confirmed at the meeting. They took baby Maxine away without any reason or justification. The policemen disappeared to an unknown destination with their baby.

NCWS later informed the parents that their baby would be put into foster care. The parents had no right to know where their daughter was, or with whom. They could submit an application for visits to the court, but they were not allowed to see their baby before the end of the trial. The reason given for taking Maxine away was the lack of eye contact in the video and the mother's childhood, which was perceived to be reflected in the mother's parenting abilities. By far the most significant reason for taking Maxine away was that the child's parents and grandmother were thinking of moving to Slovakia. Yes, that was the most serious concern for NCWS!

A normal human being would never imagine that this could happen in what is supposed to be a civilised country. Have we gone back to the days when human rights were weak and injustice prevailed?

Free Maxine

At the time of writing, Maxine was still being held at a secret address in Norway's child welfare system, but a new campaign has been organised to highlight the serious human rights abuses committed against the Ladická family. The press release reads:[ii]

> …The family won in September 2016 before a district court that called into question NCWS' practices and pointed out that the girl's parents are fully competent to take care of her. NCWS, however, appealed the decision due to the alleged bias of one of the lay judges, who had expressed a negative opinion on the work of NCWS in the past in the daily Aftenposten. The regional court admitted that NCWS was right and returned the case to the district court.
>
> The desperate family had to wait exactly nine months for the next trial. In October 2017, the district court reversed its previous decision and admitted that NCWS was right. Maxine had to stay with the foster parents at

a secret address. The family keeps on fighting and, after some consideration, they have decided to publish their story, being in a desperate and hopeless situation. The case has already been raised by media in the Czech Republic, Slovakia and other European countries.

The initial proposal to take the baby away from parents for suspected child neglect was submitted by NCWS' workers on 20th January 2015, immediately after Maxine's birth. This was at a time when the family was still at the maternity ward and the social workers could not predict how the family would cope (they left the hospital on 23rd January).

The child was removed, after persistent NCWS bullying of the family, on 26th March 2015. The removal decision states the following: concerns about the mental health of the mother, who was raised in foster care in her childhood and is deaf; the parents' refusal to stay with their child at a family monitoring facility; and a fear that the family would leave for Slovakia, where NCWS' officials "could not observe the child's development".

The immediate reason for "concern" was the alleged lack of eye contact with her parents on the part of the two-and-a-half-month-old baby, and her alleged rejection of them. The officials were concerned, for example that the baby closed her eyes while being breastfed. These accusations were made by the NCWS officials after harassing the family through unannounced visits, often at night, from the moment of the baby's birth. During those visits, the parents had to repeatedly change nappies or breastfeed the baby, even outside regular times, under the supervision of the workers and their video camera. Analysis of the individual footage and proving whether or not the child maintained eye contact later constituted a crucial part of the evidence during the individual court proceedings.

Marica Pirošíková, Agent of the Slovak Republic before the European Court of Human Rights said: "The Office of the Agent of the Slovak Republic before the European Court of Human Rights has been pursuing, in the long term and with great concern, cases concerning the taking of children from the care of their biological parents without relevant reasons in some Council of Europe countries, contrary to the existing human rights standards. The reason is, among other things, that the office has been informed in detail of many such cases of Slovak children being taken from the custody of their parents in foreign countries, in which the office may, after exhausting national remedies, intervene in proceedings before the European Court of Human Rights as a third party in the case of notification of the complaint to the respondent government.

"From the very beginning, we have also followed the Ladická case. We have provided the family with the relevant case law of the European Court of Human Rights, and if the family turns to this international court we will certainly ask for an intervention. It is recalled that in this case several Slovak public authorities – the Commissioner for Children, the Commissioner for Persons with Disabilities, the previous Minister of Justice of the Slovak Republic, the Minister of Labour of Social Affairs and Family of the Slovak Republic as well as the Chairperson of Slovak Delegation of Parliamentary Assembly of the Council of Europe – have also been active. Given the situation in Norway, the Slovak Republic is already intervening in the case of K. O. and V. M. v. Norway, and is also requesting third-party intervention in the case of Strand Lobben and Others v. Norway, which will be decided by the Grand Chamber of the European Court."

"We know the story of the Ladická family in detail. It is a daylight kidnapping of a child which Norway is responsible for. There was not even one objective reason in the case to remove a healthy and breastfed baby from her loving parents and family. The proceedings of the district court in September 2016 showed NCWS had based its argument on clear delusions. Still, they let the family suffer for another year just to tell them ultimately that the child had got used to foster care. It is time to mobilise public opinion in Norway and other countries to hold Norway accountable for such a procedure, to make it apologise to the family and return the child,' said Jitka Chalánková, a paediatrician, a member of the Petition Committee in support of the Michalak family and a former Czech MP.

Monika Onderková, a long-term activist and member of the preparatory committee of Slovak NGO Right to Family said: "Since 2012, many cases of children being taken away from their parents without a relevant reason have occurred abroad. However, this case is much more alarming, as the baby was taken away from a breastfeeding mother, who, despite being deaf, was able to care for her daughter with love, together with her partner. For more than three years NCWS has left Maxine with her foster parents, at present enabling contact with her biological parents only three times a year for an hour.

"This is absolutely unacceptable for the parents, and obviously in sharp contrast with standard rule of law procedures; not to mention the immense suffering of the parents, who cannot obtain a decision to get Maxine back for good. The NCWS psychologist proposed such a contact arrangement just so that Maxine would recognise her biological parents. The reasons why Maxine had been taken away from her biological parents have already been circulated in the media and are so absurd that it is pointless repeating them. What is needed, however, is an increase in public pressure and discussion, as in the case of the Bodnariu family. This way we can help not only the family of Maxine, but also many other families. I would like to be an optimist and say that our aim is to stop such practices of state authorities, and I believe we can do this with the help of European citizens."

An application was recently sent to the European Court of Human Rights (ECtHR) for Maxine's case to be heard, and hopefully for justice to be served.

Thrust into the spotlight

Psychiatric nurse, and father of Vibeke Vedvik, Inge Charles Vedvik, wrote the following commentary about his experience of NCWS for inclusion in this book:

> In my psychiatry work in Norway I meet many people who have been under the child welfare system, foster care and residential care on a daily basis. These people are often persecuted as adults by the system that was supposed to help them in the first place.
>
> They are like nomads roaming through life, stigmatised in their families and seen as potential contributors in helping to increase the child welfare budget. Their children also get thrust into the spotlight because of their parents' past.
>
> Last year, NCWS removed two children from newlywed parents two days after their wedding. The reason given was that they had been given a tip-off by social services with regards to the mother searching for better housing at some point in the past. The couple had not even met at this stage.
>
> Her husband had at one time been in child welfare care during his childhood. So, because of the wife's innocent request for better housing and the husband's past, NCWS took the children. To make matters even worse, if that's possible, they were advised to divorce, so now they are divorced and still childless.
>
> NCWS had no intention of helping them. Instead, it chose to take their children, who were torn from their mother's arms.
>
> I personally know the people around them. Her now ex-husband had a good job and was doing well, so why take the children two days after they were married? They had everything in order with their housing and finances, and she was happily married. But that didn't stop NCWS intervening and removing these children from their parents.

Aria's story

At 10:53 am on January 13, 2015, baby Aria was born to proud and loving parents Ken Joar Olsen and Vibeke Morrissey. Within two days Vibeke and Aria were forcibly confined to a mothers' home by NCWS and the police.

After the first week of observation, NCWS decided that Aria's mother was not good enough at parenting, although the staff at the home had noted that Vibeke was a good and loving mother. NCWS claimed that Aria's father Ken Joar, a former foster child himself, who had served prison sentences but had left his past behind, was dangerous to both the mother and the child, which was completely unfounded. Baby Aria was removed without warning and placed in a temporary foster home before she was ten days old.

All accusations against Vibeke and Ken Joar were proven to be completely false, and many professionals vouched for their good parenting skills from the beginning. Several psychologists, social workers, child welfare employees, family therapists, physicians, journalists and even the head of department at the child welfare office found Ken Joar to be reformed and believed that he was not a threat to anyone.

The courts also ruled that NCWS had made a mistake in removing baby Aria from her parents, but despite this gross injustice she was kept in a foster home. Aria's parents were allowed to see their daughter for just a couple of hours a few times a year. Sadly, removing Aria from her parents has caused her significant trauma. Ken Joar and Vibeke cut short one precious visit with their baby as they could see how traumatised she was. It is obvious that Aria wanted and needed to be with her mummy and daddy.

According to Solveig Horne, former Minister of Children, Equality and Social Inclusion, and Mari Trommald, Directorate for Children, Youth and Family Affairs, it is "guaranteed" that no baby will be taken from their parents without a thorough assessment. In baby Aria's case, no such assessment took place before she was put up for adoption. Horne also said that taking a child into care was only a temporary measure, and that all steps would be taken to reunite the child with its biological family. This rarely happens in Norway, and it has certainly not happened in Aria's case. NCWS didn't even offer the family any help. There was no guidance; not even a home visit. There was no effort to bring Aria home, even though every visit went smoothly, and the parents had sought counselling, even though there were no mental health problems or substance abuse issues, and their home was very stable.

NCWS became concerned that Ken Joar was fighting for his daughter on social media, and thereby concluded that he was not cooperating with them. At two years old, Aria was said to be 'attached' to the foster carers based on Attachment Theory, which, as discussed earlier, is an unfounded, unscientific, evolution-based theory. This is just one tactic NCWS uses time and time again: keep the child away from the parents long enough, and when the parents win their case it doesn't matter. It's too late because the baby is now attached to its foster carers.

On May 24, 2017, Ken Joar and Vibeke received an encouraging letter from the ECtHR. Ken Joar Olsen writes:[iii]

> They have asked the state to respond to our complaint about violations of human rights.
>
> The response concerns the question of whether or not the case should be promoted for the court.
>
> Our lawyer says: "This does not mean that the case has been admitted, but we are an important step further. Most cases are being rejected before this stage in the process."
>
> So I hope you are reading this, all of you who have done this to our family and our child, and inflicted such great pain: child protection in Lørenskog, municipality management, especially the municipal directors, the Court of Justice, the Court of Appeal and the Supreme Court that did not allow our appeal, and also to the highest degree Horne, who is not taking her responsibility seriously, which would be to clean up this inhuman system that has been created.
>
> Today we have eight highly qualified professionals who have spoken out in writing, stating that child protection in Lørenskog was wrong. We are good parents.
>
> Still, Aria has suffered from this trauma of being removed from us, and was robbed of the joy of spending her first two and a half years with her parents. This injustice can never be undone! We are nevertheless pleased that ECtHR is taking a stand on this, and it will hopefully lead to changes in the system.

One thing is still guaranteed: we will never give up! If it's the last thing I do in life, I'm going to fight for my child and the other innocent children!

Abuse of power

A specialist Norwegian psychologist observed how Ken Joar and Vibeke were prejudged after hardly any investigation had taken place, and claimed that serious errors were exposed in this case. The local authority was declared incompetent with regard to reporting and record-keeping, and a new local authority took over. Two new experts investigated the case and spent more than 400 hours working on it. They found Ken Joar and Vibeke to be highly competent parents and concluded that a return to the family was in the child's best interests. Many mistakes and serious abuses were revealed in this case.

The mayor, county governor, local politicians, MPs and Minister Horne were informed, but they all turned their backs and said they couldn't intervene. The reunification case was dragged on and on by the local authority. The county council's handling of the case was nothing short of scandalous, and the parents received no help or support after their baby daughter was removed from them.

On May 1, 2018, after a three-year battle, Aria was eventually released back into the arms of her loving mother and father, to their overwhelming joy and relief. The healing process has finally begun for this family.

First resort

Deutsche Welle, a worldwide multimedia network that reaches more than 157 million people weekly, reported on the overzealous nature of NCWS, particularly in relation to Ken Joar and Vibeke's case. Anne-Kathrine Eckbo-Fangan, a former child welfare employee, expressed in the video that the agency removes children from their homes as a first resort, not as a final option. She left her job because she could no longer condone its practices.

As a social worker she was under constant pressure. Rather than supporting parents long term, she had to quickly wrap up each case and move on to the next. Eckbo-Fangan commented:[iv]

> The child welfare office is only concerned with removing children from the families as quickly as possible, then not helping to bring them back again quickly. They stay with foster families until they are eighteen years old, no discussion.

She added:

> We had lists of mothers who we specifically targeted: single mothers, or ones with children from several fathers; poor, sick, unemployed parents; or families without relatives – that is, uncles, aunts and grandparents.

Child welfare reports

Author, anthropologist and historian Yngve Nedrebø is division executive for the regional State Archives in Bergen (Statsarkivet i Bergen), which holds twenty-five kilometres of public archive material on its shelves. The following commentary written by Nedrebø analyses and briefly summarises some important points made by researcher Lars B. Kristofersen, who was research director at NOVA before it became part of HiOA in 2016.

Nedrebø writes:[v]

High death rates in care

NOVA's 9/14 report shows the ages of the 1,797 children and young people who had been under child welfare measures between 1990 and 2009 (of whom there were 45,165 males and 38,585 women in total).[vi] The number of deaths increases rapidly from the age of sixteen, and when they reach the age of eighteen and become 'no one's children', the numbers soar. This child welfare population was compared with a population from the same age groups who were not registered with child welfare. The child welfare population totalled 83,750 people, while the non-welfare population totalled 95,051.

Disability pension

The report found that 6.5 per cent of the child welfare population received a disability benefit compared with 0.7 per cent of the non-welfare population. The report also showed that in the 25 to 41 age bracket 11.1 per cent in the child welfare group received a disability benefit compared with 1 per cent.

Suicides

The report showed that suicides account for 2.81 per cent of child welfare deaths compared with 0.58 per cent in the non-welfare group, making suicides 4.8 times higher among the child welfare group. The risk of being killed was twenty-seven times higher for the child welfare population. Even the chance of dying from cancer was 93 per cent higher. Most child welfare deaths were connected in some way to drugs or alcohol.

Reasons given

The report also explains why those from the child welfare population who died ended up in child welfare in the first place. It shows that fairly low numbers were taken because of alleged sexual abuse (1,466 children of the total 83,750 included in the survey) which equates to 1.75 per cent. Physical abuse accounted for 2 per cent and psychological abuse for 1.9 per cent, while 23,193 children (or 27.7 per cent) were taken on subjective grounds; issues NCWS claim to have observed that no one else had.

The highest risk of death for the child welfare population was related to drug abuse, although this was still a rather small group of 3,119 children (5.87 per cent) of those included in the study. The lowest mortality rate was recorded among those who had been sexually abused (1.75 per cent). It must be noted that all categories of welfare children had a much higher risk of dying than the non-welfare population with which they were compared.

Mothers and fathers

NIBR's 2005:12 report studied the parents of children removed by NCWS.[vii] Between 1990-2002, 3,683 mothers and 6,892 fathers died, with 438 mothers and 953 fathers committing suicide during this period. This represents an average of 116 suicides per year, a shockingly high percentage given that around 500 and 600 suicides are recorded in total each year in Norway. This indicates that around 25 per cent of all suicides in Norway involve parents of child welfare children.

Why?

NCWS will undoubtedly say that the high numbers show how badly these children were treated before they were removed from their families. Meanwhile, critics of the system will claim that the deaths are the result of NCWS' involvement. It is a mix, and Kristofersen's studies do not give us conclusive answers. We need more studies to be conducted, and they must be carried out properly. NCWS and the authorities will not be in favour of doing such studies, as they most likely already know that they will be blamed!

But I think we know that children taken into the child welfare population and their parents suffer severely. The process is very stressful, and many children and parents suffer from post-traumatic stress disorder (PTSD) afterwards. I have no doubt that most of the deaths can be blamed on NCWS.

Child welfare children generally end up without a proper education, with only 8 per cent achieving a higher education compared with around 50 per cent of the total population. Job prospects are also very bleak. Children are very often introduced to drugs, sexual abuse and prostitution for the first time while they are in the 'care' of NCWS. Dagbladet, a daily newspaper in Norway, has published several stories recently that resulted in the closing down of various child welfare institutions.

Child welfare children have a much higher risk of dying at a young age, and by the age of eighteen NCWS is no longer responsible for them. After this they are often offered a disability benefit, enabling NCWS to keep them under its control for another five years!

When NCWS takes children away from their parents and out of their homes, the children's life expectancy drops from around eighty to less than sixty. Even the risk of being murdered increases by 2,700 per cent!

They told me my parents were criminals

You are on your own now, they said...

And left me alone

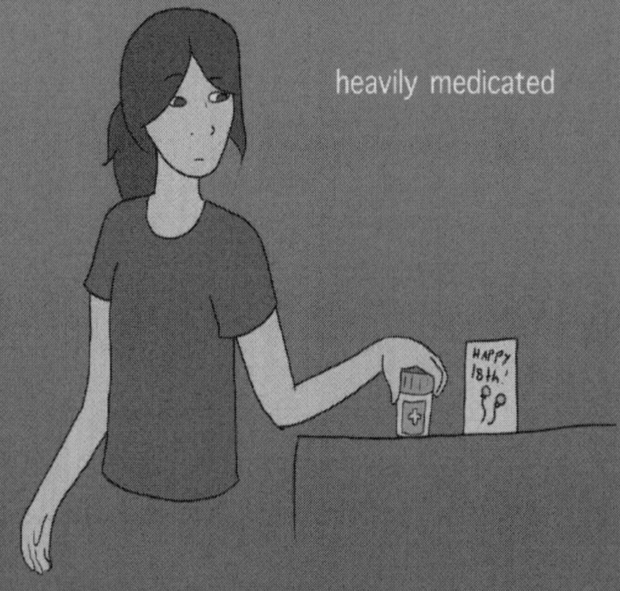

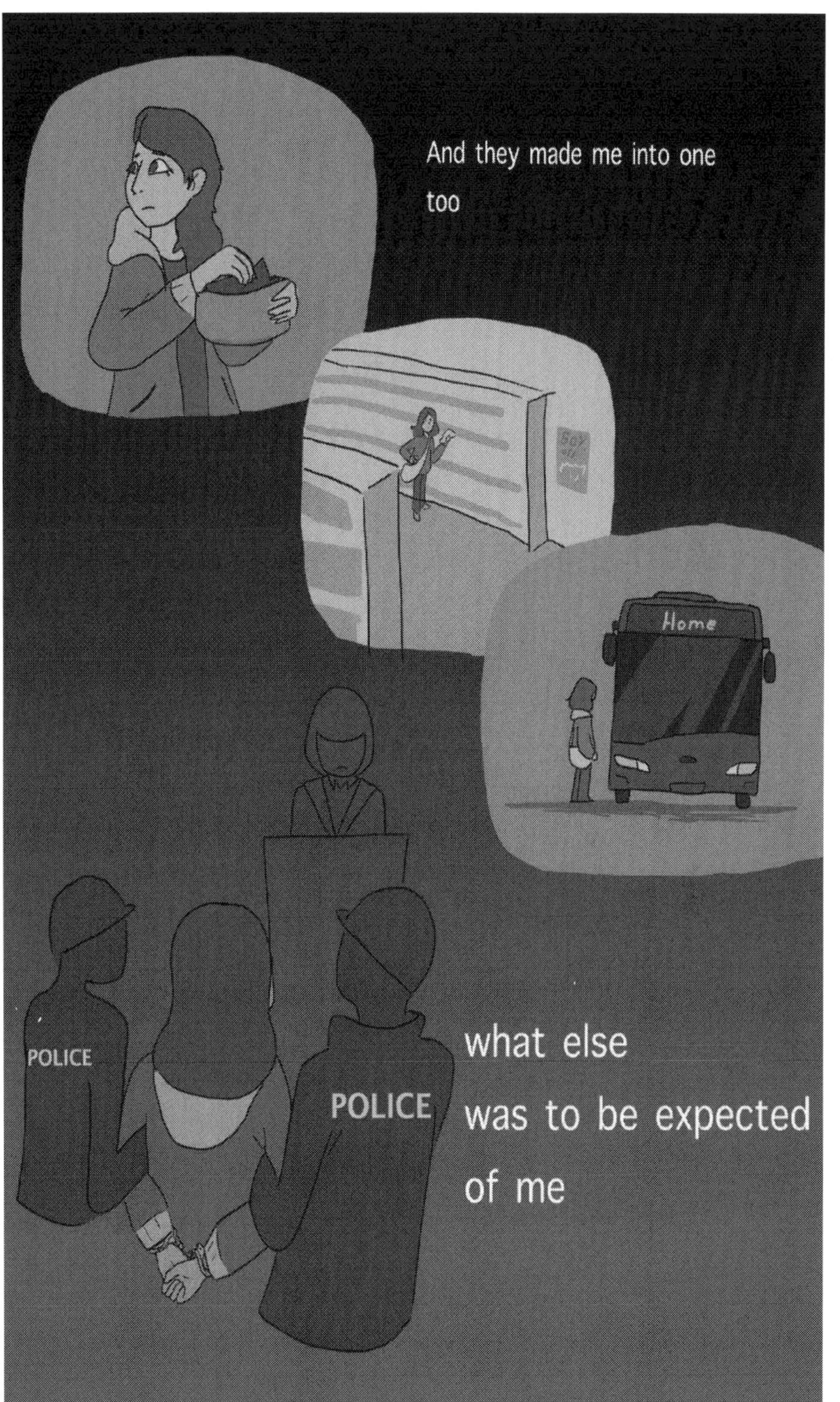
And they made me into one
too
Home
POLICE
POLICE
what else
was to be expected
of me

Can I handle myself otherwise?
I found a place to live
I found someone to love
I found myself a life
I found confidence in me
I quit the drugs
They had
made me think
I needed them
florist

I didn't

I found out there was life in me

Inside me

a tiny me

...a baby

After nine months

They told me they were worried

They told me to forget I ever gave birth

It would be easier that way...

You are on your own now, they said...

And left me alone

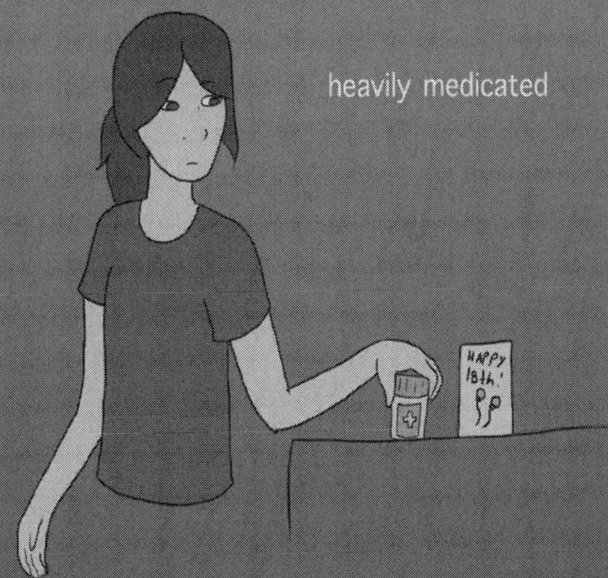

because they never could have handled me otherwise

These sketches, which show the NCWS cycle of misery, were created and sent to the author of this book by a Norwegian creative arts team called TNP.

Cycle of misery

Despite NCWS' theory that suggests people cannot learn and do not change, many people who have experienced trauma in the past use their bad experiences to create a better and brighter future for themselves and their families. The social engineering system that took Aria and Maxine away from their parents – parents who had at one time been in foster care themselves – had the effect of a 'humanitarian' shelling on the family. This type of action is senseless and totalitarian in nature, with the so-called 'superior group' asserting its power over the 'not-quite-good-enough' parents.

Chapter 13 notes

[i] Zdechovsky, T., "Under Surveillance", Step Up 4 Children's Rights: https://stepup4childrensrights.com/under-surveillance

[ii] Staff writer, "Strasbourg is facing another application against Norway", Step Up 4 Children's Rights: https://stepup4childrensrights.com/strasbourg-is-facing-another-application-against-norway

[iii] Olsen, K. J., "Not without my daughter-a father's struggle for his family" Baby Aria and the Fight for Justice: https://baby-aria-and-the-fight-for-justice.webnode.com

[iv] Eckbo-Fangan, A. K., interviewed on a documentary entitled "Child services under fire in Norway", DW English: https://www.youtube.com/watch?v=4tpcbeJjDtI&feature=youtu.be

[v] Nedrebø, Y., "Children taken into Norway's child welfare system suffer severely", Step Up 4 Children's Rights: https://stepup4childrensrights.com/children-taken-into-norways-child-welfare-system-suffer-severely

[vi] Backe-Hansen, E., Madsen, C., Kristofersen, L. B. and Hvinden, B, "Child welfare in Norway 1990-2010" ("Barnevern i Norge 1990-2010"), HiOA: http://www.hioa.no/Om-OsloMet/Senter-for-velferds-og-arbeidslivsforskning/NOVA/Publikasjonar/Rapporter/2014/Barnevern-i-Norge-1990-2010

[vii] Kristofersen, L. B., "Child welfare health: infertility and mortality in the period 1990-2002" ("Barnevernbarnas helse: Uførhet og dødelighet i perioden 1990-2002"), HiOA: http://www.hioa.no/Om-OsloMet/Senter-for-velferds-og-arbeidslivsforskning/NIBR/Publikasjoner/Publikasjoner-norsk/Barnevernbarnas-helse

14

Uncovered

Of the child welfare 'experts' living in Norway, one in particular is hailed by NCWS as a hero: Professor Lars Smith. In 2004, Smith published a book titled *Barn med Atferdsvansker: En Utviklingspsykopatologisk Tilnærmingsmåte* (*Children with Behavioural Difficulties: A Developmental Psychopathological Approach*).[i] He has also written many articles and co-authored various other books in the area of developmental psychology.

In 2015, an article written by Smith was published in the *Morgenbladet*, a weekly Norwegian newspaper. The article was titled "Child welfare failure", with a by-line that read: "Everyone will agree that physical abuse and sexual abuse do not fit the concept of good care. But what is emotional abuse?"[ii]

Smith describes situations in which parents neglect their children and talks about how we can "break the evil circle". He also admits that NCWS gets things wrong and neglects some of the children it is supposed to rescue and help. However, the article contradicts itself in places, and a question arises in the mind after reading it as to whether the author truly wants the abuse to stop. He acknowledges NCWS' repeated failures, but comes to a shocking conclusion in the last sentence of the article:

> It's better that ten innocent parents should be subjected to care decisions than one small child has to grow up with violence or abuse.

As far as Smith is concerned, it is perfectly fine to destroy the childhoods of ten children from innocent, caring and capable homes so long as that one child – who may or may not need help – is 'rescued'. Most Norwegians would have seen things the way Smith does back in 2015, and would have wholeheartedly believed that what he describes in his article counts as legitimate child protection. However, things are beginning to change and statements like Smith's no longer go unchallenged.

In real-life scenarios – which this article has consciously ignored – it is not about ten parents being "wrongfully targeted" and expected to accept this destruction on behalf of "all the children suffering". It's about ten children being wrongfully taken into the same system Smith admits is not good enough. Is he genuinely interested in saving children, or is he openly displaying his underlying hatred for biological bonds and parenting? Does he truly care about children's rights and the "best interests of the child"?

The fact that NCWS hails Smith as a hero should concern us all. He puts into words what the whole system stands for, yet no one from within NCWS stands up to him; not even when it comes to questioning his printed words. The madness of his ten children philosophy is still not recognised by those in child welfare circles.

Ironically, Smith refers to the parents' fight to get their children back as "harassment", with absolutely no consideration for the hypothetical ten families that have needlessly been destroyed and the ten children whose childhoods have been ruined.

Standing up!

In 2016, Björn Korf, a Christian radio station manager at ERF Vienna, interviewed a former Norwegian headmistress who worked at a public school in Norway. For fear of further persecution, she has asked to remain anonymous. Here is the transcript from their conversation:[iii]

> **Björn Korf:** Tell us a little more about your perspective. You were kind of criticising NCWS. What have you observed?
>
> **Headmistress:** Well, before my own experience with the system I thought the NCWS system was working well; that they really were protecting children and only made an intervention with a family when it was really needed. Then, while working as a headmistress, NCWS suddenly came for a meeting and told me that five children would be taken

away from their parents. This came as a shock because we had received no questions from NCWS beforehand and we didn't have a chance to tell them our story – how we saw the children and how they were – so this was really shocking. I tried to make them extend the process and do some investigation. I wanted to tell them our story and contact other institutions that might give documentation that could help the parents, because I knew the kids were OK. The parents were from Afghanistan and the children were born in Norway. They had some problems, because this was a very small place and they were the first foreign family ever to live there. So, yes, the children had some challenges, but psychologically, socially and emotionally I had no worries about them. And then, when I was asking critical questions and trying to slow the process down, NCWS really attacked me and tried to get rid of me. In fact, I was put on leave two days later while they were kind of investigating whether I had made any mistakes. This is how it started, anyway.

Björn Korf: How did the process continue from there?

Headmistress: Well, the children were taken. I had organised some of the teachers to accompany them in the cars. This was my worst day ever. I was putting some clothes into plastic bags… changing clothes we had at school, because of course the parents didn't know anything and hadn't thought anything. Three of the children were at school, so we had three of the children, and the babies were at home. They were taken on the same day at the same time, so this was their "action" – that's what they call it.

So the three children went away in one car each. I didn't know where they went; everything was very secret. They went away, and I know that for three months the parents didn't have the possibility to even talk to them on the phone. After three months they met at a gathering for two hours, then several months later another gathering, always with guards and always just for a couple of hours. Always with directions from NCWS not to talk about the case; that means not even trying to explain to the kids what was happening. They were also told not to show too much emotion, not to make the children cry and so on, because if they did this would worry the children and be an example of their incompetence as serious or responsible parents.

Björn Korf: What reason was given? Why did they take the children? Did you hear anything?

Headmistress: Every time I asked them, they told me, "No, this is none of your business. This is a matter of confidentiality." They gave us the impression that the parents had done something really serious, and that was the reason. At the same time I just couldn't believe it because the children were normal, and I know children from experience, both professionally and as a mother. If something serious like violence or sexual abuse was happening I would see that and the symptoms. So I immediately understood that something was wrong. I thought it was a big mistake that had happened, and later I found out that this mistake was not a singular example, but really the tendency in NCWS' work. So many families tell the same story and I had reason to believe that this was a kind of systemic error, not just a single case.

Björn Korf: And then you started to basically criticise the system, and from that you lost your job?

Headmistress: Well, when they came to my office two days before the "action", and I understood that they would in no way stop the process I contacted a lawyer in Oslo because I did not trust the local lawyers to be good enough. My mistake was not keeping the parents anonymous. So by telling the lawyers, who I knew had this rule of confidentiality, I was breaking this rule by telling the lawyers the parents' names, even if, of course, the lawyers had the same rule of confidentiality. This was my mistake, and that's what NCWS used to try to fire me.

So I was put on leave, and for two months the police were investigating me. I was not charged, and I didn't have a fear of anything. I got something like a warning, but it was not enough to lose my job, so I came back and continued working as a teacher, and then my employer tried to find other reasons to get rid of me. My new headmaster told my colleagues to write down any mistakes that I made. I remember I was coming in late, ten minutes, and a colleague was writing it down to deliver it to the headmaster. If I said things during the lesson that were somehow controversial the children reported it at home, and then the complaints came. It happened twice. The small things they tried to put together… it didn't work. It was not enough, and I had a good lawyer.

In the end they had to pay me to quit, so they paid me half a year's salary almost – half a million krone – and I accepted this, because by then the situation was that it was not possible for me to work with the children. The relationship between me and the children was destroyed, really. They were in a dilemma of who to believe: me or their parents? Because it was really me against the whole village, kind of, because of the others at work. So it was not possible to continue working.

This was all because of a single case, because I was then too scared to continue helping the family. It was really a massive abuse of power that I felt. In all my body I was really shocked and scared and afraid for my own children. Standing alone like that, it made me not strong enough to continue helping the Afghan family. But my mother was worried about them and wanted to help them, and she started talking to the father and gradually I came back on side. So my mother and I have been kind of a support group for the family now for two years. And together with that I am known to other parents on the internet and I met some of them. I am talking a lot to many of them on Skype and so on, and have given free therapy for some, and I've been making some videos.

I want normal people to understand what I did not: that the system is not working for the children, but for itself. And that children are abused, and it's the NCWS system that's really hurting the children, not their parents. Of course parents make mistakes, and some of them may not be competent enough to have full responsibility, but at the same time what I see is that people seem very honest in talking about their mistakes, and they change. They get an education and jobs, they quit using drugs, they find better friends and they really become very good parents, as I see it.

And at the same time, I want to say that even if the parents are really in trouble, a reaction like this, as we see in almost all cases – the total isolation of the kids, and no normal gatherings; these few hours, sometimes in strange places, like shopping centres or offices – it's so insane. It's so unprofessional to organise the gatherings, the social contact between the parents, like this, whatever has happened. That's not an excuse for how bad the parents are. The system is supposed to be professional, to take care of the kids, and what I see is the complete opposite. And, it really upsets me. I just swallow my fear as much as I can and continue, because too few people in Norway hear that. Most people keep quiet as they are afraid themselves, and at the same time it's just not possible for me to do nothing.

Björn Korf: We know about the Bodnariu case, which is going around the world, especially through the internet. What we have learnt so far is that the whole thing basically started with one of the girls, I think she was eight or nine years old, singing a Christian song in school and the teacher, or maybe even the leader of the school, got suspicious about it and called NCWS. Why would a teacher ever do that?

Headmistress: Well, what I know from my own experience is that the school system and also the kindergartens quickly make contact with NCWS when they are worried, and from my own experience I understand this as a plus to the system. This is how it should be, of course, if a teacher really is worried. It should be possible to discuss it with other professionals. At the same time, I think it is so strange not to talk to the parents in the first place, because what we see is that instead of talking to the parents about what's worrying the school or the teachers, they go directly to NCWS and this is a lack of competence when it comes to communication and relations, and that's a bad problem in the schools in Norway.

When it comes to religion, I also know that in this very secular society people are prejudiced against Christians. Many really think that Christianity indoctrinates kids, and, well, to some extent they may be right. I personally know it from the inside. I'm a Christian myself, and of course I sometimes ask myself: do I remember to say that this is what I believe? Most people in Norway don't believe in the same way. Of course, indoctrination can be irrelevant and criticised, but taking away the children for such reasons is really just insane. It has nothing to do with professionality at all. This is what we see: instead of an investigation they take the children, and this is what makes the people of Norway afraid because you really don't have a chance. They take the children, and nine out of ten children never come back.

Björn Korf: What we see on the internet are a lot of stories from migrant families, and you even said yourself this first case you ever encountered was a family from Afghanistan. Are there also stories from, let me put it this way, 'normal Norwegian families' where kids have been taken away? Are Norwegians also afraid of Barnevernet?

Headmistress: Yes. Maybe a little less so than foreigners, but we are also afraid. There are so many people being investigated each year, and this process is enough to scare people because they have to go to meetings and meet these people, and many of them really have a great deal of power. You don't feel very confident coming into that office. You really know this is dangerous for you and your children, and the case workers I have met really communicate this. It's like, you can believe that they kind of enjoy the power they have, because they really have enormous power compared to their educational level, which is very low. These people would never have the chance to have personal power like that in any other job except for the NCWS system.

Björn Korf: Do they also visit families at home to do these investigations?

Headmistress: Yes. They are increasing the numbers of children taken based on emergency measures, without warning, but they are also taking children after years of investigation. I know a family that was followed for up to eight years and then the children were taken. I know a mother who had three visits a day for six weeks. So this is another form of terror, because the children in these families become very afraid.

Not long after the interview this former headmistress personally experienced some of the terror other families are currently going through. Her children were taken and flown two hours away from their home. After being interrogated for six hours they were released. When the children returned from this traumatic experience they informed their parents that the only question NCWS really wanted them to answer was: does your family hate NCWS? This form of terror and bullying has stopped the mother helping other families who find themselves in desperate need of help. Like many other families in Norway, they are desperate for an international intervention and for the abuse of power to stop.

Christians beware!

An article titled "De kristne spiser barn!" ("The Christians eat children!"), published in Christian newspaper *Vårt Land* (*Our Country*) in 2011, describes how the authorities were using scaremongering tactics to convince people that all Christians beat up their children.[iv]

The article writer suggested that when criticising people from particularly large demographics in such a serious way, good documentation is needed to support the claims put forward. Where is the evidence to indicate that children in Christian communities are beaten any more than in other environments, if at all? The article suggests that those who believe in God and are responsible to him for how they live their lives should create greater barriers to hurting their fellow human beings. The writer compares these scaremongering tactics to when the Romans spread rumours that Christians ate their offspring.

Other leaflets have been handed out to NCWS employees warning them to keep an eye out for children who are raised in Christian families. The information contained in these leaflets could quite easily condition recipients to believe that Christianity is dangerous in general, instantly pitting NCWS employees against any Christians they come across and choose to target.

The leaflet describes the experiences of children who most likely grew up in cults rather than Christian families. If these extreme cases, for example where psychological and physical punishments are used against children if they want to leave a denomination, are propagated in this way, it could easily paint the entire Christian community in a negative light. Therefore, all Christians could become targets, including those who have truly made Jesus Christ the Lord of their lives.

The following is an English translation of the "Warning against Christians" leaflet seen by the author:

> **For you, the grown-up**
>
> Through the project Go On, many children and adolescents who have grown up in an isolated denomination, and those who have left or been thrown out of these denominations, have sought help from Save the Children. Go On has helped these children and young people who have severed ties with these societies. The help given has been based on children's personal rights in Norwegian society and the UN Convention on the Rights of the Child. An isolated denomination can be identified by its members shielding themselves from the rest of the society and distancing itself from aspects of mainstream societal norms and ways of living.
>
> We have reason to believe that there are huge unrecorded numbers of children and young people who do not share their parents' beliefs, but who do not dare to bring this up with anyone within the denomination or outside it. The ones who have been in contact with Go On explain that it was a huge step to take. They all say that the transition

to mainstream society has been very hard, and some have become seriously ill in the process of establishing an independent life outside the denomination.

A lot of them speak of a very strict religious upbringing, where contact with children and young people outside their society is forbidden, and where everyday life and their spare time is dictated by religion. Humility and self-effacement are seen as virtues, and breaking the accepted norms of the denomination is punished both psychologically and physically.

Most of these young people lack all knowledge of everyday life in mainstream society, in spite of being part of state schools for many years. Many are also bullied by their classmates for their beliefs. Most either have a lack of education or no education at all. To many it is more important to prepare for the next life than to learn how to function in Norwegian society.

Advice to those of you who meet with these young people:

- Listen to their story
- Believe their story
- Try to understand their story
- Acquire knowledge about the denomination in question
- Dare to ask questions about religious experiences
- Consider the fact that:
- Many of these adolescents do not know much about mainstream society and do not know how to behave in secular circles
- Many have never been allowed to make their own choices or to have their own opinions
- Many do not have a social network outside the denomination
- Many are taught not to trust anyone outside the denomination
- Many are taught that they will end up in eternal damnation if they seek help from those in secular society
- Some of their lives are overshadowed by a constant fear of judgement day and the devil

How do you meet with children and adolescents who have been brought up in isolated Christian denominations?

"When I was fourteen I decided to leave the sect. It took another two years before I was able to do so. At first it was an enormous relief. Then came the hardship. I did not fit in anywhere and I knew nothing about the society I was part of. People expected me to have opinions, but that had never been allowed inside the sect. So what was I supposed to do? I had only been in state school for half a year when I was eight years old, and I had to start from scratch. I missed my parents and I cried myself to sleep every night. The experience of relief and freedom I had at first was transformed into a maze I could not find my way out of for many years."

"Then the alarm went off… There was not enough room for all nine of us on the floor at the same time when the door was supposed to be opened. We had been taught to evacuate the upper bunks first, then the middle and finally the lower bunks. However, there was sometimes still crowding. Some of us were scared and hid. Maybe it was for real this time. Maybe today was the day when God returned to take us with him: us, his chosen children. Am I one of the chosen ones? And where are Mum and Dad? Are they going to heaven too? But most probably this was only the weekly rehearsal."

"People at social services, doctors and others do not understand what I am talking about. Some think we are exaggerating and lying. And I have only shared a tiny fraction of what happened."

Cult characteristics

The following characteristics are helpful in identifying what a cult actually is:

- When the organisation is not accountable to any authorities
- When questioning and doubting are discouraged within a group

- When the group's leadership dictates how its members should act and feel
- When conditioning and brainwashing techniques are used
- When leaders and the 'experts' within the group claim a special elitist position
- When a system preaches an 'us and them' mentality that places its members in a superior position, causing conflict with wider society
- When the group teaches or implies that its 'superior' ends justify the means, which members would have considered unethical before joining the group (for example, picketing at the funerals of homosexuals)
- When members display extremely zealous, unquestioning loyalty to the group

Disturbingly, NCWS exhibits most of these characteristics in some form or other.

Chequebook diplomacy

It's no secret that many governments around the world are very concerned with the way children and their parents are being treated in Norway, especially given the incredibly low thresholds used to take children away from their families. Is it mere coincidence that the countries that once made the most noise regarding the inhumane way Norway treats its targeted population, but no longer do, are the ones Norway gives the most money to? Are Norwegian funds being used to blindfold other nations to the human rights abuses currently taking place?

For example, Norway continues to pour money by the bucketload into Romania. The EEA Grants website states that 2,696 legal professionals and court staff in Romania have received training from the Norwegian authorities in new criminal codes, human rights and court management.[v]

The European Court of Human Rights has been telling Norway for years to train its judges and other legal professionals in the basics of human rights, but to no avail. The response that comes back from Norway is usually, "We don't need any help." This arrogant and dismissive attitude toward any governing body beyond its borders is very telling.

The website states that EEA Grants aims to help Romanian organisations fight for human rights, democracy, active citizenship, transparency, equal treatment, social justice and the inclusion of vulnerable groups. Aren't single parents vulnerable? Aren't minority groups vulnerable? Aren't former foster children vulnerable? Aren't deaf parents vulnerable?

The echoes of desperate cries from parents and children in Norway are ringing out around the world as the chains of freedom rattle in its district courts through the silencing and blackmailing of its citizens. Transparency has been replaced with confidentiality, and social justice and equal treatment have become nothing more than an illusion.

In light of this, how can Norway help other countries like Romania? Or is this another way of creating the impression of looking down on other countries from a superior position?

Everything Norway is offering other countries should work effectively on home soil first, but sadly it often doesn't. Of course, sending money around the world and offering training keeps the illusion going that Norway is somehow better than the countries it funds.

The funding proposal from Norway to Serbia states:[vi]

> The overall goal of Norway's assistance to the Western Balkans is to contribute to development of rule of law and stability through initiatives that promote:

A Stability

- *Closer regional cooperation*
- *Implementation of transitional justice in the region*
- *Reconciliation*

B Socio-economic development at country level and in the region

- *Increased economic growth and competitiveness*
- *Increased capacity in the field of environment/climate/energy*
- *Increased social and economic inclusion of marginalised groups*

C Good governance

- *The rule of law strengthened through capacity-building of courts, prosecuting authorities, independent control bodies and the police*
- *A more democratic and effective defence sector*
- *Strong, vibrant and independent civil society and media*
- *Minorities and marginal groups ensured rights in accordance with international agreements, both formally and in practice*
- *The fight against organised crime and corruption established as a top priority for the authorities.*

So the government is proposing stability, socio-economic development and good governance, but at what cost? We know what the cost is for families targeted in Norway, and for the thousands of children who have been needlessly taken into 'care' without any good reason. Love is certainly lacking in Norway, but what is also missing is truth, integrity, honesty, rule of law, freedom and privacy. This environment will eventually raise its ugly head in other countries following years of funding and training from Norway. We are already starting to see this happen, especially in Eastern Europe.

In April 2018, Norway signed a billion-kroner (c.€100 million) agreement with Lithuania via EEA Grants.[vii] The money was to be spent on various projects within the justice sector and in industry, research and healthcare, according to the Ministry of Foreign Affairs.

It could be argued that the money is being used to remind Lithuanians that they need teaching and that Norway can provide that teaching. Is it possible that the money has been given in an attempt to condition the minds of Lithuanians to believe that Norway respects the rule of law and human rights? Is it being spent in the hope that this 'generous' offer buys the silence of Lithuanians concerning the current lack of justice for Lithuanian children and families in Norway?

There has been a great deal of media coverage and debate in Lithuania in relation to the many Lithuanian children who have been unjustly taken away from their families in Norway. One

Lithuanian mother has not seen her eight-year-old son for almost two years. Her son has been kept at a secret address and the whole family, including a very heartbroken grandmother, is afraid for his well-being. It is possible that his name has been changed in an attempt to Norwegianise him, and to tear him away from his culture and heritage.

In June 2018 Slovakia accepted €113 million in funding from Norway. The Slovakian president, Andrej Kiska, who was on a three-day official visit to Norway at the time, sounded very happy about the situation. After a meeting with the Norwegian prime minister, Erna Solberg, Kiska stated:[viii]

> We have a wonderful relationship with Norway. It is a country with which we have no problem. Rather, it is a question of how we can develop our relationships; what we can do better.

Media sources in Slovakia have been exposing Norway's abuses for some time, especially around the heartbreaking case of baby Maxine. English author Barnabe Rich once stated that: "Honesty stands at the gate and knocks, and bribery enters in."

EEA Grants signed a new deal with Poland in December 2017, allocating the country €809.3 million in funding.[ix] In fact, Poland receives the highest allocation of funds from Norway, followed by Romania. These two countries have also been most active in highlighting Norway's ongoing human rights abuses in the past, but as the money flows in the criticism seems to be growing quieter and quieter. Nevertheless, while it seems to be working at a government level, people's silence is harder to buy in Poland.

It states on the EEA Grants website that:[x]

> The Norway Grants are financed solely by Norway and available in 13 EU member countries that joined in 2004, 2007 and 2013.
>
> In the previous period of 2009-2014, Norway set aside €804.6 million. For the 2014-2021 period, the funding is €1.3 billion. The decision-making body for the grant scheme is the Norwegian Ministry of Foreign Affairs. Norway also provides 96% of the funding to the EEA Grants.

Norwegian grants have also supported Bulgarian judges at the ECtHR.[xi] Some of the aims of the project are to help Bulgaria come into line with European standards, providing legal aid for vulnerable groups, especially for Roma people, and to help contribute to a more transparent and efficient judicial system. Yet the Roma people in Norway still suffer to this day, and transparency within the legal segment of Norway's child welfare system is very poor.

But if Norway is so concerned about human rights, why do we so often see the rule of law thrown aside, human rights trampled on and good families destroyed within its own borders? The list goes on, and it should be remembered that he who pays the piper often calls the tune.

Silence

For many years the Norwegian media had opportunities to publicise child welfare cases that could have encouraged a broader debate in Norway. The massive increase in reports of concern and emergency decisions, the extremely low threshold for taking children away and the lack of competence in areas such as risk assessment could have all been raised. In democracies it's important to have a broad debate, especially in relation to children's rights.

So why does the Norwegian media stay so silent when it comes to the injustice and abuse perpetrated against families by NCWS? Even when victims of abuse share their stories with a full disclosure of case papers and all the facts, media outlets are still only interested in securing a brief comment from an NCWS employee rather than pressing for answers. And because of its confidentiality get-out clause, NCWS' employees do not comment on individual cases.

Media representatives will then ask for the county court judgement, and when they find out the decision went against the family, which in the vast majority of cases it does, the story never goes to print. Media outlets naively believe everything the Norwegian courts and authorities say. When journalists stand up and ask questions they are usually stopped by their editors from publishing something that would go against the state's narrative.

The Norwegian media could investigate the serious issues at

various levels within the child welfare system, for example the vast difference between the amount of money and resources NCWS has with its many salaried individuals compared with the lack of resources and limited opportunities families have to defend themselves against its accusations of 'neglect'; a word that is often used but is very vague, subjective and lacking in any real substance.

Every week, influential media outlets in Norway promote NCWS-friendly feature articles and programmes, astonishingly even claiming at times that criticism of NCWS can harm children, although this has never been backed up by any genuine research.

At one point in 2016, media reports focused on estimates of 'unrecorded cases' of children in abusive and/or criminal homes. There seemed to be quite a high number. The reports went on to say that they needed the children's help in dealing with these hundreds of unknown cases that had recently surfaced. This could be considered as a cold-hearted attempt to sculpt the minds of Norwegians who hadn't yet engaged in this area to make it even easier to remove children from capable and caring parents with very little fuss. These types of reports usually lead to more funding for NCWS to help tackle the 'issue'.

When media outlets in Eastern Europe criticise NCWS it is often because they recognise the similar behaviour of totalitarian regimes that once ruled in their own countries, for instance: family surveillance; family observation; unannounced home visits; harassment; interrogation using leading questions; conflict creation within the family in an attempt to convince parents to divorce, so as to weaken the family unit; dehumanising; false accusations; reports written about the family from many different sources; causing trouble within the workplace; intelligence reports covering medical records, school reports, police records and so on in an attempt to find weak points; blackmail; breaking in without a warrant; spreading slanderous rumours to isolate families; slowing down processes to frustrate the family further; and eventually forcing families into submission.

For the sake of our children, it's time the Norwegian media started to reveal what is really going on within its child welfare system.

Chapter 14 notes

[i] Smith, L., *Barn med Atferdsvansker: En Utviklingspsykopatologisk Tilnærmingsmåte* (Children with Behavioural Difficulties: A Developmental Psychopathological Approach: Cappelen Damm Høyskoleforlaget, 2004).

[ii] Smith, L., "Barnevernet failure" ("Barnevernets feil"), Morgenbladet: https://morgenbladet.no/ideer/2015/barnevernets_feil

[iii] Bennett, S., "A New Form of Terror in Norway", Step Up 4 Children's Rights: https://stepup4childrensrights.com/a-new-form-of-terror-in-norway

[iv] Kvalbein, A., "De kristne spiser barn! ("The Christians eat children!"), Vårt Land: http://www.verdidebatt.no/innlegg/200057-de-kristne-spiser-barn?side=8#svar-

v Staff writer, "Where we work: Romania", EEA Grants: https://eeagrants.org/Where-we-work/Romania

[vi] Staff writer, "Call for Proposals from Public Institutions and International Organisations by the Norwegian Embassy in Belgrade", Norway in Serbia: https://www.norway.no/en/serbia/norway-serbia/news-events/news2/call-for-proposals

[vii] "Norge undertegner milliardavtale med Litauen" ("Norway signs a billion agreement with Lithuania"), ABC Nyheter: https://www.abcnyheter.no/nyheter/verden/2018/04/24/195390663/norge-undertegner-milliardavtale-med-litauen

[viii] TASR correspondent, "Kiska: Norwegian Funds Should Be Earmarked for Innovations", TASR: https://newsnow.tasr.sk/foreign/kiska-norwegian-funds-should-be-earmarked-for-innovations

[ix] Staff writer, "Strengthened Cooperation with Poland", EEA Grants: https://eeagrants.org/News/2017/Strengthened-cooperation-with-Poland

[x] Staff writer, "Norway Grants", EEA Grants: https://eeagrants.org/Who-we-are/Norway-Grants

[xi] Staff writer, "Bulgarian judges trained at the European Court of Human Rights", EEA Grants: https://eeagrants.org/News/2013/Bulgarian-judges-trained-at-the-European-Court-of-Human-Rights

15

Devastated

In an article titled "The shameful, lonely and forbidden sorrow", Norwegian mother and specialist nurse Målfrid Synnøve Schartau Viken writes of the mourning process parents experience when their children are taken away:[i]

> According to statistics, the biggest trauma a parent can experience is losing a child. This loss refers to a child dying either through illness or injury. The parents experience an acute and severe crisis. Physical and psychological reactions can occur, both instantly and on a long-term basis.
>
> It is statistically more likely that both parents will experience prolonged loss of quality of life and meaning; disturbed sleep; lack of nutrient intake and prolonged ostracism from society. Mental disorders such as severe depression also become more likely.
>
> Marriage and cohabitating relationships fall apart more frequently than if the child had not gone away. Job loss, with a reduced income and therefore strained finances, follow in the wake. Physical symptoms such as fatigue, with various painful conditions – and in more severe cases, various types of cancer – can occur. Many people experience memory problems and have attention deficit issues.
>
> It is one of the greatest ordeals a person can be subjected to in life. One thing that is eventually accepted is that at least the child is not suffering. The child knows no pain or sorrow. It is only you who does.
>
> There is no mention of what happens to a parent who loses a child or children to NCWS. There is very little focus and research on this. Why? Is it because no one wants to

join such a research project, or because there is too little interest in the field?

When a child dies, the family is connected to the acute crisis team in the local authority. The priest pays them a visit, if this is desired. Family and friends put their lives on hold for a while to be there for the ailing family. Neighbours come with hot meals, condolence cards and flowers, and stand on the stairs with the newspaper retrieved.

The elderly man down the street offers to shovel the snow away for free. Warm hands and understanding hearts listen, comfort and share fond memories of the baby; cry with and for the family, drying their tears; get siblings to school and vacuum floors. At the store, acquaintances and strangers nod compassionately at them. The kindergarten or school organises a remembrance ceremony, and classmates read works of poetry.

But what happens to a parent when their child is just as abruptly and painfully dragged away from their arms while two large police officers hold them back and the NCWS caseworker they have barely seen before takes the terrified and screaming child into a waiting car?

Does anyone take any notice of you then? Does the priest come to the door? Will the kindergarten or school remember? Will anyone bring hot soup?

The reality for many parents who lose their children to NCWS is that they expect you to return to work the next day.

They deliver no flowers or condolence cards to your door because it was your fault. You were not good enough. You were less worthy than the others. You did not reach up to the sky-high threshold that you, as a parent, must meet in Norway if you are to satisfy those who think they know what is best for your child.

Instead, words such as "lack of mental ability", "no ability to collaborate", "no ability to make use of support or assistance", "lack of supportive and developmental care" and "inability to see the child's perspective" are written on a piece of paper and will pursue you for the rest of your life, like a death sentence.

These are words you barely understood before you met the snide and condescending NCWS caseworker. Examiners believe in the administrative county board, where the yawns of weary judges who think it's in the child's best interests are barely concealed behind their hands. You are doomed to lose in approximately ninety-six per cent of cases, according to government statistics. It is David versus Goliath, and David will almost certainly not win this time round.

You get that searing, clammy feeling in your chest. Your eyes are cast down when you walk outside. In meetings you rarely gaze at anyone, your eyes stinging behind dark glasses after another sleepless night in the pitch black all alone. There is constant pressure in the chest and terrible thoughts never stop flooding your mind.

There is a ringing in the ears, a numbness in the fingers, a racing heart. You have nightmares when you're not lying awake all night. You feel a yearning, a sorrow, a numbness, a powerlessness and a deep shame. Friends turn their backs on you and the family cannot cope.

You hear nothing more from the snide and condescending caseworker. You no longer exist for NCWS. You are left to yourself and the emptiness. Only the silence exists. Then they will be there like hawks, looking for errors in everything you say or do. Next they will claim that you and your child are difficult.

Do not show emotion; it is dangerous to do so. Do not tell your child that you disagree with this situation and are fighting tooth and nail so you can be together again. You must smile, pretend and play the game. Act the fool; that's what they expect of you. They cannot understand that your children will see through the pretence because they know you and are troubled that Mummy's expression does not match how Mummy really feels. NCWS supervisors do not care about that.

You forget the smell of your baby. Your child smells of fear. He has a different hairstyle, or she is dressed in a different way with sad, staring eyes. "Mum, can we go home now?" the child asks. "No dear. Not now, but maybe soon," you say calmly. "We'll enjoy ourselves together today."

By all means, never give your child the wrong food or drink, or an inappropriate gift. Everything is written down and interpreted. Most things you do will be wrong according to those who are looking to find fault with their distorted eyes.

If your child protests at the renewed separation when the two short hours are up, and the supervisor looks at his watch and then at you, it is you who is doing something wrong. Then the meeting is deemed harmful to your child and future meetings may be cancelled. You already know this because they have given you careful instructions outlining what will be tolerated and what will not, so you try to make the goodbye as quick as possible before racing away from your child.

All you want to do is hold your child tight and cry and promise that everything will be fine again, but you cannot do or say that. You are not allowed to. Loyalty should be at system level, not at individual level, according to the so-called child welfare system.

You feel emptiness afterwards, when you can finally breathe and cry again. You scream out in rage and are left with a paralysing fear. Worry and endless grief numbs you to such an extent that you think you cannot handle it any more or fight it any longer.

The grief of losing your children to the child welfare system is not only the biggest trauma you are ever likely to experience. It is also shameful, lonely and taboo.

There are no flowers at the door when you're at your two-hour supervised Christmas visit at an NCWS office in March. Flowers that once flourished on the windowsill are now dead. You stopped watering them in December when life suddenly became your worst nightmare and the foundations were brutally torn out from beneath you in a brief second.

There is no underestimating the devastation this separation brings when a family is torn apart. It is impossible to overstate the pain, trauma and grief children and parents experience from being away from each other for eighteen hours, eighteen weeks, eighteen months or even eighteen years.

The main reason emergency takeovers are executed is not that the child in question is in a life-threatening situation or that the circumstances are in any way exceptional. It is usually an attempt to make an impression on the courts that something incredibly bad must have happened in the family, when in most cases there isn't anything extraordinary or convincing enough to justify the emergency takeover.

According to a study carried out by the Department of Psychology at the University of Oslo's Faculty of Social Sciences, eight out of ten removals are emergency takeovers.[ii] Only twenty per cent of takeovers are scheduled, with the family receiving warning in advance.

The study found that children who were taken away unexpectedly through emergency measures were significantly more stressed, displaying higher cortisol levels than children who were scheduled to be placed outside the family home. Scheduled placements were shown to be far less stressful.

Cortisol is a steroid hormone produced by the adrenal glands. Whenever we experience something our bodies perceive as a threat, for example being removed from our parents or having our children removed from us, a chemical known as adrenocorticotropic hormone (ACTH) is released in the brain, causing the adrenal glands to release cortisol and adrenaline.

The fact that eight out of ten placements are emergency takeovers should concern everyone. This is especially true as we already know that the majority of children who are taken away from their families in Norway were not in a life-threatening position to begin with, unless you consider poor eye contact or a lower-than-average IQ evidence of a life-threatening situation.

The researchers of this psychology study naively believe that these emergency takeovers are necessary, with no questions asked. Despite this, the report suggests that NCWS should take things slower for the sake of the family. In its current setup this will more than likely never happen, as it will be harder for NCWS to convince the court to support a takeover in advance of the event than to go along with it after the child has been removed.

NCWS will do everything it can to avoid allowing a cortisol test on a baby or child, as it knows from experience that it will have to give the child back to its parents if the level is dangerously high and the child was not in a life-threatening situation to start with, as in the vast majority of cases. It is therefore advisable that parents demand a cortisol test be carried out on their children if they are taken away.

Isolation

After an emergency takeover, older children, for example teenagers are often sent to an institution before they are moved elsewhere. Emergency institutions are built like prisons in many ways, and some include a room known as a *sluse* (sluice). Children who have been through the system compare it to a prison cell, and some claim to have been left in the sluse for twenty-four hours. Some have been placed in rooms where they can hear other children screaming and crying. This is such a frightening experience, and many find it very difficult to speak about these events afterwards. There have been numerous stories of a cruel 'welcome' from children who have been sent to institutions.

NCWS often won't even allow children a quick call to their parents while they are in isolation. Withholding this right requires an agreement from the county board, but NCWS usually ignores the law and avoids telling the children about their rights. Children normally receive no information about what will happen to them within the first twenty-four hours.

After a short period the children become so insecure and afraid that they often agree to do whatever NCWS says, keeping quiet about their own needs. When the parents try their best to inform NCWS that it has all been a terrible mistake, NCWS often doesn't listen. Child welfare employees have been trained to deliberately stress the parents out; even expectant parents. Any signs of stress exhibited by the parents are used against them in court. NCWS' actions are not dissimilar to those used in a genuine kidnap situation. Parents are rarely informed about where their children are or what they should do next.

The background to some of these emergency situations is that the parents have criticised NCWS during a meeting. Many reports have confirmed that NCWS does not follow the law when carrying out these takeovers. As a survival strategy, and after spending time in isolation, children often start to sympathise with NCWS in an attempt to develop a psychological alliance with them, just as we see with Stockholm Syndrome.[iii]

What can happen during the next step is that NCWS puts pressure on the children, using leading questions and informing them that unless they confirm what NCWS claims the parents have done wrong they will not be allowed out of the interrogation process and will have to stay in the sluse for longer. What sometimes happens is that NCWS forces children to make up stories, and in many instances the children do so in order to get out of the sluse and take a breath. These fabricated stories about the family situation are then used in court to destroy the parents and any chance they had of getting their children back.

PTSD

PTSD is one of the most common diagnoses for children in foster care, and unnecessary emergency takeovers can create decreased levels of cortisol that are often associated with occurrences of PTSD.[iv]

Typical reactions from children after they have been needlessly taken away from their parents are: signs of fear, being on edge, overwhelming feelings of helplessness, depression or anger, emotional numbing, headaches, a loss of appetite, self-blame, irritability, sleeping difficulties and flashbacks. Children who are taken into 'care' often start experimenting with drugs for the first time between the ages of twelve and seventeen, while nightmares, avoidance of any reminders of the event, suicidal thoughts and confusion are other typical reactions to the traumatic takeover.

Research from Northwest Foster Care Alumni Studies found that reducing the number of placements and placement moves, and shortening lengths of stay in foster care, can help prevent the onset of PTSD.[v]

When children are picked up from school by strangers, whisked away to an unknown location, and then isolated and moved around a number of times, the risk of developing chronic PTSD increases. This is due to the severity or number of post-trauma symptoms, and the condition usually manifests around one to two weeks after the event. However, PTSD may also appear weeks, months or even years after a traumatic event.

Many pregnant women and expectant fathers in Norway also experience PTSD. When NCWS starts a pre-birth investigation the joy most couples experience turns into stress, torment and fear. The anxiety a pregnant woman may experience due to a case being opened against the family can also have major health implications for the unborn baby.[vi] The stress can cause a preterm delivery or a lower birth weight,[vii] and the mother becomes more vulnerable to developing postnatal depression.[viii] When NCWS puts families under unnecessary stress during pregnancy it can cause long-term damage for the family as a whole.

The Change Factory

Another cause for concern in Norway is the Forandringsfabrikken, the "Change Factory", also known in some circles as the "Propaganda Factory". This is a youth program that incorporates foster children, children in the juvenile justice system, and those in institutions or under NCWS care.

When children enter the Change Factory they are greeted with open arms and lots of smiles. They are expected to share all the good and bad things about NCWS and are told that their feedback will help to improve the system. This rarely happens. In fact, testimonies of the good and bad are bottled up, and then the main task begins.

The Change Factory is used as a kind of enclave; a place where NCWS beliefs are forced upon unsuspecting and impressionable children. At the same time, every child's story that can be used to encourage more funding and attract more child welfare employees will be put forward.

It is important to note that the Change Factory is merely an extension of the ideology NCWS follows. Some children consider it to be a bit like a brainwashing and conditioning centre; a place where children are convinced the agency has consistently acted in their best interests.

Many children who enter the Change Factory truly believe it is a place where they will be listened to, respected and helped, but increasing numbers of those who eventually leave say they felt fooled by it. It is not uncommon to hear the names 'Change Factory' and 'Hitlerjugend' spoken in the same sentence.

Ken Joar Olsen knows all too well how it feels to grow up in a system. Olsen has done his own research on the Change Factory and has tried to help children who are part of it who have reached out to him. He wrote:[ix]

> There was a time when children in the change factory were allowed to tell their stories, give their suggestions and share their opinions. The idea of children telling their own stories is now being replaced more and more often with a script that is written for them.
>
> To help promote the need for more funding and further strengthening of NCWS, children are often carted off and used at gatherings to give talks about their sad experiences. When 'pros'[12] are on stage giving a talk they feel pressured to answer with the 'main answers',[13] supposedly collected from young people all over Norway. However, many of the pros are not really sure who wrote these main answers. Was it really young people, or was it Marit Sanner[14] or someone else…?
>
> Instead of the Change Factory helping vulnerable children, it often destroys them in many ways. Children are led to believe that everything NCWS does has been done out of love. Really, with love? The type of love NCWS administers is not love at all. Children are often told that

12 'Pros', short for 'professionals', is the name given to children when they enter the Change Factory.

13 'Main answers' are the 'correct' answers children have been programmed to use when they are out on Change Factory assignments. These answers are supposedly their own, but are in fact NCWS'.

14 Leader and co-founder of the Change Factory.

their parents are bad for them, and many children believe this, when in reality it's usually not the case.

Leaving the Change Factory is no easy business either. It's a bit like leaving the Jehovah's Witnesses or the Church of Scientology. Peer pressure is like a constant force within the Change Factory and manipulation is also very extreme. When a pro conforms and uses the main answers as their answers, as the grown-ups tell them to, they can stay. If they don't use the main answers they are considered to have made bad choices, and in some instances they are kicked out.

They destroy the children by telling them they are there to help, and the children become so grateful to be included in that. Most of the children are so vulnerable and impressionable they just go along with everything. But this is changing. More and more children are recognising how destructive this system is and what the real agenda of the Change Factory is: to force NCWS ideology on them and expect them to accept NCWS' actions as love.

Humanitarian crisis

On July 26, 2014, clinical psychologist Einar C. Salvesen was interviewed by Jolanta Miškinytė, a journalist from Lithuania. Miškinytė was writing about a specific case (N.N.) in Norway, where a child had been taken away from the mother. Salvesen was involved as a psychologist and witness in this particular case. Here is a transcript of the conversation:[x]

Miškinytė: Would you be so kind to explain to me in a few sentences what your thoughts are regarding the N.N. case?

Salvesen: There is no reason to believe that the Norwegian law concerning child-rearing and child protection was not developed with the best intentions. However, the law far exceeds the competence of the expert. Therefore, the law results in a 'machinery of evil' in far too many instances.

N.N.'s case is just one example. The assessment of this case has serious flaws. Assumptions and conclusions are biased, one-sided and speculative, without alternative interpretations.

Just a few incidents about the mother and her interaction with her child are referred to, while a more complete picture of the mother herself is missing and not taken into account. From a narrow, factual base, serious conclusions about the mother as a person and her ability to raise children have been drawn.

Conclusions are coloured by narrow bourgeois or ideological standards for child-rearing. N.N.'s case is heartbreaking and very tragic, both for her and the child.

Miškinytė: What do you think about the quality of NCWS' work concerning the removal of children from their families?

Salvesen: There is a lot to say about that. In a few words, I can say that when the actual abilities of parents concerning child-rearing practices are clarified, the child welfare office responsible for investigations frequently shows a striking lack of competence concerning 'the human factor'.

There is a catastrophic lack of processing and dialogue skills, as well as poor ability to understand and clarify what is factual and what are interpretations.

In too many cases we observe that the ability and the character of a person are judged on a few incidents alone. Measured by the child-rearing standards of many other cultures, these incidents seem to be unclear and partly linked with ideological standards of child-rearing practice.

There are, of course, a number of cases where the system of protection works according to its intention, which is to secure the upbringing of children and to decide if they should stay with their families or be removed to institutions or foster homes. However, far too many children are removed from their parents based on false premises.

Miškinytė: What are the roots of this phenomenon, and how did this form of practice become legitimate in a civilised and democratic country such as Norway?

Salvesen: This is a very important and interesting issue. We observe that children are removed from their families by

Norway's child welfare system due to incompetence, a lack of ethical foundations, greed and subservience by people who are part of the control mechanism or institution involved.

This applies to child welfare offices in Norway; the first institution to assess or evaluate the situation of the child, and the ability of the parents. It applies to the expert, usually a psychologist, whose role it is to evaluate what has been done so far, as well as making a further assessment or re-evaluation of the case. It applies to the final institution of appeal, the county court system, which almost always bows down to the conclusion of the state-appointed expert. This even applies when the conclusion has been based on speculation, a lack of evidence, narrow standards for child-rearing, a lack of common sense and so on.

I have, as an expert witness for private entities, experienced cases where not only the child welfare office, but all the other control mechanisms that come into operation when the destiny of the child has to be decided – such as the expert report and the court – fail to meet simple scientific standards of clarification of the actual situation the child has in the family, therefore seriously violating justice standards and human rights.

I have experienced child welfare offices that have become bureaucratic and authoritarian systems of experts following narrow and ideological standards for child-rearing practices who, with a striking lack of empathy, humanity and common sense similar only to local political bureaus, act as a state within a state, and the division of power is fully set aside.

As one politician (the former director of a Norwegian child welfare office) once told me: "We are driving into the ditch both ways: removing the children we should not, while not removing the children we should!"

Miškinytė: How and why does this happen in Norway?

Salvesen: From my point of view, Norwegian social democracy has been deteriorating in quality due to a rich and strong state system, heavily influenced by socialist thinking, which, as we all know, involves state control rather than the driving force being the individual or the family.

The state has, due to oil income, become enormously rich compared with earlier years, enabling it to finance a bureaucracy of control, which has evolved gradually over a period of let's say twenty years.

What made this development possible may also be connected to a population that, until recently, has had a rather naive confidence in the Norwegian state. Traditionally, what the state decided seemed to be good for us and served us well.

The serious flaws we see in Norway's child welfare system may also partly be explained by the fact that child protection law, with its general concepts and good intentions, points toward very high standards concerning child-rearing practices in families.

This, coupled with socialist philosophies of control and expertise, has enabled the state to develop a bureaucracy of 'experts' who are supposed to be able to assess or control the families'/caretakers' ability to fulfil or not fulfil the standards set for child-rearing.

To further complicate the matter, the law, with its general terms, opens up several different interpretations of child-rearing standards for local offices, or even for a particular child welfare officer in charge of the case.

Miškinytė: We are frequently told that children are being taken away only from the families where 'healthy discipline' is often similar to violence. Is that true, and are native families also encountering this phenomenon?

Salvesen: Native as well as immigrant families are suffering due to the incompetence of the Norwegian system in dealing with families where the parents use what we in Norway define as violence as part of their child-rearing practice, while parents of other cultures define their practice as a way of disciplining the child. I have experienced cases where there has been no discussion, no dialogue process and no qualified supervision of the parent concerning their child-rearing practices before they removed the child from the family.

Foster industry

Many businesspeople have seen great opportunities for wealth generation in Norway, and many have become multimillionaires working for NCWS.[xi] Foundations and business owners are making big profits from the foster care industry. The municipalities or child service agencies pay these private companies to recruit new foster homes. The foster homes receive their salaries through the private companies. Alternatively, foster carers may be recruited by NCWS and receive their salaries directly from the municipality or child service agency. Foster carers basically become government employees, which helps to improve employment figures, all funded by the taxpayer.

A never-ending avalanche of articles and advertisements about Norway needing more foster homes is appearing everywhere, and each year the foster care industry adds in excess of 1,000 new foster homes. Vast sums of money are spent on convincing the public of the desperate need for more and more homes, and a great deal is also being spent on related training courses.

Taking on foster children in Norway can be very lucrative indeed. In some cases, foster carers have been able to leave well-paid jobs to take up fostering full time. In some counties where oil sales have slumped and thousands of people have become unemployed, job hunters are now being tempted to become foster carers.[xii] Annual earnings for taking in one child are advertised at up to 500,000 kroner (€50,000). In light of this, is it surprising that nobody is asking whether these children have been deprived of their own homes and families without justifiable cause?

Why aren't relatives of the children who have been 'neglected' the first choice as caregivers? Because NCWS knows that if the children are taken to live with relatives the parents will try to see their children as often as possible. It then becomes very clear to everyone involved that there was no just cause for taking the children away in the first place. Apart from in the relatively few cases where a child's life is in danger, for example when the parents end up in prison, informal arrangements with relatives could be made without any conditions being imposed. The main reason why grandparents and other relatives are hardly ever considered as foster carers is that NCWS would lose its control over the situation.

NCWS often uses the excuse that the child needs a stable environment to justify taking it into care. When parents divorce, for instance, and a child at first wants to stay with the father but after a while wants to stay with the mother, NCWS claims that both parents are incapable of giving their child the stability it needs. An investigation is often set up if the parents move around a lot, despite the fact that foster children are often moved many times even in the first year after being removed from the family. NCWS gives absolutely no credence to the biological bond between parents and their children, or to the invaluable experiences one can gain from moving to different places and seeing new things. It is all about exerting control over the family.

A news report published in early 2018 revealed that many child welfare employees had double roles, selling private childcare services as well maintaining their main 'child protection' duties.[xiii] The report found that 211 employees employed by NCWS also hold key roles in private child protection companies. Therefore, an NCWS employee could authorise the taking of five children, as in the Bodnariu case, and send them to an institution that he or she manages and profits from. The more children there are in an institution the more financial support they get from the Norwegian authorities, and the more profit they make. NCWS employees may be sitting on both sides of the fence when decisions are being made to take children away and contracts are being written up, which raises serious ethical questions.

Tupperware-style foster parties were quite the trend in Norway at one time. Naturally, many families really want to help children in need. They sincerely want to be a blessing to a child they believe will have a better life with them than with their biological parents. As there is so much secrecy in the way NCWS operates, the prospective foster carer is usually totally unaware that the child they are about to take on would, in the vast majority of cases, have had a better life at home with their biological parents.

Some Norwegian parents who already have children also apply to be foster carers. This is not always out of love for the children, or for the wages they can earn. Some add a foster child to their existing families with the main objective of safeguarding themselves from having their own children taken. They see it as a form of security. Sadly, this doesn't always work out.

A mother sitting in the audience at a debate in Bergen spoke about taking on a ten-year-old foster son who subsequently blamed the foster dad for an incident he had been responsible for himself. NCWS used the foster son's accusation to place the foster child elsewhere and also took away the couple's three biological daughters, who were eleven, five and two at the time. The mother asked the panel how NCWS could destroy a whole family just because they had asked for help in solving a dispute between them and the foster child. At that point the streaming of the event hit a technical issue and the video cut off.

Not only do foster children and their biological families have unfinished business with NCWS, but many foster parents have also become enraged, having witnessed first-hand the devastating actions committed against children and families by NCWS.

Another couple who had their children taken away unfairly applied to become foster carers. They completed the short training programme without mentioning that their children had been confiscated by NCWS. They successfully passed the training to become foster carers, yet they weren't considered to have good enough parenting skills to raise their own children.

'Wanted' children

At a local shop there is a noticeboard near the checkout with a dozen or so advertisements on it. People are selling kittens, someone has lost his bike and a tiny company is looking for employees. Among these adverts, one stands out. It reads: "Someone ask me how my day was – WANTED!". It looks as if it was written by a child of no older than seven or eight years old who is crying out for a foster home. On another noticeboard in a different shop, a similar advert reads: "Holding hands together" accompanied by a child's drawing of a foster carer holding the hand of a child. If one takes a closer look, these children's adverts have ten pull-off slips at the bottom that read: "fosterhjem.no" ("fostercare.no"). These ads are not really made by children; they have simply been designed that way to attract more people to sign up as foster carers.

'Sadvertising' is very manipulative, as it plays on an emotional reaction and a compassionate response from the consumer. It is like something unattractive that is dressed up to look good. Many good people with the right intentions feel very drawn to the foster care industry through these adverts, and any criticism is seen to be a lack of compassion for the welfare of our children.

Jitka Fialová is the mother of three children and one of the administrators of Norway, Give Us Back the Children You Stole. She writes:[xiv]

> I joined the team to help persecuted families in Norway after I was informed about the story of Eva Michaláková. In Eva's case, her two children were taken by NCWS after false accusations were made, and were separated not only from their mother and father but also from all other relatives, their language, their culture and from each other.
>
> I found out that children's rights in Norway were not valued as you would expect, especially after hearing reports that claim Norway to be one of the most democratic countries in the world.
>
> An arrested criminal has far better legal protection in Norway than small children who are being taken away from their families without any provocation and placed with total strangers. Criminals can be held in custody for only a few hours and must be evaluated by an experienced police lawyer. A small child who is taken after an emergency decision may have to wait several months for a careful evaluation of whether the legal conditions for taking them were met!
>
> Adverts pop up everywhere in Norway on Twitter and popular websites that read: "Looking for foster parents." They also pop up as Facebook adverts and are often found in newspapers. Some private organisations do not know how to find foster carers, so they advertise children online, with sentences like: "Do you want a child? We have more than a thousand to choose from." Some parents even find

out where their children are by spotting them on a "child for sale" site.

The annual salary for fostering is very high in Norway, with non-taxable bonuses, paid vacations, grants and so on. The salary and other conditions correspond to the kind of job role where a person normally has to be a university graduate with ten years of experience. The adverts are intended to find long-term foster carers who foster children as their main role and stay at home with the children; however, having a second form of employment or entrepreneurship is also permissible.

To become a foster carer in Norway, a 30-hour Parent Resources for Information, Development, and Education (PRIDE) course is required. In general, the requirements for foster carers, according to Bufdir, are agility, integrity, and good health and background. This could apply to an unmarried couple, a single man or a homosexual couple. Interestingly, the entitlement is much higher for temporary foster parents (for placements of up to sixty-one days), but they are not allowed to have a second job during this time.

If many rewards are on offer, coupled with low demands and training of an unknown quality, it is clear that sooner or later things will fall apart. NCWS employees commonly believe that foster carers can do no wrong. They are treated as infallible.

A newspaper in Norway provided information about fifty-two children who had been grossly abused while in foster care, and forty-two child welfare employees who had been punished to some extent. The NCWS employees were found to be lacking in terms of supervision and follow-up of the foster carers. They also ignored the children's reports, and in two cases it turned out they had not even recorded them.

With every day that passes, more incriminating evidence piles up against Norway's child welfare system.

Who is protecting the children from the 'protectors'?

Added to this, more and more stories of abuse are being reported by children in care. In 2017, a foster father was sentenced to six years and six months in prison for rape and serious sexual assault against the foster daughter.[xv] The abuse began when the girl was twelve and continued until she was fifteen.

NCWS was the subject of another scandal in early 2018 after it was reported that a quarter of all children who taken into care (forcibly in the majority of cases) were not given adequate supervision and follow-up.[xvi] Around 2,100 children were more or less forgotten about.

Signing up to Article 3[xvii] of the European Convention on Human Rights should mean that the authorities protect their citizens from torture (both mental and physical), as well as inhumane and degrading treatment. False accusations, character assassination, dehumanisation and isolation techniques can all be considered to be mental torture of the family.

Divided

In an article titled "Child Welfare", Øistein Schjønsby, a Norwegian lawyer with thirty years' experience explains how NCWS tends to worm its way out of existing rules and regulations.[xviii]

He observes that public interest in neglected children and the perceived need to protect them grows when NCWS has to present its budget time for the following year. At this same time, NCWS increases its monitoring of families under consideration for intervention. NCWS gives the impression that it plans to help the family in the way it is obliged to by law, but in reality it doesn't happen. Instead, NCWS removes children via emergency measures, and in doing so the outcome of the case is more or less guaranteed.

Schjønsby argues that when children are taken from their homes, the county committee on social matters and the county court, which are supposed to make sure the population lives under the rule of law, do nothing of the kind. Instead, they nearly always accept the proposed transfer of the child into the welfare system.

There is also a rule of law that NCWS firmly goes against. The second paragraph of section four in the regulations concerning foster homes states that child welfare should always consider whether someone in the child's family or close network could provide a foster home. Schjønsby criticises NCWS on this issue, pointing out that the child's family members are very rarely considered. The child is invariably placed in a temporary foster home while NCWS goes out looking for foster parents who are complete strangers.

Foster parents can be hard to find, so a permanent placement can be a long time coming. Schjønsby suggests the child could have been given a permanent home with its family, for example with the grandparents or aunts and uncles, but NCWS is not interested in going down that route.

Schjønsby states that the family can demand that section four be applied but explains that NCWS gets around the rule in several ways because it is not interested in the family having anything more to do with the child. He concludes his article with the question: "Is it really any wonder that people are afraid of the child welfare system in Norway?"

In another article titled "Are we bad at child welfare?" Schjønsby highlights the monotonous charade of families being put through the system when NCWS sends the case to the county board, followed swiftly by the district court.[xix] He says that the judgement will almost certainly be a carbon copy of the initial decision from the county council and questions whether this can be right.

The county council and the courts never seem to ask whether the family has been offered any help measures because the law states that a takeover will not happen if the family can be aided by auxiliary measures. Schjønsby reminds us that the experts always seem to be in the same boat as NCWS, making little or no time for dialogue with the parents.

Schjønsby recommends that relief measures be set up in cooperation with the parents. It does not help, he argues, if NCWS is exclusively able to choose what it considers to be auxiliary measures because the so-called guidance given is: "If you don't get it together we will take your children away." Such action is of no help at all, but it acts as an obvious threat.

The lawyer goes on to say that grandparents offer a valuable relief measure when it comes to taking care of the children, but this suggestion is regularly rejected by NCWS. He wonders why the board doesn't ask whether this option has been considered or tried, and why the experts don't contact the grandparents themselves.

Schjønsby also reminds us that the law stipulates children must be returned to their parents when the conditions at home are good enough, though this doesn't generally happen. "With more than thirty years of experience in the field I have never noticed Barnevernet 'delivering' the children they have taken back home. And, I've covered [the whole area] from south to north for all these years," he writes.

Schjønsby also recognises that the county councils and courts naively believe NCWS without even thinking to question or criticise its action. He argues that the local authorities need to be courageous enough to instruct NCWS to do its job without undertaking these unstoppable removals as it's just too expensive, not to mention being of absolutely no help to the children or parents whose families are torn apart forever.

Norwegian human rights advocate Tor Åge Berglid claims that family placements – where children are placed with members of their extended family – just don't happen. He writes:[xix]

> Barnevernet only considers shipping children out to strangers and leaving them there until they are eighteen years old. The whole thing is a big joke. There are zero family placements in Stryn. Barnevernet says that everything is working fine and the reason for the low numbers of people reporting problems is that they get into the families at an early stage. But the fact is, many people have stopped assisting Barnevernet by not reporting because of the genuine fear and lack of trust they have in Barnevernet.

Human rights expert Gro Hillestad Thune told *Aftenposten*:[xx]

> We see several examples that demonstrate how NCWS has developed an authoritarian and closed system that exposes vulnerable children and families to abuse by the authorities.
>
> We also hear of how parents whose children have additional health challenges, such as Asperger's, Tourette's and ADHD, are often not met with support or respect for their difficult parental roles, but instead have their children taken away and are deprived of their parental rights.

Chapter 15 notes

[i] Viken, M. S. S., "Den skamfulle, ensomme og forbudte sorgen" ("The shameful, lonely and forbidden sorrow"), Trude Helen Hole: https://trudehelenhole.no/2017/08/31/den-skamfulle-ensomme-og-forbudte-sorgen

[ii] Staff writer, "De fleste barn hentes uanmeldt" ("Most children are taken unannounced"), UiO: https://www.sv.uio.no/psi/forskning/aktuelt/aktuelle-saker/2012/de-fleste-barn-hentes-uanmeldt.html

[iii] Westcott, K., "What is Stockholm syndrome?" BBC: https://www.bbc.co.uk/news/magazine-22447726

[iv] Staff writer, "Children's Services Practice Notes: Posttraumatic Stress Disorder", Jordan Institute for Families: http://www.practicenotes.org/vol10_n3/cspnv10n3.pdf

[v] Pecora, P. J. et al, "Improving Family Foster Care", Northwest Foster Care Alumni Studies: https://caseyfamilypro-wpengine.netdna-ssl.com/media/AlumniStudies_NW_Report_FR.pdf

[vi] Lilliecreutz, C., Larén, J., Sydsjö, G. and Josefsson, A., "Effect of maternal stress during pregnancy on the risk for preterm birth" NCBI: https://www.ncbi.nlm.nih.gov/pmc/articles/PMC4714539

[vii] Wolpert, S., "Women with impaired stress hormone before pregnancy have lower-birthweight babies", UCLA: http://newsroom.ucla.edu/releases/women-with-impaired-stress-hormone-before-pregnancy-have-lower-birthweight-babies

[viii] Qobadi, M., Collier, C. and Zhang, L., "The Effect of Stressful Life Events on Post-partum Depression: Findings from the 2009–2011 Mississippi Pregnancy Risk Assessment Monitoring System" NCBI: https://www.ncbi.nlm.nih.gov/pmc/articles/PMC5290058

[ix] Olsen, K. J., "Norway's Change Factory", Step Up 4 Children's Rights: https://stepup4childrensrights.com/norways-change-factory

[x] Staff writer, "Norway's humanitarian crisis", Step Up 4 Children's Rights: https://stepup4childrensrights.com/norways-humanitarian-crisis

[xi] Mikkelsen, M. S. and Majid, S., "FosterhjemsKongen" ("The foster industry"), *VG*: https://www.vg.no/spesial/2017/fosterhjem

[xii] Laugaland, J. M., and Evensen, M. R., "Ønsker arbeidsledige som fosterforeldre" ("Unemployed wanted as foster parents"), *NRK*: https://www.nrk.no/rogaland/onsker-arbeidsledige-som-fosterforeldre-1.12951593

[xiii] Majid, S., Nærø, A. F., Mikkelsen, M. S. and Norman, M. G., "Ansatt i barnevernet – selger privat barnevern på si" ("Employed in child welfare – sells private child welfare services"), *VG*: https://www.vg.no/spesial/2018/dobbeltroller-i-barnevernet

[xiv] Fialová, J., "Mizerní norští pěstouni" ("Poor Norwegian foster parents"), iDNES: https://fialovajitka.blog.idnes.cz/blog.aspx?c=493016

[xv] Rovick, A., "Jente ble voldtatt av fosterfaren – nå tar barnevernet kraftig selvkritikk" ("Girl was raped by the foster father – now the child welfare office takes strong self-criticism"), TV2:http://www.tv2.no/nyheter/9450260

[xvi] Majid, S., "2100 fosterbarn uten lovpålagt tilsyn" ("2,100 foster children without statutory supervision"), *VG*: https://www.vg.no/nyheter/innenriks/i/a24VJ7/2100-fosterbarn-uten-lovpaalagt-tilsyn

[xvii] Staff writer, "Article 3: Freedom from torture and inhuman or degrading treatment", Equality and Human Rights Commission: https://www.equalityhumanrights.com/en/human-rights-act/article-3-freedom-torture-and-inhuman-or-degrading-treatment

[xviii] Schjønsby, Ø, "Er vi slemme mot barnevernet?" ("Are we bad at child welfare?"): norgesavisen.no: https://norgesavisen.no/er-vi-slemme-mot-barnevernet

[xix] Berglid, T. Å., "Many people fear Norway's child welfare service", Step Up 4 Children's Rights: https://stepup4childrensrights.com/many-people-fear-norways-child-welfare-service

[xx] Skogstrøm, L., "Fagfolk melder bekymring om barnevernet" ("Professionals report concern about child welfare"), *Aftenposten*: https://www.aftenposten.no/norge/i/Q9rP/Fagfolk-melder-bekymring-om-barnevernet

16

Proceedings

Amy Jacobsen is an American citizen who lives in Norway. On July 23, 2013, her worst nightmare began.[i] Without any advance warning, and accompanied by police officers, NCWS knocked on the door and told Amy her nineteen-month-old son Tyler had to be taken to hospital for an urgent examination.

In the weeks preceding this event, Amy, like any caring mother, had become increasingly concerned about the growth rate of her son. Tyler didn't seem ready to move on to solid food, so he continued to be breastfed. Tyler was Amy's first child, so she did not have first-hand experience of children developing individually and at different times. Being a concerned mother, she took Tyler for medical check-ups three times a month to monitor the growth process very closely.

Over the summer, Amy took Tyler to America on a two-week holiday to visit friends and relatives, but as soon as they returned child welfare and the police turned up. She later found out that someone had reported her to NCWS for malicious reasons. Feeling completely overwhelmed by the situation, Amy agreed to go to the hospital with them, and the child's Norwegian father, Kevin, also went along. One of the hospital doctors diagnosed Tyler as being slightly underweight. Tyler should have weighed 10 kg but only weighed only 9.6 kg, though this shouldn't have been cause for concern according to the weight charts. The doctor also criticised Amy for continuing to breastfeed her son.

Instead of offering advice, the NCWS employees wanted to intervene and remove the child from his mother on the basis of the medical diagnosis. This led to a verbal confrontation that the father filmed on his smartphone.

"When will I see my son again?" he asked.

"We can't tell you that yet," replied a child welfare employee.

Kevin was eventually escorted away from the hospital as the argument became louder and louder.

What followed next sounds like something from a movie scene. Kevin went back to the hospital and put on a doctor's uniform. Using his disguise, he was able to enter the room where his son had been temporarily placed. He took his son, unnoticed, left the building in a hurry and drove aimlessly around the area, knowing these might be the last moments he would get to spend with his precious boy. He was finally pulled over by several police cars. One officer at the roadside even threw a large stone at the car, which nearly hit the child and could have caused a great deal of harm to both father and son.

Kevin was detained overnight for attempted child abduction. He was released the next day as a judge ruled that Kevin was the biological father and still had parental rights. However, Tyler remained with NCWS. For a short time Amy and Kevin had the right to visit him, albeit at a police station behind double-locked doors.

Amy was originally allowed to visit Tyler weekly. This was reduced to fortnightly visits, and eventually she was deprived of all visitation rights. NCWS saw Amy as a potential 'abduction' risk as she is an American citizen and the agency didn't want her taking Tyler to America. This was the main argument for removing parental rights from both Amy and Kevin in the court cases that followed. Amy saw her son for the last time on September 22, 2014. She and Kevin have no idea where he is now or how he is doing.

In order to conceal Tyler's new whereabouts, the authorities changed his name twice. By the age of four Tyler had already been given three different names. But why? NCWS stated that it had acted only in the child's best interests, but how can such a traumatic experience really serve his interests? The love and affection of the biological parents in the first few years of life are known to be of great importance in the healthy development of a child.

Meanwhile, Amy has been down all the legal routes in Norway to get her son back. In the spring of 2016 the case was rejected by Norway's Supreme Court, but she will never give up. Through a Christian initiative called Step Up 4 Children's Rights in Vienna, Amy was able to make contact with international lawyers. They discovered seven human rights violations in her case documents and helped her file her petition at the European Court of Human Rights. CitizenGO also launched a campaign on Facebook to raise awareness about this case. They challenged people to post selfies holding up a poster that says: "Norway, return Tyler to Amy."

It is still not clear how Tyler's case will end. Once again, a family in Norway has been torn apart for no justifiable reason. Once again, a child has been put through an extremely traumatic experience by NCWS. And once again we are expected to believe that this action has served the best interests of the child.

A petition was set up for Tyler in May 2018.[ii] The petition has already garnered over 47,000 signatories. It was also sent to Norway's newly elected Minister of Children and Equality, Linda Hofstad Helleland, asking her to ensure that Tyler is freed immediately.

As Norwegian lawyer Erik Bryn Tvedt pinpoints in his article, "A legal risk", most people who lose their children to NCWS have done nothing wrong.[iii] He goes on to highlight the fact that losing a child is a far greater a punishment than being sent to jail. "When the threshold is so low in the area of family life, one would think the media would be concerned by the issues," he observes.

Tvedt goes on to remind us that confidentiality laws are used by the authorities to mask the actions they take against small children in Norway. "The child welfare authorities will not explain their motives within one of the most basic human rights: the right to family life under the European Convention on Human Rights, Article 8," he writes.

One of Trondheim's most prominent lawyers, Venil Katharina Thiis, states that between 1991 and 2009 she won only two cases at the county board that allowed a family to stay together: her first case and her last.[iv] She believes NCWS should be replaced by a new system built on completely different principles.

Never giving up!

Two children run up to their mother and ask her, "When will our brother come home?" Their mother, Trude Lobben, answers "One day" as heartfelt tears run down her face. All those around you – except NCWS and those being paid to support them – are aware that this was a miscarriage of justice and an abuse of power.

Fast-forward nearly ten years and the Lobben case had eventually made it to the European Court of Human Rights, far away from the mockery the Norwegian 'justice system' had made of it. Seven judges gave their verdict on December 1, 2017. Three judges voted in favour of Trude and four voted against her. But the story doesn't end there. The fourth judge, and the one who swung the vote, was Norwegian and is allegedly still connected in some way to the Supreme Court of Norway. How can this be legal?

The result shocked a lot of people, both in Norway and internationally, because it challenges the very notion of fairness and justice, which the European Court of Human Rights has the biggest responsibility to preserve and protect.

The judges who supported this mother and son are from Azerbaijan, Ireland and Bulgaria; countries that strongly uphold family values. These judges were bemused by the verdict reached by the other four, who were from Austria, Germany, France and Norway. They drew attention to the manner in which the other four judges seemingly distanced themselves from the concrete facts of this case.

In May 2018, Marius Reikerås, a human rights proponent and legal expert, reported some encouraging news about Trude's case at the European Court of Human Rights. The case was heard again at the Grand Chamber in October 2018. Let's hope justice is finally served for Trude's family and that her son is returned to his biological mother soon.

In a news report titled "Norway under scrutiny for its child welfare policies", ADF International, an alliance-building human rights organisation that defends freedom and seeks justice through legal advocates, stated the following:[v]

> The case is one of a number of cases where the authorities have removed children from their parents without proper justification. For example, a three-week-old child was taken away from his mother [Trude] in 2008 based on doubts about her 'parenting abilities'. The child was placed in foster care and the mother was allowed only twelve hours of contact per year with her son. Ultimately, all visitation rights were denied, the mother's parental rights were

removed, and the child was put up for adoption.

Parental rights under international law

"Removing children from their families should always be a last resort. This is one of a number of cases where the Norwegian authorities have failed to prioritise the reunification of families. Every parent has the fundamental right to raise their child in accordance with their convictions as protected by international law. Such separation can have long-lasting damaging effects on children and families. Putting a child up for adoption against the mother's will, as in this case, is an irreversible and extreme measure, which was initiated without evidence of parental abuse or violence," said Jennifer Lea, Legal Counsel for ADF International based in Strasbourg.

The Fifth Section had previously found no violation of Article 8 of the European Convention of Human Rights which protects the right to family life. Now the Grand Chamber has agreed to review the decision. ADF International was granted permission from the court to intervene in the case.

Norway's poor track record

A recent report by the Parliamentary Assembly of the Council of Europe (PACE) into the practices of the Norwegian child protection agency, Barnevernet, revealed a number of troubling discoveries. For example, it showed a high frequency of 'emergency' interventions by the agency. The reasoning behind these interventions were of particular concern as well as the exceptionally short visitation times which usually followed.

"The primary purpose of child protection agencies is to support families. Even when child removal is truly necessary, family reunification should be a central aim. The investigation into Norway has shown that without effective safeguards, child protection agencies can cause long-term damage to families and undermine the prior right that parents have to raise their children according to international law. It is very encouraging to see the Council

> of Europe highlight the importance of keeping families together," said Laurence Wilkinson, Legal Counsel for ADF International and expert in international law.
>
> "The case of Strand Lobben v. Norway reminds us of the Bodnariu case, which ultimately resulted in an international outcry and the family fleeing the country. We hope the Grand Chamber will affirm the right to family life as described in Article 8 of the European Convention. It is time for Norway to act on the recommendations made by the Council of Europe and respect the right of parents to raise their children unless there is evidence of a serious breach of the parents' duties," said Jennifer Lea.

According to Norwegian lawyer Fridtjof P. Gundersen, the reason the Lobben case reached the Grand Chamber at the ECtHR in Strasbourg is probably due to the public perception of injustice and abuse on the part of the Norwegian authorities. The title of Gundersen's article reads "Many of us are actually quite stupid and bad when we get power".[vi]

Gundersen comments that the Lobben situation is a typical Norwegian child welfare case, where a mother has asked NCWS for help. After asking for help, Trude and her child were placed in a mothers' home. And, ignoring the midwife's support for the family, NCWS recommended an emergency placement for Trude's son because it was perceived that Trude was not meeting her son's emotional needs.

After Trude subsequently got married and had two more children, no one talked about the good care her children were receiving. Gundersen states that this is how Norway is starting to go backwards, because there are now strong indications that it was wrong to take Trude's son away from her. "It does not seem right to take a baby away from an obviously competent mother," writes Gundersen.

At the time of writing, the Lobben case is still waiting to be determined by the Grand Chamber. The following commentary from the ECtHR about this case offers a very powerful dissenting opinion on the shortcomings of the Norwegian courts:[vii]

> Nowhere in the file does it emerge clearly that the domestic

> authorities considered the long-term effects on the child of the permanent and irreversible cutting of de facto and legal ties with his biological mother. The court has repeatedly held that severing such ties cuts a child off from its roots, a measure that can be justified only in exceptional circumstances…
>
> Furthermore, it is difficult to avoid the impression that assessment of the first applicant's competence and conduct was influenced throughout by the very fact of her conflict with the child welfare authorities and foster mother. The city court highlighted the fact that "nothing had emerged… to indicate that the first applicant had developed a more positive attitude to the child welfare authorities or to the foster mother". However, conflict of this nature is hardly exceptional. Since both the foster parents and domestic authorities were deemed to be acting in the best interests of the child, by challenging or being in conflict with them the first applicant was perceived to be doing the opposite. The mother's behaviour in relation to the authorities and her express determination to fight until her child was returned were factors that played against her…
>
> A review of the court's case law demonstrates the existence of legal standards: the need to establish particularly weighty reasons, to limit the breaking of de facto and de jure ties to exceptional circumstances and to apply stricter scrutiny when the latter occurs. They are standards with legal meaning and which should, in our view, have legal consequences.
>
> An excessive focus on procedures risks rendering banal what are far-reaching intrusions in family and private life. In addition, the court's general principles when read in the abstract risk providing false hopes of reunification, which, as this case demonstrates, are unlikely to be fulfilled once a child has been taken into care, access rights have been significantly limited, time has passed and domestic proceedings formally meet Article 8 procedural standards.

This reflects the thinking in the recent case of Jansen v. Norway (decided on December 6, 2018) concerning a young Roma mother whose child was taken away by NCWS at a very young age. In this case, the European Court found that Norway had indeed violated

Article 8 of the European Convention on Human Rights:[viii]

> The high court's decision did not focus on reuniting A and the applicant, or on preparing for reunification in the near future, but rather on protecting A from a potential abduction and its consequences. Taking into account the circumstances of the present case, the court considers that there was a risk that A could completely lose contact with her mother. According to the court's jurisprudence it is also imperative to consider the long-term effects a permanent separation of a child from her natural mother might have...
>
> In conclusion, although the court accepts that the decisions of the national authorities were made in what they considered to be the best interests of the child, and bears in mind that perceptions as to the appropriateness of intervention by public authorities in the care of children vary from one contracting state to another, the court holds that, in the instant case, the potential negative long-term consequences of losing contact with her mother for A, and the positive duty to take measures to facilitate family reunification as soon as reasonably feasible, were not sufficiently weighed in the balancing exercise.

Overridden

In an article titled "The local lawyer's prayer wasn't heard", Norwegian lawyer Olav Sylte explains how NCWS tried to tear apart a family because the mother, a Bible-believing Christian, was perceived to have extreme religious views.[ix] Sylte notes that the prosecuting lawyer said the mother was listening only to God and that everything else – including her son's care – was being overridden, so the prosecuting lawyer asked the county council to permanently separate the child from his family. Fortunately, this request was not supported by the county council.

Section 4-12 (a) of the Child Welfare Act was cited in this case. While Sylte highlights the fact that absolutely none of the conditions for removing the child were met, he was placed in emergency care for at least three months.

According to Sylte, the county board's biggest concern was unpredictability of the mother's 'extreme' religious convictions and mental health, as she had said she would be prepared to serve in mission either in Norway or abroad if God called her to do so. The fact that the mother indicated a desire to travel certainly does not indicate irresponsible parenting.

Sylte claims that the child is looked after by a warm and caring person, and that he is at an age where he is able to take care of himself. When the mother has to travel she always prepares freezer meals for him and another caregiver looks after him. The child did not want to be forced into a foster home, so it was decided that it was in his best interests to stay with his mother.

The prosecuting lawyer still tried to force the issue that the mother had a mental disorder because of her faith and couldn't give the child adequate care. Furthermore, this lawyer argued that the mother did not share NCWS' views, complaining that she was denying that she had a mental illness and would not take medication or follow the treatment recommended by the health service. As far as we know, there was no evidence of a mental illness, and this allegation was linked to the mother's 'fanatical' Christian views rather than scientific fact.

In September 2018, Sylte, wrote about twelve child welfare cases in which his law firm had defeated NCWS within twelve months. He asserts that NCWS' actions should be investigated much more closely, since each case shows signs of serious miscarriages of justice. He writes (text translated):[x]

> I could have written about more cases, too. To take children away from their families by force is just as serious an intrusion as it is to jail people. It is unclear whether Helleland [Minister of Children and Equality] sees the problem in this way. I have never heard of anyone who, having been the victim of a serious miscarriage of justice, thinks this was all right because the child welfare service supposedly did something good for other people in other cases.

Breached

On Friday May 13, 2016, when the Bodnariu children were still being held by the Norwegian authorities, a group of more than 100 attorneys from various countries around the world, including four MEPs, submitted an International Attorney Petition to the Prime Minister of Norway, Erna Solberg, demanding the immediate and permanent release of the Bodnariu children to their biological parents.[xi]

The petition was delivered via email and fax, and through the offices of Norway's Ministry of Foreign Affairs. It was also delivered to the Norwegian Embassy in Washington, DC, to coincide with King Harald V of Norway's trip White House visit. It's impossible to say whether this played a key part in securing the eventual return of the children, but it certainly made some people sit up and pay attention to what was happening.

Cristian Ionescu is the senior pastor at Elim Pentecostal Church in Chicago, and was the main architect behind the global pro-Bodnariu movement. Along with a team that included Pastor Daniel Bodnariu, Steven Bonica, Peter Costea, Timotei Dinică, Vinicius Sabău, Dennis Stoia, Paul Susman and the extended Bodnariu family, he helped initiate the worldwide demonstrations and created media awareness in support of the Bodnariu family. The protests created a very negative image of Norway, and this shaming of Norway more than likely had a major impact on the decision that led to the release of the Bodnariu children.[xii]

After the worldwide demonstrations on April 16, 2016, the Norwegian media went into full propaganda defence mode. Norwegian newspapers focused on criticising Ionescu rather than addressing the serious concerns of the worldwide pro-Bodnariu movement. Following the demonstrations, former children's minister Solveig Horne wrote the following on her Facebook profile:

> We take criticism towards child welfare seriously and give the board of health now the mission to go through a selection of issues in child welfare.

Ionescu was not impressed with this half-hearted response. In his article "God forbid they don't return the kids… We do not play tic tac toe with Norway", he elaborates:[xiii]

> I am not patient with Norway. They should have given the [Bodnariu] kids back long ago. All this procrastination

> proves that we are dealing with a system in survival mode, which will damage itself if it admits its mistake. It is an evil system, and evil cannot be reformed. It must be destroyed.
>
> This system committed more abuse than it did good. It exploits crisis to create greater crisis. We are not here to represent a strategy. We do not play tic tac toe with Norway. Strategy is out the door now. We tell Norway what we will do, and we will do it. We proved that we are credible.
>
> Everything we announced, we did, and we will do. If Norway does not hurry up and give the kids back, there will be an avalanche of actions. We hope we do not get to 30 May to 2 June when [Barnevernet] is preparing a court hearing; God forbid that there will be an unfavourable decision for the Bodnariu [family], because there will be protests and actions against Norway that Norway cannot imagine. We came [to Norway] to open their imagination and tell them exactly what will happen. If they want us to fight against the image of Norway abroad, then they should keep the kids.
>
> This is a fight of two painful realities: Norway's pain of recognizing its mistake and giving the kids back, or Norway's pain of international shame. Which painful reality prevails will be the one which will determine Norway's action. We must make the international shame so painful that Norway will resort to returning the kids.
>
> If the children are not returned, then we will communicate our actions at that time. All countries involved in this protest will have a blueprint of action, and this will cause great headaches for Norway. Once we get this going, it will be unstoppable.

In 2016, Peter Costea, a civil rights attorney practising in Houston, Texas, presented some interesting findings in a report that centred on the Bodnariu case. This is an excerpt from the report, which exposes grave breaches of the UN Convention on the Rights of the Child:[xiv]

> Though Norway savvily projects internationally the image of a rational, peaceful and polished system, it is far from it. Its ugly side, as here, never makes the news. Barnevernet has gravely

violated the 1989 International Convention on the Rights of the Child, which Norway has signed and ratified. Here's how.

Article 5 of the convention imposes an obligation on Norway and on all signatories to uphold parental rights. ("State Parties shall respect the responsibilities, rights and duties of parents…") This obligation is restated in **Article 14**. **Article 7** grants children "the right to know and be cared for by his or her parents," and **Article 8** the right to "preserve his or her identity, including nationality, name and family relations as recognised by law without unlawful interference."

Article 9, however, is less straightforward and allows for subjective interpretation. It states, in relevant part, that "state parties shall ensure that a child shall not be separated from his or her parents against their will, except when competent authorities subject to judicial review determine, in accordance with applicable law and procedures, that such separation is necessary for the best interests of the child. Such determination may be necessary in a particular case, such as one involving abuse or neglect of the child by the parents…" Even where the child is separated, however, the child still has the right "to maintain personal relations and direct contact with both parents on a regular basis, except if it is contrary to the child's best interests"…

In the case of the Bodnariu family, Norway's secular state scored at the expense of parental rights, parental autonomy and the welfare of the children. For now. Because, in the long run and for generations to come, millions of Romanians, Poles, Czechs, Slovaks, Turks, Russians, Ukrainians, Brazilians, Filipinos, Iraqis, Indians and many others from other nationalities will recount their horrific encounters with Norway's Barnevernet.

In an article published in January 2018, Olav Sylte, writes that, because of the current legal setup in Norway, only those with more or less unlimited funds are able to fight against the system. Sylte states that in a recent decision the authorities made it impossible for private parties to investigate whether an infringement of the ECHR had taken place in child welfare cases. He writes (text translated):[xv]

> The consequences of this new decision are that private parties will never get the opportunity to investigate whether there is a violation in child welfare cases without bringing an independent action against the state or the public prosecutor. There is no free legal aid in such cases, and the cost rapidly reaches hundreds of thousands of kroner. Consequently, only those who earn millions and lose their children will get a real opportunity to have their cases investigated for an infringement of Article 13 in the ECHR. I do not think there are many of them.

In order to win back people's trust, Sylte believes the government must immediately propose a change in the law, as this is the only way to ensure that private parties have their rights respected with regard to what is laid out in Article 13 (the right for children to express and educate themselves, and to search for, receive, and share information and ideas). Sylte and many others believes that the government should immediately appoint a committee to investigate this issue.

Proposed new Child Welfare Act

A newly proposed Child Welfare Act was sent to the Norwegian government in early 2017.[xvi] If implemented, the new proposal would result in even more human rights violations for families.

One provision in the proposed act states that NCWS is entitled to deny parties access to documents if this could cause injury or danger to a child or others. Again, the authorities will be able to use the child as a pawn to get the new law passed. They will do all they can to convince a conditioned Norwegian public that the act will benefit the child, but it is not about protecting children. This is about using children to pass a law that will totally control families without any repercussions.

It could be argued that family lawyers will no longer be necessary as they will have little or no power to help parents fight for their children if all the case documents are hidden. Had this law been in place while the Bodnariu children were being held, the likelihood is that they would not have been released until they were eighteen.

How will parents and families defend themselves if they are denied access to documents that are used within the court system?

Who is this proposed law really going to protect? Certainly not the child or the parents! It would be another nail in the coffin for Norwegian families if this new law were ratified.

How will it help the family if the parents' right to appeal to the higher courts is removed? How will it help children if the current duty to tell parents about the opening of investigations after reports of concern have been made is removed? How will it help the family if they are denied the right to read case documents?

Totalitarian authorities disguised as democracies will make every effort to communicate how hard they work to benefit children. They know that when this idea is accepted by the majority people will endure almost any violation of their freedom. On top of all this, the Norwegian government will refuse Norwegian children the right to appeal to the UN Children's Committee as they can in Denmark, Finland and Germany.[xvii]

Kirsta Fontanilla, a Christian musician from British Columbia, wrote the attached song for Kevin, Amy, Tyler and the many families in Europe who are suffering unjust separation.[xviii]

Forever Home

Your forever home is in my heart
No matter how many years, how many miles apart
I pray the day is coming soon I'll hold you in my arms
Your forever home is in my heart

They changed your name more than once
Tore you from my loving arms
Ignorance!
Arrogance!
Their "help" only harms

Their love so cruel
Hearts so blind
They are the rule
They don't mind
Tearing us
Breaking us
To get their deal signed

Your forever home is in my heart
No matter how many years, how many miles apart
I pray the day is coming soon I'll hold you in my arms
Your forever home is in my heart

The fight is fierce
All seems lost
I hold back tears
Count the cost
Loving you
Losing you
Giving all I've got

Truth is rising
All will see
The unmasked lies
They decree
We cry out
Together shout
Set our children free!

Your forever home is in my heart
No matter how many years, how many miles apart
I pray the day is coming soon I'll hold you in my arms
Your forever home is in my heart

Deep inside do you know
The sound of my voice,
The light of my eyes?
Could I find you in a crowd
If you smiled
Or laughed out loud?
Can you cure the pain I hide?
Years we lost, dreams that died?
I lift my eyes to the highest one
Breathe a prayer for help to come

Your forever home is in my heart
No matter how many years, how many miles apart
I pray the day is coming soon I'll hold you in my arms
Your forever home is in my heart

Chapter 16 notes

[i] Elizabeth, L., "'Norway Took My Child': Child Protective Services Takes Baby from American Mom", Faithwire: http://www.faithwire.com/2018/06/21/norway-child-protective-services-unfairly-targeting-immigrant-families-takes-baby-from-american-mom

[ii] Staff writer: "Petition to: Norway's Minister of Children and Equality Norway seized this child. Help free Tyler!", CitizenGO: http://citizengo.org/en/sc/161492-norway-stole-mothers-child-help-free-tyler

[iii] Tvedt, E. B., "En rettssikkerhetsrisiko" ("A legal risk"), *Dagen*: http://www.dagen.no/dagensdebatt/synspunkt/synspunkt/En-rettssikkerhetsrisiko-296768

[iv] Thiis, V. K., "Jeg har fått nok" ("I have had enough"), adressea.no: https://www.adressa.no/nyheter/trondheim/2009/01/10/Jeg-har-f%C3%A5tt-nok-1483738.ece

[v] Staff writer, "Norway under scrutiny for its child welfare policies", ADF International: https://adfinternational.org/news/european-human-rights-court-to-hear-parental-rights-case

[vi] Gundersen, F. P., "Mange av oss er faktisk ganske dumme og slemme når vi får makt" ("Many of us are actually quite stupid and bad when we get power"), *Dagbladet*: https://www.dagbladet.no/kultur/mange-av-oss-er-faktisk-ganske-dumme-og-slemme-nar-vi-far-makt/70395228

[vii] Staff writer, "Case of Strand Lobben and Others v. Norway", ECtHR: http://hudoc.echr.coe.int/eng?i=001-178877

[viii] Staff writer, "Case of Jansen v. Norway", ECtHR: http://hudoc.echr.coe.int/eng?i=001-185495 Jansen v. Norway

[ix] Sylte, O., "Kommuneadvokaten ble ikke hørt med sin 'bønn'" ("The local lawyer's prayer wasn't heard"), Advokatfirmaet Sylte: http://advokatsylte.no/artikkel/9/barnevernsaker/728/kommuneadvokaten-ble-ikke-hort-med-sin-bonn

[x] Sylte, O., "Etter 12 måneder: 12 nye justismord" ("After 12 months: 12 new legal words"), Advokatfirmaet Sylte: http://

advokatsylte.no/artikkel/9/barnevernsaker/805/etter-12-maneder-12-nye-justismord

[xi] Staff writer, "International Attorney Petition for the release of Bodnariu children", Bodnariu Family Fighting Barnevernet: http://bodnariufamily.org/international-attorney-petition-for-the-release-of-bodnariu-children

[xii] Ionescu, C.; "Official communication: Bodnariu case – Latest developments", Popaspentrusuflet: https://popaspentrusuflet.wordpress.com/2016/03/11/comunicat-oficial-official-statement-cazul-bodnariu-ultimele-stiri-latest-developments

[xiii] Ionescu, C., "God forbid they don't return the kids… We do not play tic tac toe with Norway", Delight in Truth: https://delightintruth.com/2016/05/05/cristian-ionescu-bombshell-to-norway-god-forbid-they-not-return-the-kids-we-do-not-play-tic-tac-toe-with-norway/

[xiv] Costea, P., "A Norway gone Berserk", Costea Law: http://bodnariufamily.org/4794

[xv] Sylte, O., "Umulig å få dom på EMK-brudd" ("Impossible to get them on EMK violations"), Advokatfirmaet Sylte: http://advokatsylte.no/artikkel/9/barnevernsaker/737/umulig-a-fa-dom-pa-emk-brudd

[xvi] Staff writer, "Proposal for a new child welfare act handed over to the Minister of Children" ("Forslag til ny barnevernslov overlevert barneministeren"), regjeringen.no: https://www.regjeringen.no/no/aktuelt/forslag-til-ny-barnevernslov-overlevert-barneministeren/id2512893

[xvii] Foss, A. B., "Regjeringen vil ikke gi norske barn rett til å klage til FN" ("The government will not give Norwegian children the right to appeal to the UN"), *Aftenposten*: https://www.aftenposten.no/norge/i/RBXM8/Regjeringen-vil-ikke-gi-norske-barn-rett-til-a-klage-til-FN

[xviii] Fontanilla, K., "Forever Home" © 2018

17

Principle

Norwegian mother Ronja Ophaug was harassed by NCWS throughout her pregnancy and her precious baby was removed from the labour ward. Foster parents who were unable to have children had allegedly been lined up in advance after ordering a baby boy through a pre-adoption company. Below is Ronja's account of events:[i]

> My name is Ronja Ophaug. I'm twenty-one years old and live in Norway. NCWS brutally took my child away from me within one hour of me giving birth at a hospital in Trondheim, Norway.
>
> I had also been part of the child welfare system in my youth due to a difficult period during my childhood. I dropped out of school and partied for a short period, something I decided to stop doing before I fell pregnant. A few months after I had changed my lifestyle, my boyfriend and I found out we were expecting a baby boy. This was a turning point; a time of great enrichment for us. The past was behind us and we were very optimistic about the future of our little family. A new start, we thought.
>
> I had frequent pregnancy check-ups due to my previous lifestyle, so I had to take regular drug tests during the pregnancy. I wholeheartedly agreed to this because I wanted to cooperate and prove my innocence. I also quit smoking on my own initiative because I wanted to protect my child from all the toxins. I had already received threats from NCWS about taking my baby away from me, and one nurse at the healthcare centre, who was working with

NCWS, tried to pressure me into having an abortion. They said that if I didn't they would take my newborn baby away.

All the other mothers who were going through a pregnancy received care and psychological support with the hospital doctors via the healthcare centre. I spent my pregnancy under constant threat and observation! The idea from NCWS to impose an emergency decision was most likely made in advance of the birth, as I was informed before the birth that they would take my child from me.

I thought I would be met with understanding and empathy when I was open with them, humbly cooperating all the way. I realise today that I was naïve to have trusted these people who work at NCWS. NCWS has so much power in Norway. It has the power to execute orders via the police without question. It has power over the nurses and midwives in hospitals, and can tell them exactly what to do.

When I was in hospital I experienced some very bad labour pains. At this point there were police officers sitting in the hospital corridor waiting. The 'child welfare guards', who were dressed as nurses, constantly disturbed me by walking in and out of the birthing room, putting more and more pressure on me. I found it terribly invasive, offensive and traumatic.

In my life's greatest moment, when I was about to bring my precious child into the world, I was treated very poorly, like a subhuman who has no rights to even exist, let alone give birth. I cannot find the words to describe the immense pain and fear I felt at this time.

I had to beg them just to let me hold my son for a short hour. After forty-five minutes they snatched him out of my arms. I did not even get the opportunity to breastfeed him. I had to pump breast milk out while I sat there crying. After they had taken our baby boy they ran out of the hospital and drove away. My boyfriend and I just fell to pieces in total grief, traumatised and in absolute shock. And we still feel this way.

But we are fighting to get our son back because we have done absolutely nothing wrong! I cry for my son every day. He was torn out of my safe arms and carried away by strangers. It's inhumane treatment for a newborn baby to go through such a thing. Not even animals are treated like this in Norway. We are still in shock and deep sorrow. It all feels incomprehensible, like a bad dream. We only get to see our baby four to six times a year, for two hours and under supervision. We are not criminals and we don't really understand this, but it is standard procedure in Norway these days.

Foster parents who were unable to have children had already been lined up and were waiting for a baby boy. They had allegedly ordered a baby boy via a pre-adoption company. I felt so exploited and was treated like a lesser being in an incubator. That's not how a human being should feel. I had every opportunity to be a good mother from the start, but they didn't give me a single chance, even though I did everything I could to follow their demands. I also said I would go to a home for mothers and babies, but they even took that possibility away from me.

I was so focused on preparing a good start for my beloved son's life. I have the resources and the strength, but NCWS didn't acknowledge this. It seemed as if its staff just wanted to, and even enjoyed, keeping me down and exerting their power over me. They never worked with me or helped me in any way so that our little family could get a good start in life.

According to human rights laws in Norway, NCWS should be working to keeping families together, and it is obliged to do everything it can to help parents take care of their own children. Laws are constantly broken, as we have seen in our case with the many laws that were broken when they took our baby boy.

But even worse than this, human rights are not just being broken. They are being broken in the most brutal and terrifying fashion. There is hardly any justice to be found in the court system. We have now been to every court possible in Norway's 'justice system', so our last chance of getting our baby boy back is in the European Court of Human

Rights (ECtHR) in Strasbourg. We have now started with the application process, and we are going all the way. We will never, ever give up on our son.

How can it be possible for a government-supported system to abuse so many human rights laws? The Norwegian media try their best to make NCWS look good, and the new children's minister has, to date, simply ignored what is happening within Norway's child welfare system. Many children die in foster care every year. Some are diagnosed with psychiatric illnesses and others are highly medicated. They are forced to live apart from their families, whom they desperately long to be with. Many children and parents sadly choose suicide because of the way NCWS has treated them. The children and their parents are not listened to, and the parents are ridiculed, bullied, manipulated and treated like subhumans.

NCWS was not interested in my caring skills, even refusing to have an expert psychologist evaluate my caring skills for my child. I still want an expert to evaluate me, and the formal recommendations in these cases confirm that it should be allowed. But I did not get any evaluations. I have never had the chance to experience the joys and challenges of motherhood.

Two young women with no child psychology education who work as social workers at NCWS have condemned me, and have forcibly taken my baby away from me and my partner. How can they commit such violations without considering the law for one minute? And how can a local lawyer, county councillors and district court judges manage these matters in such an undemocratic way and without the support of any experts with competence in this area? The abduction of newborns in Norway should be a high-priority issue for the media. I think it is of great public interest.

It is today's situation that should apply, not the parent's past. And being judged for neglect of care based on subjective views and the prediction of future events should be strictly prohibited. It is unscientific, unprofessional and irresponsible.

According to Jerzy Kwaśniewski, attorney and president of law firm Ordo Iuris ("Legal Order"), the support mechanisms within Norway's current child welfare system work toward destroying the children's emotional attachment to their biological parents, siblings and relatives in an attempt to create new relationships with strangers inside the foster care industry instead. Ordo Iuris has observed various radical ideologies that are being used to aggressively change the existing social order, but instead of helping to improve society these ideologies seek to destroy its very foundations.

The following excerpts from a report written by Ordu Iuris explain human rights from a legal perspective with regard to the international conventions that have been set up. Kwaśniewski also explains the aforementioned change to the Child Welfare Act in 2012, which violates international guarantees of respect for the family. Human rights violations are discussed with examples of how culture, language and heritage are systematically denied to children who are taken away from their biological families and Norwegianised:[ii]

> The principle of primacy of the natural (biological) family in the process of raising a child is one of the basic principles of the universal system of human rights. It is confirmed in Article 16 of the Universal Declaration of Human Rights, the UN Declaration of the Rights of the Child and the Convention on the Rights of the Child. These acts of international law confirm the character of family as a natural and fundamental unit of society, protected against arbitrary actions of public authorities, whose task it is to protect biological family and to support it in the implementation of its natural upbringing functions, while respecting the principle of subsidiarity of the state and the autonomy of parents to raise their children in accordance with their beliefs.
>
> The right of the child to be brought up by the parents and to remain under their care, guaranteed directly in Article 7 of the Convention on the Rights of the Child, strengthened by the prohibition of separating a child from the parents as stipulated in Article 9 of the Convention, has been repeatedly

confirmed as being in itself a manifestation of the child's welfare in documents written by international organisations working to protect human rights. Broader right to respect for family life, guaranteed in Article 16 of the Convention, is interpreted extensively in the General Comment No. 14/2013 of the UN Committee on the Rights of the Children on "the right of the child to have his or her best interests taken as a primary consideration (article 3 para. 1)".

Moreover, in light of the standards of international law, the family gives the best guarantee of raising the child in the spirit of national traditions and cultural values, which promotes child protection and harmonious development. The importance of the right to upbringing in the biological family is greater if the child comes from an ethnic, religious or linguistic minority.

The rules mentioned above complement the content of the standard contained in article 8 of the European Convention on Human Rights, confirming the right to respect for private and family life. According to the uniform case law of the ECtHR, the convention must be applied in line with the general principles of international law, in particular with the principles that apply to the international protection of human rights.

A growing number of media reports mostly concerning families of migrant workers affected by the proceedings conducted by the NCWS is a stimulus to undertake an analysis of the system of national provisions in force in Norway, their practical application and the compliance of such a system with international guarantees of human rights, in particular with the European Convention on Human Rights, the Convention on the Rights of the Child and Norway's other international obligations.

The Official Norwegian Report of 2000 (*Norges offentlige utredninger: NOU 2000:12*), commissioned by the government and prepared by a committee of experts, stressed the importance of biological kinship and continuity of contacts with biological parents as circumstances that support the child's welfare (*bilogiske prinsipp*). The report pointed to the close relationship between biological kinship and respect for family life stemming from the convention. Experts stressed that the task of social welfare services after placing a child in foster care is to carry out continuous assessment of the situation of biological parents, including verification of whether the circumstances that result in the termination of custody are still valid. The task of social care is to support biological parents in the process of assuming full responsibility and care for their children.

Interpretation of the current provisions of the 1992 Child Welfare Act (*Lov om barneverntjenester*) changed as a result of the publication of another official Norwegian report in 2012 entitled "Better protection of children's development – report of the committee of experts on the principle of biological kinship in social childcare". In the opinion the government experts presented, the value of biological kinship was limited to the value stemming from the bond and strong relationship between the child and his or her biological parents. Ending this relationship would lead to a loss of importance of biological kinship between parents and their children.

As a consequence, the report introduced a new principle called the 'principle of the most beneficial relationship for development' ('*Utviklingsfremmende tilknytning*') and Barnevernet introduced this new rule into their practices. According to this principle, 'child welfare' should be assessed without taking into consideration the biological kinship of the child, based on the assessment of development benefits that may stem from a stable relationship between the child and various caregivers, whereby no presumed developmental benefits are related to the child staying in the care of his or her biological parents.

Rejection of the importance of biological kinship for the welfare of the child is accompanied by a tendency to allow two, four or six parent-child contacts a year. Each contact lasts no more than a couple of hours. The right to contact is perceived as a burden, especially if the child is placed in long-term foster care, because contact with parents can make it difficult for children to build relationships with new caregivers. The aim of these contacts is not considered to be the retention of an emotional bond with the biological parents, but the child's right to knowledge about his or her parentage. According to the NOU report (2012:5), contact between biological parents and the child should be more and more limited timewise in order to create space to establish the primary relationship between the child and its foster carers.

Infrequent contact leads to a weakening of emotional ties, and consequently – in line with the 'principle of the most beneficial relationship for development' – the court then finds the child's return to his or her biological parents groundless, even if the parents have already tackled any behavioural defects identified previously. This was the sequence of events in the case of Terje Pedersen et al. v. Norway, pending before the ECtHR, in which the Norwegian Supreme Court permitted the deprivation of parental rights and adoption of a child, pointing to the superiority of a stable emotional relationship with foster parents (applying for adoption) over the value of relations with biological parents demanding custody.

The superiority of attachment to foster parents over the biological bond is reflected in article 4-21 of the Child Welfare Act of 1992, according to which "the municipal social welfare council will revoke the foster care order when it finds high probability of exercising proper care by the parents. The order, however, will not be revoked if the child is so attached to the person or environment in which he or she stayed that revoking it could lead to serious problems for the child". At the same time, article 4-8 of the act introduces the presumption that after two years of alternative care the attachment of the child to the person or environment in which he or she was staying is such that its revocation could lead to serious problems for the child.

From the perspective of opinions and guidance contained in the Official Norwegian Report of 2012:5, it is justified both to limit contact between parents and children, and to exclude the child's contacts with grandparents (if the parents are alive), or to permit the separation of siblings in the course of searching for the 'principle of the most beneficial relationship for development' with new carers for each child. However, such activities violate international guarantees of respect for family life.

The stated direction of the Norwegian law and its practice clearly contradicts international human rights standards, including the right to respect for family life. According to the jurisprudence of the European Court of Human Rights: "The mutual enjoyment of each other's company by the parent and the child constitutes a fundamental element of family life." In A. Schultz and M. Schultz v. Poland, the court stated that: "Mutual enjoyment by parent and child of each other's company constitutes a fundamental element of family life and that domestic measures hindering such enjoyment amount to an interference with the right protected by Article 8 of the Convention."

The Monory v. Romania and Hungary ruling emphasised – apart from the obligation of non-interference of public authorities in private and family life – the existence of positive obligations of the state to ensure the implementation of the fundamental right to contact between parents and children. At the same time, the 'principle of the most beneficial relationship for development' promoted in the Norwegian Official Report 2012:5, which marginalises the value of natural, biological family ties, preferring the assessment of developmental benefits of the child, has already been – albeit in a different form – the subject of criticism of the European Court of Human Rights in K. and A. v. Finland.

The Norwegian government also recognises the problem of rare contact weakening the child's emotional bonds with biological parents and, subsequently, leading to decisions – taken in the name of the 'principle of the most beneficial relationship for development' – to keep the child in a foster family. A new government report from the NOU expert committee (2016:16) called "The new social childcare law: ensuring the rights of the child to care and protection" pointed to the area of potential conflict between the applicable law and the norm described in Article 8 of the European Convention on Human Rights. The reason behind this incompatibility was supposed to be an insufficient – in order to maintain the family relationship – number of contacts granted to biological parents and children in foster care, and the lack of grounds for ruling out contact with other members of the biological family, including grandparents. The first change in the Norwegian legislation on children's contact with their parents postulated by the committee is the introduction of a general principle of the right of the child in foster care to contact with biological parents, siblings and other close relatives. The committee justifies the need for such a change, citing, among other things, the decision of the Norwegian Supreme Court, which examined the case law relating to contact and stated that "the number of visits in the case of long-term foster care varied at between three and six a year".

Following the opinion of the committee, doubts regarding the compatibility of the law and its practical application with the right to respect for family life stemming from the convention were also emphasised by Christian Børge Sørensen, chairman of the NOU expert committee (2016:16). A similar position was presented by the [former] Minister for Children and Equality, Solveig Horne, who did not rule out the need to change the Norwegian law and its practical application along the lines of the European Convention on Human Rights.

Marius Emberland, lawyer of the office of the Attorney General of Norway, which represents Norway before the European Court of Human Rights, called the decision of the European Court of Human Rights to hear a series of cases against NCWS a cause for concern. Supporting the line of defence of Norway, which points to the conflict of the rights of the child to protection and the rights of the child's relatives to respect for family life, Emberland notes that until now Norwegian courts had not given the deserved status to guarantees of human rights arising from the European Convention on Human Rights. Proposed changes to Norwegian law that would include the respect for family life laid out in the convention, have not yet been adopted.

Limiting contact with biological parents has obvious consequences in the form of a violation of the child's right "in community with other members of his or her group, to enjoy his or her own culture, to profess and practise his or her own religion, or to use his or her own language" (Article 30 of the Convention on the Rights of the Child). An overview of the practice shows, however, that children from ethnic and religious minorities are only sent to foster care with Norwegian families.

As a result of the application of these legal standards and their practical interpretations, the Norwegian mechanism of foster care systematically violates the right to respect for family life that is guaranteed, among other things, in article 8 of the European Convention on Human Rights and in related international guarantees to the rights of the child. The adopted solutions are aimed at extinguishing children's emotional attachment to their biological parents, siblings and relatives, and at shaping new relationships with foster carers instead.

Cut off and tortured

Experienced Norwegian psychiatrist and former high jump champion Leif Roar Falkum believes that it should come as no surprise that the Norwegian authorities are attracting so much negative attention at home and abroad.

He claims that in present-day Norway biological parents are being totally cut off as human beings and that NCWS inflicts such deep trauma on children and their parents that they never completely recover from it.[iii] "What's happening in Norway is unnecessary and ugly," says Falkum. "It reminds me of how vulnerable groups have been treated in the past in our country, or in the totalitarian society we do not like to be compared to."

In 2008, Gro Hillestad Thune, published a book that featured the personal accounts of seventy former patients and relatives who described their negative experiences within the Norwegian psychiatric system.[iv] Thune points out that the mentally ill are among the most vulnerable to human rights violations. Many tell their stories, but they are not being heard. The purpose of her book was to create a debate on how psychiatric patients can be given better protection against abuse from the authorities. Thune explains that current legislation allows health professionals to use physical force, which can lead to an abuse of power.

Following visits to Norway, the European Committee for the Prevention of Torture (CPT) has reported several instances of significant human rights violations at psychiatric institutions.[v] Though it is impossible to carry out in-depth investigations during a short visit, the reports are useful and should provoke discussion about the use of coercion and the patient's legal certainty (a principle in national and international law, which holds that the law must provide those subject to it with the ability to regulate their conduct).

A report from We Shall Overcome (WSO), an organisation that supports those in the field of psychiatry, includes personal testimony from a patient on the subject of forced psychiatry:[vi]

> What is tragic is that something that begins as care, and should ensure the patient the right to treatment and follow-up, allows for the use of police transportation, forced drugging, restraints and solitary cells... Conduct that in other houses is called torture, infringement and punishment is given other names when it is carried out by medical doctors... Patients in psychiatry have to relate to a health system where the same hand that comforts you and says it wants to help is also the one that puts you into restraints. Dealing with such a situation is inhuman and leads to chaos in a human mind. When the trauma is a fact, you have nowhere to turn other than back to the

place where they inflicted the injury on you but refuse to give it legitimacy.

Hans Magnus' story

According to TV2, Norwegian couple Sylvia and Trond Rikard Ensby were hoping to get some help when they agreed to stay at a mothers' home in Norway, but instead NCWS took away their precious baby boy because he allegedly failed a baby IQ test.[vii] There is nothing in Sylvia's history to suggest that she has ever been diagnosed with learning difficulties, and the parents appear to be loving, caring and capable. They also have a supportive family around them, including grandparents who were close to their only grandson.

The court of appeal ruled that Hans Magnus' mother and father will not see their precious baby boy again, and their son has now been put up for adoption without any of his relatives being considered. This story is similar to many others, highlighting the serious negligence that so often takes place in Norway.

Trond commented (translated): "Even though we were prepared, it was a shock to get the verdict. For us it is incomprehensible. The first few days after the sentence I felt completely empty. The entire experience has been very tough, but we've got through it."

The couple's first lawyer, Marie Sølverud, stated (translated): "It's a very serious, sad and wrong judgement. The verdict will be appealed. I think it is hard to say anything about how the Supreme Court will deal with the matter. If it's necessary we will appeal to the ECtHR."

Sølverud reacted strongly to the fact that the court did not take into account the reports of two expert psychologists who believe the child should be returned to his parents.

Toward the end of 2017, Trond wrote (translated): "Our son has been denied any contact with his parents and his biological family. The state has decided that it is necessary to go ahead with a forced adoption. The adoptive parents have determined that our son will never get to know of his origins. There is a visitation ban to ensure that his grandfather can never bring him any presents or give him hugs."

Human rights proponent and legal expert Marius Reikerås, who is now representing the family, revealed that a complaint has now been sent to the European Court of Human Rights.

Anti-family

Pastor Jan-Aage Torp from KKN believes that instead of making a constructive effort to replace the current dysfunctional child welfare system, the Norwegian authorities are using bullying techniques to silence those who are fighting for families' and children's human rights.

In the following comment he describes how people have been isolated and excluded from society just for speaking up against those who are blindly supporting NCWS' attempts to destroy the family unit (translated):[vii]

> Poland has experienced extraordinary development in terms of economics, culture, religion and politics since the fall of communism in 1989. There are many opinions in Poland and outside Poland about the Polish people. They are certainly setting a standard.
>
> Christian Coalition World is making a strong statement about the Polish people, as we did in 2017 when the Family Defense Award was given to the beautiful Romanian-Norwegian Bodnariu family. At KKN we support and honour people of principle, character and love.
>
> The 2018 Family Defense Award went to Katarzyna Jachimowicz, a Polish medical doctor who was fired for exercising her right to conscientious objection in relation to pro-life issues, and to Ordo Iuris, the mighty Polish legal thinktank in Warsaw led by president Jerzy Kwaśniewski, which has, for several years, been winning huge battles in support of family and pro-life values in Poland, and which is now fighting on behalf of families in Norway who are being abused by NCWS.
>
> The award to Mrs Jachimowicz represents a case that has barely been debated in Norway. Most medical doctors have bowed down to Baal. She has received support from some Christian medical doctors and from the Christian

newspapers. Their positive words represent a low risk to themselves; however, she has personally paid a high price for her heroic stand, even losing her job. We believe that in the long run this will bring deep change to our nation, allowing others to exercise their right to conscientious objection in the workplace.

However, the government does not care about this situation. KKN has received no protest whatsoever against our award to her because Norway's government and people consider this fight a far-fetched dream. But we know that it will redefine reality!

The award given to Ordo Iuris and Dr Kwaśniewski, however, has been a hot potato. We should rather say a burning potato! KKN has received threats of exclusion and isolation, even from 'conservative' Christians from whom we ought to expect more. It is all because of NCWS, the pride of Norwegian social democracy, secularism and feminism, which has so infiltrated the evangelical and Lutheran churches that hardly anyone dares confront the evils of this system. A lot of Norwegians make a living from governmental interventions instigated against thousands of families.

Both awards were collected during a formal ceremony that was broadcast live on the popular *Studio Direkte* program on TV Visjon Norge, Scandinavia's largest Christian TV channel. The 2017 award given to the Bodnariu family was also broadcast live on this channel.

We thank God for the Polish people who came through the evils of communism to become a nation that esteems God and the family. We believe the same will happen in Norway. We love the Polish people, and we sure love our own people as well!

Chapter 17 notes

[i] Bennett, S., "Emil's abduction at birth", Step Up 4 Children's Rights: https://stepup4childrensrights.com/emils-abduction-at-birth

[ii] Kwaśniewski, J., "Rejection of protection of natural (biological) family", Ordo Iuris: https://ordoiuris.pl/rodzina-i-malzenstwo/odrzucenie-ochrony-rodziny-biologicznej-jako-zrodlo-naruszen-miedzynarodowych

[iii] Staff writer, "Vi Er I Ferd Med Å Få Et Sorteringssamfunn, Sier Psykiater" ("We are ready to become a tiered community, says psychiatrist"), Barnefjern: http://www.barnefjern.org/vi-er-i-ferd-med-a-fa-et-sorteringssamfunn-sier-psykiater

[iv] Thune, G. H., *Overgrep søkelys på psykiatrien* (*Abuses: spotlight on psychiatry*), Abstrakt, 2008: https://www.bokklubben.no/boeker/overgrep-gro-hillestad-thune/produkt.do?produktId=3060294

[v] Thune, G. H., "Menneskerettigheter også for psykiatriske pasienter i Norge?" ("Do human rights laws also apply to for psychiatric patients in Norway?"), Tidsskriftet: https://tidsskriftet.no/2006/06/kronikk/menneskerettigheter-ogsa-psykiatriske-pasienter-i-norge

[vi] Staff writer, "Forced psychiatric interventions as disability-based discrimination", WSO: https://tbinternet.ohchr.org/Treaties/CESCR/Shared%20Documents/NOR/INT_CESCR_NGO_NOR_15310_E.doc

[vii] Øyhovden, A., "Trond (40) og Sylvia (44) kjemper for å beholde sønnen – barnevernet sier nei" ("Trond (40) and Sylvia (44) fight to keep their son - child welfare says no "), TV2: https://www.tv2.no/nyheter/9209112

[vii] Torp, J-A., "We love Poland", Christian Coalition World: https://christiancoalition.world/news/read2/we-love-poland

18

Reform

Reform can only take place when the Norwegian authorities recognise the destructive nature of their child welfare system and become open to change. The big question is, does NCWS truly want to help children and their families, or would it rather focus its efforts on controlling, persecuting and punishing them? If NCWS chooses to continue with its dysfunctional strategy, any suggestion made in favour of a new service will fall on deaf ears.

Children must be protected against violence and a serious lack of care, and a new family-orientated service brought in to replace NCWS would support this. The idea that anyone who criticises NCWS is of an extreme, child welfare-hating opinion is not only ridiculous but also a reactive form of deflection away from the real problem. The key issue is that untold numbers of children are being taken away from their families every week in Norway for no justifiable reason, with no evidence of abuse or violence provided.

NCWS can either continue to spend most of its energy on targeting easy prey, for example poor families, single mothers, former foster care children, those with health problems, the unemployed, those with a lower-than-average IQ, families with a small social network and those with language learning difficulties. Or it could put all its resources into stopping serious abuse, for example when a child's life is at risk from violence or sexual abuse at preschool, school or at home, or in their foster care or adoptive family settings. Of course, confronting a pathological person who is abusing a child is much harder than confronting a poor single mother with a small support network who isn't quite reaching the expected standards.

Norwegian lawyer Preben Kløvfjell states in an article titled "'Manglende foreldreferdigheter' som grunnlag for inngrep"

("'Missing parenting skills' used as a basis for intervention") that taking children away from their parents due to a perceived lack of parenting skills is dramatic and potentially dangerous.[i] Yet he claims that, according to government statistics, this is the most frequently cited reason for taking children away from their parents in Norway.

Kløvfjell believes that the consequences of these wrong decisions may be irreversible. He also recommends that parents check the credentials of 'experts' who may have close ties with NCWS. Kløvfjell concludes his article with a reminder of the number of occasions Norway has been found by the European Court of Human Rights to have broken the law in cases where NCWS has separated children from their parents.

Inter-parliamentary meeting

In a press release published in 2017, MEP Tomáš Zdechovský highlighted the following:[ii]

> At the 33rd inter-parliamentary meeting, held in Oslo and attended by an EU delegation and members of the Norwegian parliament, NCWS services became the primary topic for debate. The EU's concerns about NCWS were on the official agenda, and Norwegian MPs promised to investigate the situation.
>
> Zdechovský said: "It is a breakthrough in further negotiations that the topic of NCWS got on the program list of such an important meeting, which [had been] planned for a year. Norwegian MPs were very surprised. They anticipated that the European politicians could solve this agenda, but the increasing number of petitions by European citizens and up to nine lawsuits against Norway, recognised by the European Court of Human Rights, speaks quite uncompromisingly."
>
> Polish MEP Julia Pitera addressed the situation during the meeting. According to information Zdechovský received from other members of the delegation, Barnevernet's actions were not only talked about in general terms, but specific cases of injustice were also discussed.
>
> "My colleague Julia Pitera proved that she knows

> Norway's child protection system and specific cases better than Norwegian parliamentarians. Norwegian parliamentarians subsequently declared that they will discuss the situation with the relevant ministers and consider further negotiations when the theme returns," Zdechovský said.
>
> "Norwegian colleagues have demonstrated that they are interested in changing the system, so I'm cautiously optimistic. But we will continue to deal with the situation," commented Pitera.

In September 2018, an article titled "Propaganda or reality about the Norwegian Child Welfare Service?" was written by clinical psychologist Einar C. Salvesen.[iii] Salvesen highlighted the huge discrepancies between what Linda Hofstad Helleland is trying to promote with regard to NCWS and the destructive reality that thousands of professionals and ordinary people have encountered.

Salvesen comments that there has been massive criticism against NCWS from academic environments based on detailed knowledge of how the agency works, particularly when it comes to emergency care takeovers. He highlights the importance of keeping families together and slams the soaring number of care takeovers, where children in foster care lose contact with their networks, are subjected to a traumatising lack of visitation access and are given a poor prognosis by NCWS.

According to Salvesen, NCWS lacks basic human values such as humility, transparency and self-understanding, and common practices such as an error-handling strategy. In conclusion, he calls for an independent investigation into NCWS that would investigate the many 'casualties' of the system that support the widespread criticism. "Following a plane crash, one does not look at a random selection of aircraft for answers, but at the plane in question," he writes.

In September 2018, Norwegian lawyer Nathalie Helene Brinkmann wrote an article titled "Ministeren fraskriver seg ansvaret" ("The Minister declines any responsibility")[iv] in response to one written by Hofstad Helleland titled "Barneministeren: Norsk barnevern går foran. Snart vil andre land komme etter oss" ("Norwegian child welfare is the best and soon other countries will follow us").[v] Brinkmann almost finds Hofstad Helleland's claims that NCWS is the best system, and that other countries will follow Norway's example, laughable. She derides the notion that dividing so many families is a kind of pioneer work comparable to the 1970s gender quality struggle.

Brinkmann states that Hofstad Helleland's comments are at best self-centred and at worst testify to considerable ignorance, which goes to show why it is proving so difficult to improve the current child welfare system.

Brinkmann asks (text translated): "Does [Hofstad Helleland] know how many families are split up without any type of addiction, violence or serious mental illness claimed?"

She argues that a child receiving assistance from the child welfare system is among the least powerful in society, and that what this child doesn't need is a children's minister who refuses to acknowledge the problems associated with children being subjected to serious mistakes and injustice.

In conclusion, Brinkmann insists that the child welfare system needs a radical overhaul. "Child welfare educators must realise that they cannot help a child without helping the family it is a part of," she writes.

Interestingly, on June 28, 2018, after much deliberation at the Parliamentary Assembly of the Council of Europe (PACE), the report and resolution on striking a balance between the best interests of the child and the need to keep the families together, drawn up on the basis of the Bodnariu family case, was adopted![vi] There were forty-three votes in favour of the resolution, two against and fourteen abstentions.[vii] Many hope that this victory will help thousands of families whose rights have been violated.

"Children have the right to be protected from all types of violence, abuse and neglect," the parliamentarians said in a resolution based on a report[viii] by Valeriu Ghiletchi (Republic of Moldova). "But they also have the right not to be separated from their parents against their will, except when… absolutely necessary in the best interests of the child."

At the worldwide demonstration on April 16, 2016, James Hunter gave a speech. In an excerpt, he said:[ix]

> I care because it is not now, and never has been, simply about the Bodnariu family. It is not now, and never has been, simply about Norway. This is about existing in a global community, and if Norway wants to exist in that community, if they want to import and export, if they want to send athletes to the Olympics, or compete in the World Cup or sing at Eurovision, if they want to be a part of the United Nations, they must listen to people from other countries. They have to listen to me right now.
>
> Barnevernet may be able to intimidate Norwegians into cowering in a corner or whispering when they should be shouting, but they cannot intimidate me or the other speakers who are here today, and they cannot intimidate you. The Norwegian people may not be able to speak up for themselves for fear of attracting the attention of Barnevernet, but you can and you should because, like me, you care...
>
> Norway, do you want to rule in a dystopian futuristic society of Orwellian proportions? If you do, fine, we will stop you. But if you don't you should stop yourself. Submit to independent oversight.

Moving forward

Erik Selle, leader of Partiet De Kristne ("The Christian Party", PDK) has identified a number of changes that need to be made within NCWS. He says that Norway needs a child welfare service the population has confidence in, so that when hundreds of Norwegian professionals sound the alarm someone in government intervenes and takes action. Selle also shared with the author of this book that many Christians are now comparing the current situation in Norway to that of the former Soviet Union and to other totalitarian, atheistic states.

In an open letter addressed to former children's minister Solveig Horne, he suggested that the following recommendations are implemented in order to create a new and improved child welfare service:[x]

- Respect the biological principle of the family
- Create an independent commission to look into cases where

children and parents have been treated unfairly
- Monitor NCWS' actions (it needs an independent watchdog), as many children and their families are currently exposed to rough and abusive behaviour
- Re-evaluate the law and separate the economic interests of the various players
- Establish, as soon as possible, an independent appeal authority that promotes credibility within international child welfare circles

Norwegian paediatric nurse Margaret Hennum has been working with children and families in crisis almost her entire adult life. In an article titled "Norway's Dehumanising Strategy Part 7", Hennum explores the shift in power of Norway's public institutions, and the way NCWS undermines and in many ways controls public institutions that generally have far greater competency than child welfare employees. She also claims that NCWS has made attempts to gain power by eroding people's trust in other public institutions.

Hennum discusses her ideas for an alternative child welfare service with a focus on how to help the most vulnerable in today's society: the children and their families. She writes (text translated):[xi]

Where do we find experts in today's society?

- The police are responsible for handling criminal activity
- The medical industry, including doctors, dentists, specialists and pharmaceutical companies, are responsible for medical treatment
- Healthcare centres/nurses have a responsibility to follow up with parents and check on the development of children
- Paediatric nurses are competent when it comes to newborn babies, breastfeeding, nutrition and general care
- School systems are responsible for children's education, in accordance with the Education Act
- As part of its responsibility, NAV can assist financially when needed.

These professions can collaborate, ensuring considerable competency with regard to the protection of children and families. This can be achieved by sharing professional insights and referring to each other's specialist knowledge where needed. In fact, this was standard practice prior to the new child welfare reforms. Collaboration between these public institutions will make NCWS surplus to requirement, and rightly so.

NCWS has the opportunity to approach the above professionals/experts to draw conclusions in its cases if necessary. Consider the fact that an employee from one of the above fields could easily gain employment within child welfare services because they are well qualified. However, if one of NCWS' social workers applied for one of their jobs they would not be successful. So the question is: why does NCWS claim to be offering a service that no one else is qualified to do?

Social workers at all levels draw conclusions based on personal judgement and assumptions. Diagnoses may include depression, dehydration, learning disabilities, ADHD, apathy, autism, and lack of emotional and social development. In order to substantiate their diagnoses, NCWS employees carry out exhaustive and unnecessary investigations, building cases based on fragments of reality.

They observe children and parents over a short period of time in conditions of intentional and unintentional stress. Their observations are recorded as they stack up the evidence to reach a preconceived diagnosis. They then take their findings to professionals in other fields, asking them to support this diagnosis based on their observations. Without the final assessment of these professionals, the social workers have no basis for their diagnoses or decisions.

This means NCWS cannot work exclusively from experts in these professions, and therefore cannot act as an independent body. Child welfare tasks and responsibilities are constantly increasing. NCWS employees hijack the professional knowledge of experts whose skills they ultimately depend on to do what they perceive to be their job. Again, the question arises: what function is NCWS fulfilling that no one else can fulfil?

NCWS is attempting to increase its reach across the entire population. It achieves this by providing Signs of Neglect courses for those working in other professional sectors. What is it that makes other professions look up to NCWS as the expert in all of this? How does an agency with far less knowledge about neglect get to dictate to others on when and how to report incidents based on the hypothesis it has made?

The following is stated in clause 33 of the Healthcare Act:[xii]

Clause 33: Informing Child Welfare Services

The person providing healthcare should be aware of any circumstances that may lead to measures being undertaken by child welfare services.

Without prejudice to the duty of confidentiality, in accordance with section 21, health personnel shall, on their own initiative, provide information to NCWS when there is reason to believe that a child is being abused at home or there are other forms of serious neglect, as in the Child Welfare Act (sections § 4-10, § 4-11 and § 4-12). The same applies when a child has shown persistent and serious behavioural disorders (as per § section 4-24 of the act).

Healthcare professionals shall provide such information by order of the bodies responsible for implementing the Child Welfare Act. A person shall be appointed in healthcare institutions to be responsible for the disclosure of such information.

The first part of this act refers to violence, substance abuse and sexual abuse. These were the conditions that could lead to NCWS measures. However, the list of conditions has changed since the 1990s due to major developments. An 'early signs' list continues to grow. In fact, the list has become so long that courses have become necessary to explain what these 'early signs' mean!

Teachers, doctors, police officers and others can uncover serious cases of neglect without having to ask for additional information from NCWS. Neither is it wrong when a government employee feels there are people who need guidance or help in some way. For example, a doctor, nurse or police officer will be able to investigate the matter under the authority of their job and disclose whether there is any cause for suspicion or not. In this way, the need for long, professionally weak investigations disappears. In reality, the self-made proclamation that NCWS is the only organisation with the ability to decide whether something is abuse or not is a complete exaggeration.

If the police receive reports of concern they can investigate and determine whether a criminal offence has been committed. If required, they can organise a medical examination. A doctor can draw the conclusion that a child lives under adverse physical conditions based on their medical assessments. A nurse can provide guidance to a family in need by contacting a doctor, school, day care centre or the NAV. Not only that, but all these professions have dedicated departments that provide assistance to families that are in need, which proves once again that there is no need for an intermediary body without any professional competence in these areas.

A teacher is responsible for the follow-up of learning. A teacher can see the student's needs and learn what he or she needs to be able to keep up with the teaching. In order to obtain the resources this student is entitled to under Norwegian law, NCWS should not demand a full investigation into all the areas for which these other professions are responsible. It often undertakes searches, citing reasons that do not exist so that the educational responsibility is taken away from the school. The same applies if a family has to seek financial support from NAV.

Why do NCWS employees enter these families' lives to investigate whether there really is a need for financial help, while looking for other reasons behind their 'misfortune' so the case ends up in their lap instead? Isn't income minus expenses a good and easy starting point to determine whether the family should be aided by NAV? And is this not NAV's area of competence? So why does NAV have a duty to report this as a possible sign of abuse and neglect? A parent who seeks help in an emergency shows signs of good parenting, right? Why is this a matter for NCWS?

Which tasks are left for an independent body to take care of in terms of children? Criminal affairs come under the responsibility of the police, medical concerns are the responsibility of the doctor, educational issues are the responsibility of the schools and the healthcare centre links them all together.

We should point out that there is a real need for the relocation of children in some cases. A small proportion of children in Norway live with what could be classified as gross neglect. This includes situations that pose a threat to the child's life and health, such as violence, substance abuse and sexual abuse in the true meaning of these words.

This does not refer to a correctional slap on the hand or a towel being thrown that accidentally hits a child. In these less serious instances, healthcare centres can help through the courses they run. Gross neglect does not relate to a mother who has been on prescription drugs that are classified as potentially addictive. Again, the healthcare centre can intervene here. Sexual assault does not refer to a father holding the thigh of his two-year-old daughter as he manoeuvres her leg into a pair of tights or pyjamas. This does not fall under the responsibility of any public unit. It's called putting clothes on a child!

We are talking here about violence in the sense that most people perceive it: punches, kicks and ill-treatment that leads to physical and mental harm. We are talking about drug abuse in an environment where drugs and alcohol are prioritised over parenting. We are talking about sexual abuse with regard to adults who sexually assault children and adolescents. All signs of this kind of abuse should be investigated within the relevant professional environment (for example by the police or the doctor).

So what happens to the children who need to be relocated? The responsibility for responding to genuine claims of assault should fall to the police. The police should have a unit designed to protect children who need this type of intervention.

Abuse cases should not be managed by an office where money can be earned on the side through running private institutions or foster home companies. It should be a place where ordinary police officers who have taken courses in psychology and developed interpersonal skills should take turns to deal with such cases as part of their usual service in the police, not a separate unit that specialises only in child welfare. The police should work in collaboration with healthcare centres that can accommodate children at short notice. These centres are in the best position to approve families that are looking to become foster care providers, and to keep an eye on them subsequently.

If we were to pass the responsibility and professional pride back to professionals in these fields we would have no need for child welfare services at all. Instead, NCWS is being given more and more power to put other agencies under orders. Doctors, teachers and many others have a statutory duty to report the minutest deviations (such as normal life crises, learning difficulties and tiredness in newborn mothers) to NCWS. In this way, it has become a threat to the trust and function of well-established and competent public institutions upon which our communities and population depend.

Change needed

Brave, independent journalists are rarely associated with Norway, especially when it comes to commenting on issues relating to NCWS. However, one article titled "Glass Girl", written by Thomas Ergo, Rune Vandvik and Hans Petter Aass, bucked the trend and was nominated for the European Press Prize in 2017.[xiii] Journalists who write the truth are vital in forming a healthy society, so here's hoping that independent journalism makes its presence known in Norway once again, and soon.

The absence of legal certainty

As Gro Hillestad Thune elucidates in her article titled "Previous human rights judgements trigger alarm: the total absence of legal certainty in child welfare", there is a clear lack of sound legal certainty in the actions of today's NCWS. There are also significant contradictions in many child welfare cases.

Thune has more than forty years' experience working with child welfare cases, both as a lawyer and as a member of the European Commission of Human Rights between 1982 and 1998. She is widely considered to be Norway's leading human rights lawyer.

Thune paid attention to the case *Norge Idag* covered in recent weeks, where NCWS employees in the Haugesund region refused to comply with a judicial verdict stipulating that a two-year-old boy should be returned to his parents. At the time of writing it has been more than four months since the Supreme Court's appeal committee backed the district court's verdict. But NCWS has been granted permission by the county council to ignore the enforceable verdict. Instead of helping the boy move home to be with his parents it has decided to keep him in permanent foster care. Thune writes:[xiv]

> The case illustrates the main problem in child welfare: namely that the individual prosecutor has the power of attorney to use force and power without being attached to a proper complaints and control structure.

The way she sees it, NCWS was established as a supplementary support service but has started to act more and more like a government agency in its own right. This gradual change has given regional child welfare services much greater freedom to carry out tasks of their own choosing from behind closed doors. Thune continues:

> Having been given so much freedom to use force against families with children, society has irresponsibly accepted that people with so-called child-related competence can assess whether parents are able to give their children proper

> care or not. Many child welfare issues are not about child abuse related to violence or substance abuse, but about whether or not the local authority trusts that the parents will do a good enough job.
>
> Instead of supporting a child welfare system that interacts with parents around their children, we have, as a society, created an accusatory system in which schools, teachers and churches are urged to immediately report any issues related to children to NCWS. And in this system, case officers are sitting and processing reported concerns within fixed deadlines, protected by confidentiality and often without proper guidance.
>
> While the police need permission from a judge before they can search a private home, local NCWS officers have power of attorney to decide whether a child is to be urgently taken into custody with police assistance from preschool, school, a mothers' home, their own home or even a maternity ward. It may involve hauling a baby from the mother's breast or lap, or sending siblings to different and unfamiliar homes. Such moves may of course be necessary in very extreme cases. But when this is happening so often in this country without the situation being an emergency in any way it is because the child welfare officer does not need to obtain permission from a judge before the child is removed.
>
> It does not matter whether a great deal of what child welfare does is done well. As long as there are cases that are handled disastrously, society must shine a strong spotlight on the system. The lack of legal certainty and contradictions within child welfare constitute a national disaster that affects children, parents and employees who want to do a good job. Everybody is a victim of this system. It is time to start asking fundamental questions and talking about this problem.

Thune goes on to accuse politicians of failing vulnerable children:

> Through the #metoo campaign, questions about legal certainty and contradictions have appeared on the politicians' agenda for women. Now it's time to ask the same questions about the public welfare system for children."

In her opinion, ongoing revisions to the Child Welfare Act do not meet the deep need for change:

> Instead, the focus is on making the right to be loved a key part of the Child Welfare Act. This is a statement of social failure; that children should be met with love is self-evident. What we need is an independent analysis – a Gjørv Report[15] – that publicly scrutinises the system at all levels.

Thune believes it is necessary to strip local authorities of their power to make enforced decisions:

> The only viable option I can see is to make the local authority a clean auxiliary body and to establish a system in which the various staff and caregivers who know the child stand together to find out how to act in the child's best interests. The child welfare staff should be helped out of the straightjackets they are wearing today in their irresponsible double role as both helper and authority. Force and power belong to the police and the judicial system.
>
> I want to encourage all parents who need help not to contact NCWS until we get a whole new system, as it's so hard to predict what kind of treatment you will get.

15 A government report ordered after the 2011 Oslo bombing and the Utøya massacre that followed: https://www.regjeringen.no/no/dokumenter/nou-2012-14/id697260

Chapter 18 notes

[i] Kløvfjell, P., "'Missing parenting skills' used as a basis for intervention" ("Manglende foreldreferdigheter' som grunnlag for inngrep"), Advokatfirmaet Tveter: https://www.barnevernsportalen.no/single-post/2016/11/16/%C2%ABManglende-foreldreferdigheter%C2%BB-som-grunnlag-for-inngrep

[ii] Staff writer, "Barnevernet became the official topic for relations between the EU and Norway", Facebook: https://www.facebook.com/BarnevernetStealsChildren/posts/707478836090377:0

[iii] Salvesen, E. C., "Propaganda eller realiteter om norsk barnevern?" ("Propaganda or reality about the Norwegian Child Welfare Service?"), *Aftenposten*: https://www.aftenposten.no/meninger/debatt/i/l1y3VL/Propaganda-eller-realiteter-om-norsk-barnevern--Einar-C-Salvesen

[iv] Brinkmann, N. H., "Ministeren fraskriver seg ansvaret" ("The Minister declines any responsibility"), *Aftenposten*: https://www.aftenposten.no/meninger/debatt/i/9mAg0M/Ministeren-fraskriver-seg-ansvaret--Nathalie-H-Brinkmann

[v] Skogstrøm. L., "Norwegian child welfare is the best and soon other countries will follow us" ("Barneministeren: Norsk barnevern går foran. Snart vil andre land komme etter oss"), *Aftenposten*: https://www.aftenposten.no/norge/i/Mg8y30/Barneministeren--Norsk-barnevern-gar-foran-Snart-vil-andre-land-komme-etter-oss

[vi] Staff writer, "Strasbourg yesterday: PACE spells out strict conditions for removing a child from the family as a 'last resort'", Christian Coalition World: https://christiancoalition.world/news/read2/pace-strict-conditions-removal-child

[vii] Staff writer, "Vote on Resolution", PACE: http://assembly.coe.int/nw/xml/Votes/DB-VotesResults-EN.asp?VoteID=37349&DocID=16634&MemberID&Sort=2

[viii] Ghiletchi, V., "Striking a balance between the best interest of the chid and the need to keep the families together", PACE:

http://website-pace.net/documents/19855/4491159/20180427-socdoc11rev-interet-superieur-enfant-EN.pdf

[ix] Hunter, J., "Brisbane International Pro-Bodnariu Anti-Barnevernet Protest 16 April 2016 (James Hunter)", YouTube: https://youtu.be/vZsn3-EVxa4

[x] Selle, E., "Barnevernet trenger en kritisk gjennomgang" ("Barnevernet needs a critical review"), Søkelys: http://www.sokelys.com/?p=15578

[xi] Hennum, M., "Norway's Dehumanising Strategy, Part 7" ("Norges Dehumaniserende Strategi, Del 7"), Facebook: https://www.facebook.com/notes/margaret-hennum/norges-dehumaniserende-strategi-del-7/1894502537465177

[xii] Staff writer, "Lov om helsepersonell m.v." ("Healthcare Act"), Lovdata: https://lovdata.no/dokument/NL/lov/1999-07-02-64

[xiii] Ergo, T., Vandvik, R. and Aass, H. P., "Glassjenta" ("Glass Girl"), European Press Prize: https://www.europeanpressprize.com/article/glass-girl

[xiv] Thune, G. H., "Tidligere menneskerettighetsdommer slår alarm: totalt fravær av rettssikkerhet i Barnevernet" ("Previous human rights judgements trigger alarm: Total absence of legal certainty in child welfare"), *Nyheter*: http://idag.no/samfunn/nyheter/totalt-fravar-av-rettssikkerhet-i-barnevernet/19.28084

Afterword

The following tribute (translated) was written by an anonymous Norwegian poet for Norwegian Constitution Day, the official national holiday observed on May 17 each year alongside Children's Day.

My beautiful Norway

Beautiful Norway, every year you let us celebrate you in the glorious spring. You clothe yourself in your finest garment: the buds are in bloom and the warming sun gives us hope of summer and school holidays. All your introverted residents pop out of their homes and greet even those who are unfamiliar with warm hugs and happy celebrations.

They dress their children in the most imposing splendour, give them money for ice cream and film them waving flags as the parade goes by – the children's parade – the epitome of your excellence.

The children are free with their rights to hope and joy, sheltered from the injustice and deprivation that exists beyond your borders. The parade is your symbol of pride; it's what you want everyone to see and admire.

The colours you have chosen for your flag are red, blue and white. Red for the sun's heat and hearts filled with love. Blue is for the sea, the broad horizon and our dreams. White is for snow and glaciers, our famous national landscapes.

Snow and ice: the truth about Norway. The truth about the real Norwegian atmosphere under the cover of a short, beautiful spring.

On this day, the light shines out. The focus is on streets filled with life. No one notices the silent ones; those who do not rejoice; those who remain inside with their curtains closed.

They have nothing to cheer for today. They have lost all the beauty in their lives. They see this day as a mockery, as the proverbial salt in the wound. For this is not a day that fits with the truth. They have lost all faith in freedom. Their hope and joy are held in captivity.

Their children are not marching in the parade. They are not where they can see them. Their children are no longer theirs. The children have been removed; trapped and isolated from rest of the family.

In a cupboard somewhere hangs a costume that has never been used or was used a long time ago. The door to the cupboard is closed. The beautiful folk costume reminds the parents of pain. Today the blue in your flag stands for tears in helpless eyes. Maybe they asked for help and you responded by taking away their happiness, their children.

Outside stands the flagpole, which was once used a very long time ago when a child woke up in this house to celebrate its freedom and buy ice cream. There was also a feast here on this day. Maybe they did not have all the things everyone else had, but they had each other. There was a family gathering with a barbecue, and they enjoyed themselves on this Children's Day.

These are the children they love so dearly, who they never get to live with. Hearts are bursting. Blood flows from the deepest of wounds that will never stop bleeding. They have been cut up into infinite pieces and live stigmatised, and you have twisted and distorted every piece. They still hold the battered pieces together and stand up to fight, because they love. Today the red in your flag symbolises this blood.

The white stands for emptiness on this Children's Day. It also stands for betrayal. It stands for the cold you have exposed far too many people to. The cold, white mist is your breath. You are cold, Norway. Downright cold. People are freezing in darkened rooms today. They are in mourning as you celebrate yourself. Joyful shouts from the ignorant outside make them wish this day had never come.

Today is one of the saddest days for too many of us. Beautiful Norway, look around you. Do you not see the missing flags? More and more are missing with each year that passes. Your glossy print is fading, my oh so beautiful Norway.

Media coverage

ARTE/ORF 2 documentary: ***Norwegen: So schützen sie Kinder? (Norway: how do we protect our children)***
French: http://www.arte.tv/fr/videos/070086-000-A/norvege-familles-brisees
German: http://www.arte.tv/de/videos/070086-000-A/norwegen-so-schutzen-sie-kinder
French with English subtitles: https://youtu.be/BBWXhrN4AM4

BBC documentary: ***Norway: Parents against the state***
Video: http://www.bbc.co.uk/programmes/b078hfq2
Radio: http://www.bbc.co.uk/programmes/p03qylz2
Article: http://www.bbc.com/news/magazine-36026458

BBC documentary: ***Norway's silent scandal***
Video: https://www.bbc.co.uk/programmes/n3ct4f1y
Article: https://www.bbc.com/news/resources/idt-sh/norways_hidden_scandal

SBS documentary: ***Norway's stolen Children***
http://www.sbs.com.au/news/dateline/story/norways-stolen-children

DW documentary: ***Child services under fire in Norway***
English: https://youtu.be/4tpcbeJjDtI
German: https://youtu.be/lSsRNJp9tSw

Forbes article: "Norway's Government-Abducted Children, And Ramifications for Europe"
https://www.forbes.com/sites/realspin/2017/02/27/norways-government-abducted-children-and-ramifications-for-europe/#c3eb4b74f738

The Sunday Guardian Live **article: "A case exposing the double standards of Norway's CPS"**
https://www.sundayguardianlive.com/lifestyle/case-exposing-double-standards-norways-cps

The Christian Post **article: "Norway Forcibly Removes 12-Y-O Son After Christian Family Decides to Homeschool"**
https://www.christianpost.com/news/norway-forcibly-removes-12-y-o-son-after-christian-family-decides-to-homeschool-video-217663

Glaube.at article: "12 -jähriges Kind wurde seinen Eltern wie ein Schwerverbrecher entrissen" ("The 12-year-old child was snatched from his parents like a felon")
www.glaube.at/news/politik/ausland/article/1000000613-norwegen-12-jaehriges-kind-wurde-seinen-eltern-wie-ein-schwerverbrecher-entrissen

TV2 documentary *Sak om Sylvia og Trond* (*The case of Sylvia and Trond*)
https://www.facebook.com/AdvokatSolverud/videos/1156684621103599

Media coverage on the case of Amy Jakobsen and her son Tyler

***The Christian Post* article "Norway Took Baby from This American Mom; She Is Still Fighting for Her Son 5 Years Later"**
www.christianpost.com/news/norway-took-baby-from-this-american-mom-she-is-still-fighting-for-her-son-5-years-later-225028

Faithwire article "'Norway Took My Child': Child Protective Services Takes Baby from American Mom"
www.faithwire.com/2018/06/21/norway-child-protective-services-unfairly-targeting-immigrant-families-takes-baby-from-american-mom

Patriot24.net information on the case in Polish and English
www.patriot24.net/amy-jacobsen-case

Glaube.at article "Kindesentzug als Folge Behördlicher Überreaktion in Norwegen" ("Children's Dementation as a Result of Regulatory Overaction in Norway")
www.glaube.at/news/gesellschaft/weltgeschehen/article/1000001572-kindesentzug-als-folge-behoerdlicher-ueberreaktion-in-norwegen

Printed in Poland
by Amazon Fulfillment
Poland Sp. z o.o., Wrocław